STRATEGIC HRM

Michael Armstrong graduated from the London School of Economics. He is a companion of the Chartered Institute of Personnel and Development and a fellow of the Institute of Management Consultants. He has had over 25 years' experience in personnel management, including 12 as a personnel director. He has also practised as a management consultant for over 20 years, and is a former chief examiner, employee reward, for the CIPD. He has written a number of successful management books, including (with Angela Baron) *The Job Evaluation Handbook* (1995); (with Angela Baron) *Performance Management* (1998); *Employee Reward* (2nd edition 1999); *Managing Activities* (1999); *Rewarding Teams* (2000); and (with Duncan Brown) *New Dimensions in Pay Management* (2001), all published by the CIPD.

Angela Baron has a master's degree in organisational and occupational psychology, and is a member of the Chartered Institute of Personnel and Development, for whom she is currently an adviser on employee resourcing. In that role she has been involved in numerous research projects, including detailed investigations into quality management, the lean organisation and organisational culture. She is also responsible for the CIPD's work investigating the link between people management and business performance, as well as contributing to work on all aspects of resourcing the organisation, including recruitment and selection, psychometric testing, organisational design and development, career counselling, human resource planning, teamworking, flexible working, workplace relationships and management style. Her previous collaborations with Michael Armstrong were *The Job Evaluation Handbook* and *Performance Management* (also published by the CIPD).

The Chartered Institute of Personnel and Development is the leading publisher of books and reports for personnel and training professionals, students, and for all those concerned with the effective management and development of people at work. For details of all our titles, please contact the Publishing Department:
tel. 020–8612 6204
e-mail publish@cipd.co.uk
The catalogue of all CIPD titles can be viewed on the CIPD website:
www.cipd.co.uk/bookstore

STRATEGIC HRM

The key to improved business performance

MICHAEL ARMSTRONG
and
ANGELA BARON

Chartered Institute of Personnel and Development

First published in 2002
Reprinted 2003, 2005

Design by Paperweight
Typeset by Fakenham Photosetting
Printed in Great Britain by
The Cromwell Press, Trowbridge

British Library Cataloguing in Publication Data
A catalogue record for this book is available from the
British Library

ISBN 0–85292–923–4

Chartered Institute of Personnel and Development, 151 The Broadway,
London SW19 1JQ
Tel: 020-8612 6200
E-mail: cipd@cipd.co.uk Website: www.cipd.co.uk
Incorporated by Royal Charter. Registered charity no. 1079797.

CONTENTS

ACKNOWLEDGEMENTS

Books like this can never be completed without the involvement and support of a range of individuals. We are grateful to the various members of the CIPD publishing team, academics who gave advice, those who transcribed the taped interview material, and the colleagues who offered moral support. However, our most grateful thanks must go to all the busy practitioners who gave up their valuable time to talk to us at length about their personal views on HR strategy and how they go about developing HR strategy in their own organisations.

FOREWORD

by Jean Tomlin, immediate past CIPD Vice-President for Organisation and Resourcing

So when is 'people management' 'strategic HRM'? A simple enough question and one that is asked in one form or another many times through the average career in personnel and development. On the one hand there is the view that strategic HRM is a collection of policies and practices based on a simple aim to manage and develop people better. On the other is the notion that there should yet be some over-arching theme of strategic direction that will automatically lead to a business-focused and credible role for personnel specialists.

The truth is of course that neither view is entirely right and neither entirely wrong. A set of policies is not always a strategy, and a strategy is not always the route to influence and power. Even senior HR people themselves cannot always agree what strategic HRM should look like. However, most agree that it should be embedded in the business strategy and should be geared towards achieving better business performance.

What this book tries to demonstrate is that there are many ways to create a strategy. Practitioners who might have been hoping for some kind of quick fix will quickly learn there are no short cuts nor easily replicated examples of strategy. Even the most intense pressure from readers' bosses will not produce a coherent strategy overnight. A good strategy requires a bedrock of understanding of the business, its aims and objectives, the context in which it operates, the capabilities and capacities for development of its people, and the resources that are available.

Only when such understanding exists can practitioners go on to develop strategic directions that will fully realise the potential of that greatest of assets – people power.

The authors of this book have identified a number of approaches and models to assist in developing strategy, but ultimately, strategy will be unique to each particular organisation. One maxim is worth remembering, however. No matter how good the strategy may be, if people don't get paid on time, the personnel function will get a bad name. To paraphrase the much-quoted Dave Ulrich: we've got to be good at everything to achieve the power and influence in organisations that people management and people development rightly deserve.

As the general marches at the head of his troops, so ought wise politicians – if I dare use that expression – to march at the head of affairs: insomuch as that they ought not to wait for the *event* to know what measures to take but that the measures they have taken ought to *produce* the event.

Demosthenes
Athenian statesman and orator (384/3–322 BC)

INTRODUCTION

This is a book for chief executives and human resource (HR) practitioners. It aims to provide practical guidance on how strategic human resource management (HRM) processes can be used to improve business performance. Much of the book is based on the extensive research sponsored by the CIPD and other organisations into people management and development strategy, and into the impact people management policies and practices make on business performance. This research has been supplemented by 18 interviews carried out by the authors with chief executives and HR directors on their approaches to strategic HRM. In addition, the book draws on unpublished CIPD-sponsored research conducted by Marc Thompson and Ian Kessler of Templeton College, Oxford, and Kim Hoque then of the Cardiff Business School, Cardiff University.

Theme

The fundamental theme of this book is that improved bottom-line performance takes place when organisations adopt a strategic and coherent approach to people management incorporating the use of leading-edge practice. The belief underpinning this theme is that 'People management represents the catalytic condition – the fundamental "X-factor" – that combines other factors into a formula for high performance' (CIPD, 2001a). This belief has been reinforced by the considerable volume of recent UK and US research evidence on the link between people management practice and organisational performance. The research has demonstrated that a distinct link does exist, and the findings 'usher in a new era which puts people squarely at the heart of the business model' (CIPD, 2001b). Caulkin (2001) reinforced this view:

> Real managers in the real world get superior results by managing people better. These superior results help the recruitment of better people. Better people make better decisions and develop new capacities for winning customers. The business of winning customers creates better returns which reward shareholders and investors.

However, as Thompson (1998b) asserts, conclusive evidence has not yet been forthcoming on 'what works at work, how it works, and why it works'. This is the 'black box' that lies between the intention and the result, the rhetoric and the reality. When explaining the purpose of their research, Purcell *et al* (2000) referred to the need to solve the 'black box problem' – 'how the inputs are converted into results, whether these are profits or productivity, customer satisfaction or employee well-being'. At an event sponsored by the CIPD, senior personnel practitioners expressed the view that the case for HR making an impact on the bottom line is not in dispute. What they were more interested in was establishing the best means to make that impact. But the CIPD (2001b) claims that an emerging consensus favours the 'high-performance management' approach in which companies differentiate themselves through innovation and superior customer services. The rationale is that 'Investing in people increases their value to the firm, a process that in turn makes the firm more "intelligent" – quicker to react, more flexible, more decisive to spot and exploit new opportunities.'

In this book we forward the theme that an approach broadly described as strategic people management and development provides a practical framework within which to develop and implement ways to maximise the contribution of people to business performance. In doing so we refer to the process as 'strategic HRM'. There has been some debate over the use of this term and whether it encompasses anything significantly different from 'personnel strategy'. We discuss the distinction, if any, between HRM and personnel management in Chapter 1. However, because 'strategic HRM' is the expression most commonly adopted by writers in this area it is the term we are using to describe the development, formulation and implementation of strategies concerned with the management of people.

Richardson and Thompson (1999) identified three broad perspectives on the relationship between people management and business performance: best practice, contingency, and 'bundles' (HR efforts linked so as to be mutually supporting). Both the contingency and the bundles perspectives advocate that practices must fit together in a complementary way that will vary according to organisational environment and business circumstances. In addition, the best-practice perspective advocates a specific set of practices, all of which must be implemented for performance improvement to occur. The merits and limitations of these various approaches are evaluated in Chapter 5, but whichever approach is adopted, suffice to say that strategic HRM offers a well-defined route to the achievement of the aims. In this Introduction, therefore, we present a preliminary definition of strategic HRM and a brief analysis of the role of HR and the context within which strategic HRM takes place. The general structure of the book is then outlined.

Strategic HRM defined

Strategic HRM 'provides the all-important framework for applying people management practices to achieve business outcomes' (CIPD, 2001b). It is concerned with the intentions of the organisation on the overall direction it wishes to take in order to achieve its objectives through people. Because intellectual capital is a major source of competitive advantage, and it is people who implement the strategic plan, it is argued that top management must take these key considerations fully into account in developing its corporate strategies. Strategic HRM is an integral part of those strategies.

Strategic HRM addresses broad organisational issues relating to changes in structure and culture, organisational effectiveness and performance. It endeavours to match resources to future requirements, the development of distinctive capabilities, knowledge management, and the management of change. It is concerned with both human capital requirements and the development of process capability – that is, the ability to get things done effectively. It should form part of the business strategy by addressing any major people issues which affect or are affected by the strategic plans of the organisation. As Boxall (1996) remarks: 'The critical concerns of HRM – such as choice of executive leadership and formation of positive patterns of labour relations – are strategic in any firm.'

A distinction can be made between the broad-brush approach of strategic HRM and HR strategies. The latter focus on the specific intentions of the organisation on what must be done, what must be changed, and how these changes are to be made. Richardson and Thompson (1999) suggest that an HR strategy has two key elements: 'There must be strategic objectives (ie things that the strategy is supposed to achieve) and there must be a plan of action (ie the means by which it is proposed that the objectives will be met).' The issues with which these individual HR strategies may be concerned include ensuring that the organisation has the people it needs, training, motivation, reward, flexibility, teamworking and stable employee relations. On their own they may have some success in 'fire-fighting', or addressing issues which specifically inhibit corporate strategy. However, a cluster of HR strategies do not necessarily add up to strategic HRM.

According to this analysis, strategic HRM decisions are built into the strategic plan while HR strategy decisions are derived from it. HR strategy may be more passive than strategic HRM, being driven by corporate strategy rather than helping to shape and determine business focus. But the whole concept of strategic HRM requires that the thrust and purpose of HR activity should be determined as part of the process of determining overall corporate strategy, and this could well be a continuously evolving process.

To sum up, it could be said that the relationship between strategic HRM and HR strategies is comparable with the relationship between strategic management and corporate or business strategies. Both 'strategic HRM' and 'strategic management' are terms that describe an approach which may be adopted by top management that focuses on longer-term plans and on setting the overall direction. HR strategies for resourcing, etc, and functional business strategies in areas such as product/market development can be outcomes of this approach which specify in more detail the intentions of the organisation concerning key issues and particular functions or activities. However, this distinction should not be pursued too rigorously. The concept of strategic HRM can embrace both the overall approach and the manifestations of that approach in the form of specific HR strategies.

The role of HR

HR has a key role to play as a business partner in developing integrated HR strategies which support the achievement of business goals. However, as Caulkin (2001) argues, 'The *how* of people management (doing things right) is at least as important as the *what* (doing the right things).' The impact made by the HR function will be largely dependent on the quality of HR professionals and their ability to do things right.

The context

Interest in strategic HRM and the people–performance relationship has been generated within the context of a turbulent business environment characterised by intensifying global competition, ever-increasing demands to achieve higher levels of shareholder value or to deliver 'best value' performance, massive pressures to respond to and delight customers, and business imperatives to capitalise on technological developments and break new ground in activities such as e-commerce.

Consequently, as Guile and Fonda (1999) comment, businesses have had to learn how to operate more flexibly and how to integrate functionally separated tasks into horizontal work processes. Multi-functional teams are replacing management hierarchies as the primary method of delivering results. Organisations have learned to appreciate the significance of their intellectual capital and to be aware of the need to develop and nurture it. The concept of knowledge management has come to the fore. Because firms achieve competitive advantage through the unique, inimitable capabilities of their people, it has been recognised that 'knowledge displaces capital as the motor of competitive performance' (Scarbrough *et al*, 1999).

Research sponsored by Investors in People (Rajan *et al*, 1999) covering more than 2,000 UK organisations has identified some specific characteristics of organisational change over the last decade:

□ A range of new technologies has been applied to automatic routine processes to develop new products and produce a flatter hierarchy.

□ There is greater clarity in staff roles, performance criteria, accountability and monitoring.

□ There is more teamworking, there is improved communication, and there are fewer job demarcations.

□ There is greater flexibility in employment conditions and work systems.

□ There is greater willingness on the part of staff to manage their own work as well as their own learning.

It is against this background that five key people management strategic goals have emerged. These are expressed in a number of ways by different organisations and management thinkers. However they can be summarised as:

□ to invest in people through the introduction and encouragement of learning processes designed to increase capability and align skills to organisational needs

□ to ensure that the organisation identifies the knowledge required to meet its goals and satisfy its customers and takes steps to acquire and develop this intellectual capital

□ to define the behaviours required for organisational success and ensure that these behaviours are encouraged, valued and rewarded

□ to encourage people to engage wholeheartedly in the work they do for the organisation

□ to gain the commitment of people to the organisation's mission and values.

There are, however, three questions that have to be answered concerning these strategic goals:

□ What impact will the pursuit of these goals make on organisational performance?

□ Assuming this impact is positive, what approaches should organisations adopt to formulating and implementing the people strategies necessary to achieve the goals?

□ What practices or sets of practices are most likely to be effective in particular circumstances?

The answers to these questions provide the detailed themes for the rest of this book.

An overall plan of the book

Although the book is largely about the practice of strategic HRM we believe in company with Douglas McGregor (1960) that there is nothing so practical as a good theory. Part I of the book therefore starts with an exploration of the conceptual framework within which strategic HRM takes place.

□ *Chapter 1* explores the nature of human resource management with particular reference to the belief that HRM is an essentially strategic process which provides a basis for the strategic practices described in Parts III and IV of the book.

□ *Chapter 2* examines the concept of strategy. It focuses on resource-based strategy which provides the rationale for practices discussed in Part III concerned with resourcing and human resource development. Chapter 2 also examines the practical issues involved in any attempt to develop strategies, including HR strategies. One such issue is the fact that the traditional approach to strategy formulation has largely ignored the process issues of implementation and attached insufficient importance to the resource implications of developing strategies or putting them into effect. This provides the impetus for a recurring theme in this book – that strategic HRM is a meaningless concept unless it delivers results which make a significant impact on the performance of the organisation. As Armstrong and Long (1994) commented, 'A strategic HRM approach only becomes "real" when it provides the basis for integrated HR strategies which clearly declare the future intentions of the organisation about its people, which are put into effect, and which *work.*'

□ *Chapter 3* brings the first two chapters together by providing a guide to the essential practical issues that have to be addressed if a strategic approach which delivers results is to be adopted. Such issues include the need to achieve integration or fit, the importance of ensuring that HR strategy is resource-based, and the development of strategic capability.

□ *Chapter 4* deals with intellectual capital theory and its practical implications. The theme is that if strategic HRM is to be effective, it must take account of the need to recognise, retain and measure the contribution of the intellectual capital of the organisation – its people and the knowledge that they generate.

□ *Chapter 5* describes the various models of strategic HRM developed recently, including such approaches as high-performance management and bundling. The models provide guidance on the methods organisations can adopt to maximise the impact made by their human resource management policies and practices.

Part II of this book reviews the outcome of the various research projects on the impact of HRM on business performance and examines methods of measuring the impact and the role of the HR function in making that impact. These projects clearly point the way to the development and implementation of HR practices that make a significant contribution to organisational effectiveness. Part III deals with the components of strategic HRM – how the individual HR strategies which add up to strategic HRM address overall organisational issues, together with specific aspects of HRM such as resourcing, human resource development, reward and employee relations. And Part IV concentrates on the practical issues: it describes strategic HRM in action as established by the recent research, and finally spells out how HR practitioners can act as business partners to improve bottom-line performance through the use of strategic HRM approaches. Although this Part and Part III deal with practical issues, they take account also of the implications of HRM research and the resulting theory of HRM which, as spelled out in Part I, has made an important contribution to our understanding of what organisations should do to achieve success through people.

How the theory informs practice

As described above, the aim of this book is to show how the theory emerging from research about HRM and its impact informs the practice of HRM. To demonstrate the process, the links between the various key concepts and their associated practices are summarised in Table 1.

Table 1
THE IMPACT OF CONCEPTS ON PRACTICE

Concept	Practice
Human resource management as an approach which ☐ emphasises the need for strategic fit – the integration of business and HR strategies ☐ attaches importance to strong cultures and values ☐ treats people as human capital to be invested in as key assets ☐ involves the adoption of a comprehensive and coherent approach to the provision of mutually supporting employment policies and practices – ie the development of integrated HR processes	The HRM practices derived from these concepts are: ☐ ensuring that what is planned and done focuses on meeting business needs ☐ paying close attention to culture management ☐ inaugurating resourcing and development practices that increase the added value provided by people ☐ taking a holistic view of the development and use of HR practices to ensure that no innovation is treated in isolation, so that the combined impact of what is done can be much greater
Strategy as a process concerned fundamentally with both ends and means which involves: ☐ planning how to allocate resources to opportunities ☐ managing these opportunities in ways that will significantly add value to the results achieved by the firm ☐ recognising that the strategic capability of a firm depends on its resource capability, especially its distinctive resources	The HRM practices derived from these concepts are: ☐ human resource planning activities that are based on an understanding of the future needs of the business for people who have the qualities required to exploit the opportunities available in order to achieve competitive advantage ☐ adopting a strategic approach which always defines how planned practices will contribute to meeting business needs for improved performance and competitiveness ☐ focusing on the need to raise the skills base of the business and to attract and retain high-quality people

Concept	Practice
Strategic HRM as: ☐ an integrated process ☐ a resource-based approach that addresses methods of increasing the firm's strategic capability through the development of managers and other staff who can think and plan strategically and who understand the key strategic issues	The HRM practices derived from these concepts are: ☐ the use of 'bundling' to maximise the impact of HR practices ☐ the development of resource capability by recruiting and developing people who are better than those employed by competitors and providing them with rewards that recognise their contribution
The concept of intellectual capital which: ☐ distinguishes between the human, social and organisational capital upon which organisations largely depend for their success ☐ emphasises the importance of the knowledge, skills, abilities and intellect of the people of the organisation and their willingness and ability to apply this in the pursuit of organisational goals	The HRM practices derived from these concepts are: ☐ resourcing and development practices that build and maintain human capital ☐ organisational development activities that enhance the contribution of social capital (the effectiveness with which people work together and interact) ☐ knowledge management activities that capture, share and promote the use of knowledge to enhance learning and performance
The models of HRM that have been developed: ☐ the general 'best practice', 'best fit' and 'configurational' models ☐ the specific models: high-performance management, high-commitment management and high-involvement management	The HRM practices derived from these concepts are: ☐ an emphasis on the importance of 'best fit' rather than best practice, and recognition of the potential benefits of 'bundling' (linking HR strategies and practices so that they are mutually supporting) ☐ specific examples of high-performance, high-commitment and high-involvement practices and their likely impact

PART I

THE CONCEPTUAL FRAMEWORK

1   THE CONCEPT OF HRM

To understand strategic HRM it is necessary to appreciate the concept of HRM. This chapter therefore starts with a working definition of HRM and continues with sections describing first the origins of the concept and its subsequent development, and next summarising the reservations expressed about it. The differences, if any, between HRM and personnel management as practised today and how HRM has been assimilated into personnel management are then explored.

HRM defined

HRM can be defined as a strategic and coherent approach to the management of an organisation's most valued assets – the people working there who individually and collectively contribute to the achievement of its objectives.

Characteristics of HRM

There is no such thing as a generally accepted theory of HRM. A number of typical characteristics, some or all of which may be present in the various versions of the theory, may be identified as listed below, but there are different approaches to HRM and different categories of HRM, as discussed later in this section.

Typical characteristics of the various versions of HRM are that:

- it emphasises the need for strategic fit – the integration of business and HR strategies
- importance is attached to strong cultures and values
- it stresses the importance of gaining commitment to the organisation's mission and values – it is 'commitment-orientated'

☐ people are treated as human capital to be invested in as key assets – they are not regarded as a variable cost

☐ it involves the adoption of a comprehensive and coherent approach to the provision of mutually supporting employment policies and practices – ie the development of integrated HR policies and practices (configuration or bundling)

☐ employee relations are unitarist rather than pluralist, individual rather than collective

☐ it is a top-management-driven activity, and the performance and delivery of HRM is a line management responsibility

☐ organising principles are organic and decentralised, with flexible roles, a focus on process (how things are done, especially across traditional organisational boundaries) and more concern for teamwork: flexibility and team-building are important

☐ it contributes in measurable ways to the creation and maintenance of competitive advantage, and the focus is on performance and adding value, especially for shareholders

☐ there is strong emphasis on the delivery of quality to customers and the achievement of high levels of customer satisfaction

☐ rewards are differentiated according to performance, competence, contribution or skill.

However, it can be argued that HRM as a philosophy is not so clear-cut as this list of characteristics implies. It means different things to different people. Some emphasise one aspect – for example, its strategic nature – others concentrate on its emphasis on commitment and mutuality. Keenoy (1999) as cited by Legge (2001) likens HRM to a hologram:

> As with a hologram, HRM changes its appearance as we move round its image. Each shift of stance reveals another facet, a darker depth, a different contour. As a fluid holistic entity of many different forms, it is not surprising that every time we look at it, it is slightly different. This is why, conceptually, HRMism appears to be a moving target, and why, empirically, it has no fixed (fixable) forms.

Categories of HRM theories

Guest (1997) has identified three categories of HRM theory:

- *strategic theory*, which identifies key environmental influences on HRM (Hendry and Pettigrew, 1990) or classifies HR strategy in relation to models of corporate strategy such as those produced by Miles and Snow (1978) and Porter (1980)

- *descriptive theory*, which sets out to describe HRM in a comprehensive way by classifying the content, as did Beer *et al* (1984)

- *normative theories*, which are more prescriptive in their approach. These include those advanced by Walton (1985) advocating a mutual commitment approach, and the best-practice list of Pfeffer (1994).

The hard and soft varieties of HRM

A distinction was made by Storey (1989) between the 'hard' and 'soft' versions of HRM.

Hard HRM

The hard approach to HRM emphasises that people are important resources through which organisations achieve competitive advantage. These resources have therefore to be acquired, developed and deployed in ways that will benefit the organisation. The focus is on the quantitative, calculative and business-strategic aspects of managing human resources in as 'rational' a way as for any other economic factor. It adopts a business-orientated philosophy which emphasises the need to manage people in ways that will obtain added value from them. It regards people as human capital from which a return can be obtained by investing judiciously in their development. Fombrun *et al* (1984) quite explicitly presented workers as another key resource for managers to exploit. As Guest (1999) comments: 'The drive to adopt HRM is based on the business case of a need to respond to an external threat from increasing competition. It is a philosophy that appeals to managements who are striving to increase competitive advantage and appreciate that to do this they must invest in human resources as well as new technology.' He also commented that HRM 'reflects a long-standing capitalist tradition in which the worker is regarded as a commodity'.

The emphasis is therefore on:

☐ the interests of management

☐ adopting a strategic approach that is closely integrated with business strategy

☐ obtaining added value from people by the processes of human resource development and performance management

☐ the need for a strong corporate culture expressed in mission and value statements and reinforced by communications, training, and performance management processes

☐ the need to obtain the commitment of employees to the goals and values of the organisation.

Soft HRM

The soft model of HRM traces its roots to the human-relations school, and emphasises communication, motivation and leadership. As described by Storey (1989), it involves 'treating employees as valued assets, a source of competitive advantage through their commitment, adaptability and high quality (of skills, performance, and so on)'. It therefore views employees – in the words of Guest (1999) – as means rather than as objects. The soft approach to HRM stresses the need to gain the commitment – the 'hearts and minds' – of employees through involvement, communication and other methods of developing a high-commitment high-trust organisation. Attention is also drawn to the key role of organisational culture.

The focus is on 'mutuality' – a belief that the interests of management and employees can, and indeed should, coincide. It is therefore a unitarist approach. As Gennard and Judge (1997) put it, organisations are assumed to be 'harmonious and integrated, all employees sharing the organisational goals and working as members of one team'.

It has, however, been observed by Truss (1999) that 'even if the rhetoric of HRM is soft, the reality is often hard, with the interests of the organisation prevailing over those of the individual'. And research carried out by Gratton *et al* (1999) found that in the eight organisations they studied, there was a mixture of hard and soft HRM approaches. This suggested to the researchers that the distinction between hard and soft HRM was not as precise as some commentators have implied.

The development of the HRM concept

The background

Some aspects of the basic philosophy of 'soft HRM' can be traced back to the writings of Douglas McGregor (1960) who, as mentioned by Truss (1999), even used the terminology 'hard' and 'soft' to characterise forms of management control. McGregor's Theory X essentially describes the 'control' model of management as described by Walton (1985), whereas McGregor's Theory Y emphasises the importance of integrating the needs of the organisation and those of the individual – the principle of mutual commitment, again expressed by Walton. HRM was at that time perceived by some commentators as an antidote to the confrontational stance of people management dominated by a decade of difficult industrial relations.

The full concept of HRM emerged in the mid-1980s against the background of the popularist writers on management who flourished in that decade. These included Pascale and Athos (1981) and Peters and Waterman (1982), who produced lists of the attributes they claimed characterised successful companies. These popular 'school of excellence' writers may have exerted some influence on management thinking about the need for strong cultures and commitment (two features of the HRM philosophy) but, as David Guest (1993) has commented, they were right enough to be dangerously wrong. Indeed, their failure was often their inability to offer any real practical guidance on the implementation of their versions of best practice.

The concept of HRM has gone through two stages:

☐ the initial notions developed by US writers in the 1980s, christened by Boxall (1992) as the matching model and the Harvard framework

> ❑ the take-up of these ideas by British writers in the late 1980s and 1990s who were often sceptical about the reality beyond the rhetoric and dubious about its morality.

However, as reviewed at the end of this chapter, the notions of HRM and personnel management have been slowly but progressively assimilated into one another.

The matching model of HRM

One of the first explicit statements of the HRM concept was made by Fombrun *et al* (1984), part of the Michigan school. They held that HR systems and the organisation structure should be managed in a way that is congruent with organisational strategy (hence the name 'matching model'). They further explained that there is a human resource cycle (an adaptation of which is illustrated in Figure 1) which consists of four generic processes or functions that are performed in all organisations. These are:

❑ *selection* – matching available human resources to jobs

❑ *appraisal* – assessing performance

❑ *rewards* – 'the reward system is one of the most under-utilised and mishandled managerial tools for driving organisational performance'. It must reward short- as well as long-term achievements, bearing in mind that 'business must perform in the present to succeed in the future'

❑ *development* – developing high-quality employees.

Figure 1

THE HUMAN RESOURCE CYCLE

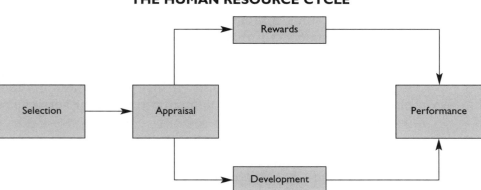

Adapted from Fombrun *et al*, 1982

Fombrun *et al* suggest that the HR function should be linked to the line organisation by providing the business with good HR databases, by ensuring that senior managers give HR issues as much attention as they give to other functions, and by measuring the contribution of the HR function at the strategic, managerial and operational levels.

The Harvard framework

The other founding fathers of HRM were the Harvard school of Beer *et al* (1984). This 'Harvard framework' is based on the belief that the problems of historical personnel management can be solved, in their words, only

> when general managers develop a viewpoint of how they wish to see employees involved in and developed by the enterprise, and of what HRM policies and practices may achieve those goals. Without either a central philosophy or a strategic vision – which can be provided *only* by general managers – HRM is likely to remain a set of independent activities, each guided by its own practice tradition.

Beer and his colleagues believed that 'Many pressures are demanding a broader, more comprehensive and more strategic perspective with regard to the organisation's human resources. These pressures have created a need for a longer-term perspective in managing people and consideration of people as potential assets rather than merely a variable cost.' They were the first to underline the HRM tenet that people management belongs to and is dependent on line managers. They also stated that 'Human resource management involves all management decisions and action that affect the nature of the relationship between the organisation and its employees – its human resources.'

The Harvard school suggested that HRM had two characteristic features:

☐ Line managers accept more responsibility for ensuring the alignment of competitive strategy and personnel policies.

☐ Personnel has the mission of setting policies that govern how personnel activities are developed and implemented in ways that make them more mutually reinforcing.

Figure 2

THE HARVARD FRAMEWORK FOR HUMAN RESOURCE MANAGEMENT

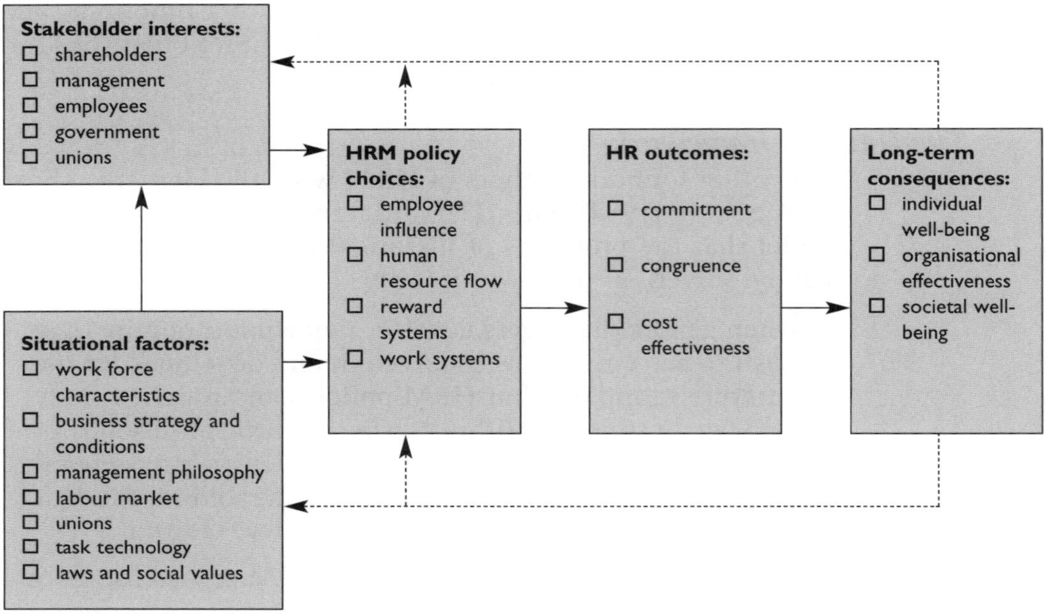

Source: M. Beer, B. Spencer, P. R. Lawrence, D. Quinn Mills, R. E. Walton, *Managing Human Assets,* The Free Press, 1984

The Harvard framework as modelled by Beer *et al* is shown in Figure 2.

Boxall (1992) believes the advantages of this model are that it:

□   incorporates recognition of a range of stakeholder interests

□   recognises the importance of 'trade-offs', either explicitly or implicitly, between the interests of owners and those of employees as well as between various interest groups

□   widens the context of HRM to include 'employee influence', the organisation of work and the associated question of supervisory style

□   acknowledges a broad range of contextual influences on management's choice of strategy, suggesting a meshing of both product-market and socio-cultural logics

□ emphasises strategic choice – it is not driven by situational or environmental determinism.

The Harvard model has exerted considerable influence over the theory and practice of HRM, particularly in its emphasis on the fact that HRM is the concern of management in general rather than the personnel function in particular.

Walton (1985), also of Harvard, expanded the concept by emphasising the importance of commitment and mutuality. He stated that:

> The new HRM model is composed of policies that promote mutuality – mutual goals, mutual influence, mutual respect, mutual rewards, mutual responsibility. The theory is that policies of mutuality will elicit commitment which in turn will yield both better economic performance and greater human development.

This commitment model of human resource management is associated with the concept of soft HRM referred to earlier.

Developments in the concept of HRM

A number of academic commentators in the UK have developed the original US concept of HRM.

David Guest

David Guest (1987, 1989a, 1989b, 1991) took the Harvard model and expanded it by defining four policy goals he believes can be used as testable propositions:

□ *strategic integration* – the ability of the organisation to integrate HRM issues into its strategic plans, and ensure that the various aspects of HRM cohere and provide for line managers to incorporate an HRM perspective into their decision-making

□ *high commitment* – behavioural commitment to pursue agreed goals, and attitudinal commitment reflected in a strong identification with the enterprise

□ *high quality* – this refers to all aspects of managerial behaviour which bear directly on the quality of goods and services provided, including the management of employees and investment in high-quality employees

□ *flexibility* – functional flexibility and the existence of an adaptable organisation structure with the capacity to manage innovation.

Guest believes that the driving force behind HRM is:

> the pursuit of competitive advantage in the marketplace through provision of high-quality goods and services, through competitive pricing linked to high productivity, and through the capacity swiftly to innovate and manage change in response to changes in the marketplace or to breakthroughs in research and development.

He considers that HRM values are:

□ *unitarist* to the extent that they assume no underlying and inevitable differences of interest between management and workers

□ *individualistic* in that they emphasise the individual–organisation linkage in preference to operating through group and representative systems.

Guest has also asserted that HRM has been 'talked up' and that its impact has been on attitudes rather than behaviour.

Karen Legge

Karen Legge (1989) considers that the common themes of the typical definitions of HRM are that:

> human resource policies should be integrated with strategic business planning and used to reinforce an appropriate (or change an inappropriate) organisational culture, that human resources are valuable and a source of competitive advantage, and that they may be tapped most effectively by mutually consistent policies which promote commitment and which, as a consequence, foster a willingness in employees to act flexibly in the interests of the 'adaptive organisation's' pursuit of excellence.

In 1995 Karen Legge distinguished between two HRM perspectives: 'The one sees HRM in a contingent light – as a strategically-orientated perspective on personnel management cohering with business strategy...The other sees HRM in absolutist terms – as a speciality of personnel management.' The contingent perspective (Boxall's 'matching model') is typified by the Michigan school (of Fombrun *et al*, 1984) and the absolutist perspective is represented by the Harvard school (Boxall's 'Harvard framework', Beer *et al*, 1984).

In 1998, Karen Legge defined the 'hard' model of HRM as a process emphasising 'the close integration of human resource policies with business strategy which regards employees as a resource to be managed in the same rational way as any other resource being exploited for maximum return'. In contrast, the soft version of HRM sees employees as 'valued assets and as a source of competitive advantage through their commitment, adaptability and high level of skills and performance'. She regards the three key features of HRM as first, various forms of flexibility; second, teambuilding, empowerment and involvement; and third, cultural management.

Chris Hendry and Andrew Pettigrew

Hendry and Pettigrew (1990) play down the prescriptive element of the Harvard model and extend the analytical elements. As pointed out by Boxall (1992), such an approach rightly avoids labelling HRM as a single form and advances more slowly by proceeding more analytically. It is argued by Hendry and Pettigrew that 'better descriptions of structures and strategy-making in complex organisations, and of frameworks for understanding them, are an essential underpinning for HRM'.

They believe that as a movement HRM expressed a mission to achieve a turnaround in industry: 'HRM was thus in a real sense heavily normative from the outset: it provided a diagnosis and proposed solutions.' They also suggest that 'What HRM did at this point was to provide a label to wrap around some of the observable changes, while providing a focus for challenging deficiencies – in attitudes, scope, coherence, and direction – of existing personnel management.'

John Purcell

John Purcell (1993) thinks that 'the adoption of HRM is both a product of and a cause of a significant concentration of power in the hands of management', while the widespread use 'of the language of HRM, if not its practice, is a combination of its intuitive appeal to managers and, more importantly, a response to the turbulence of product and financial markets'. He asserts that HRM is about the rediscovery of management prerogative. He considers that HRM policies and practices, when applied within a firm as a break from the past, are often associated with such words as commitment, competence, empowerment, flexibility, culture, performance, assessment, reward, teamwork, involvement, co-operation, harmonisation, quality, and learning. But 'the danger of descriptions of HRM as modern best-management practice is that they stereotype the past and idealise the future'.

Keith Sisson

Keith Sisson (1990) suggests that there are four main features increasingly associated with HRM:

- □ a stress on the integration of personnel policies both with one another and with business planning more generally
- □ the responsibility for personnel management no longer residing with (or being 'relegated to') specialist managers.
- □ the shift of focus from manager–trade union relations to management–employee relations, from collectivism to individualism
- □ a stress on commitment and the exercise of initiative, such that managers now take the role of 'enabler', 'empowerer' and 'facilitator'.

John Storey

John Storey defined human resource management in 2001:

> Human resource management is a distinctive approach to employment management which seeks to obtain competitive advantage through the strategic deployment of a highly committed and capable workforce using an array of cultural, structural and personnel techniques.

He believes (1989) that HRM can be regarded as a 'set of interrelated policies with an ideological and philosophical underpinning', and he suggests four aspects that constitute the *meaningful* version of HRM:

□ a particular constellation of beliefs and assumptions

□ a strategic thrust informing decisions about people management

□ the central involvement of line managers

□ reliance upon a set of 'levers' to shape the employment relationship – these are different from those used under proceduralist and joint regulative regimes typical of classical industrial relations systems.

He has written (1989) that 'In stereotyped form [HRM] appears capable of making good each of the main shortcomings of personnel management.' The HR function becomes recognised as a central business concern, and training-and-development assumes a higher profile: 'Its performance and delivery are integrated into line management: the aim shifts from merely securing compliance to the more ambitious one of winning commitment.' The concept locates HRM policy formulation firmly at the strategic level, and insists that a characteristic of HRM is its internally coherent approach.

Reservations about HRM

On the face of it, HRM has much to offer, at least to management. But strong reservations have been expressed about it by a number of academics and by a practitioner, Alan Fowler (1987).

These reservations may be summed up as:

□ HRM does not pass muster either as a reputable theory or as an alternative and better form of personnel management.

□ HRM is, in David Guest's (1991) words, an 'optimistic but ambiguous concept' – it is all hype and hope.

□ Even if HRM does exist as a distinct process – which many doubt – it is full of contradictions, it is manipulative, and, according to the Cardiff school (Blyton and Turnbull, 1992), it is downright pernicious.

□ The 'prized goals' of HRM remain unproven at best, and unfulfilled at worst (Mabey et al, 1998).

HRM as a theory

Mike Noon (1992) has commented that HRM has serious deficiencies as a theory:

> It is built with concepts and propositions, but the associated variables and hypotheses are not made explicit. It is too comprehensive...If HRM is labelled a 'theory', it raises expectations about its ability to describe and predict.

HRM is simplistic

As Alan Fowler (1987) has written:

> The HRM message to top management tends to be beguilingly simple. Don't bother too much about the content or techniques of personnel management, it says. Just manage the context. Get out from behind your desk, bypass the hierarchy, and go and talk to people. That way you will unlock an enormous potential for improved performance.

HRM as rhetoric

The HRM rhetoric presents it as an all-or-nothing process that is ideal for all organisations, despite the evidence that different business environments require different approaches. This produces the gap between rhetoric and reality referred to (frequently) by Gratton *et al* (1999).

HRM is overambitious and impractical

HRM can be accused of promising more than it can deliver. As Mabey *et al* (1998) comment, 'The heralded outcomes (of HRM) are almost without exception unrealistically high.' They imply that management has either been conned by consultants offering quick-fix solutions (which is of course what consultants always do, at least according to many academics) or is indulging in rhetoric influenced by 'extra-organisational values' such as excellence, flexibility, quality, and customer focus.

To put the concept of HRM into practice involves strategic integration, developing a coherent and consistent set of employment policies, and gaining commitment. This requires high levels of determination and competence at all levels of management, and a strong and effective HR function staffed by business-orientated people. It may be difficult to meet these criteria, especially when the proposed HRM culture conflicts with the established corporate culture and traditional managerial attitudes and behaviour.

Some commentators have claimed that the development of integrated HR strategies – a central feature of HRM – is difficult, if not impossible, in companies which lack any real sense of strategic direction. Business strategies, they say, where they *are* formulated, tend to be dominated by product-market imperatives, leading to product and systems developments. To support these, priority is given, understandably enough, to obtaining financial resources and maintaining a sound financial base. Enhancing shareholder value comes first; human resource considerations come a poor second.

HRM and industrial relations

As Fowler (1987) has stated:

> At the heart of the concept is the complete identification of employees with the aims and values of the business – employee involvement, but on the company's terms. Power in the HRM system remains very firmly in the hands of the employer. Is it really possible to claim full mutuality when at the end of the day the employer can decide unilaterally to close the company or sell it to someone else?

Contradictions in HRM

Karen Legge (1989) believes that the concept of HRM contains specific internal contradictions:

- the complementarity and consistency of 'mutuality' policies designed to generate commitment, flexibility, quality, etc
- problems over commitment – as Guest (1987) asked: 'Commitment to what?'
- the apparent dilemma between preaching the virtues of individualism (concentration on the individual) and collectivism (teamworking, etc)

□　the potential tension between the development of a strong corporate culture and employees' ability to respond flexibly and adaptively.

The morality or otherwise of HRM

In spite of all their protestations to the contrary, the advocates of HRM could be seen to be introducing alternative and more insidious forms of 'control by compliance' when they emphasise the need for employees to be committed to do what the organisation wants them to do. HRM can be – and often is – accused of exploiting people to benefit the business. As Legge (1989) pointed out:

> In its emphasis on 'strong culture', in theory HRM is able to achieve a cohesive workforce, but without the attendant dilemma of creating potentially dysfunctional solidarity. For a 'strong culture' is aimed at uniting employees through a shared set of managerially sanctioned values ('quality', 'service', 'innovation', etc) that assume an identification of employee and employer interests. Such co-operation – through cultural management, of course – reinforces the intention that autonomy will be exercised 'responsibly' – ie in management's interests.

Legge (1998) summed up her reservations about the morality of HRM:

> Sadly, in a world of intensified competition and scarce resources, it seems inevitable that, as employees are used as means to an end, there will be some who will lose out. They may even be in the majority. For these people, the soft version of HRM may be an irrelevancy, while the hard version is likely to be an uncomfortable experience.

She contends that managements only go in for HRM out of self-interest regarding employees. As she explained in 2000:

> For low cost producers, particularly operating in mature markets, investment in training, intensive communication and guarantees of job security may be seen as both unnecessary and undesirable. If behavioural compliance

is sufficient, why go to the expense of trying to secure additional commitment?

HRM is accused by many academics of being manipulative. As Willmott (1993) argues, HRM operates as a form of insidious control. It preaches mutuality but the reality is that behind the rhetoric it exploits workers. It is said to be a wolf in sheep's clothing (Keenoy, 1990a), and as Willmott (1993) comments: 'The governance of the employee's soul becomes a more central element in the corporate strategy for gaining competitive advantage.' They note that chief executives with a mission for HRM tend to adapt the principle of 'What is good for General Motors is good for America' to that of 'What is good for the business must be good for everyone in it' – in other words, like an apple a day, HRM is good for you. Such assumptions are dangerous, and the forces of internal persuasion and propaganda may have to be deployed to get people to accept values with which they may not be in accord, and which in any case may be against their interests.

Essentially, the accusation is that HRM treats employees as means to an end. However, it could be argued that if organisations exist to achieve ends, as they do, and if those ends can be achieved only through people, as is clearly the case, the concern of managements for commitment and performance from those people is not unnatural and is not solely attributable to HRM – it existed in the good old days of personnel management before HRM was invented. What matters is *how* managements treat people as ends, and what managements *provide* in return for employees, and whether employees believe their personal aspirations can be achieved.

Inconsistencies in the comments on HRM

As Guest (1999) has suggested, there are two contradictory concerns about HRM. The first as formulated by Legge (1995, 1998) is that although management rhetoric may express concern for workers, the reality is harsher. And Keenoy (1997) complains that:

> The real puzzle about HRMism is how, in the face of such apparently overwhelming critical 'refutation', it has secured such influence and institutional presence.

Other writers, however, simply claim that HRM does not work. Scott (1994), for example, declares that both management and workers are captives of their history and find it very difficult to let go of their traditional adversarial orientations.

But these contentions are contradictory. As Guest (1999) remarks: 'It is difficult to treat HRM as a major threat (though what it is a threat to is not always made explicit) deserving of serious critical analysis while at the same time claiming that it is not practised or is ineffective.'

HRM and personnel management

In the words of David Guest (1989b): 'HRM and personnel management – can you tell the difference?' An earlier answer to this question was given by Armstrong (1987):

> HRM is regarded by some personnel managers as just a set of initials, or old wine in new bottles. It could indeed be no more and no less than another name for personnel management, but as usually perceived, at least it has the virtue of emphasising the virtue of treating people as a key resource, the management of which is the direct concern of top management as part of the strategic planning processes of the enterprise. Although there is nothing new in the idea, insufficient attention has been paid to it in many organisations. The new bottle or label can help to overcome that deficiency.

And Torrington (1989) argued that:

> Personnel management has grown through assimilating a number of additional emphases to produce an ever-richer combination of expertise...HRM is no revolution but a further dimension to a multi-faceted role.

Similarities

It can be argued that the similarities between personnel management and HRM are:

☐ Personnel management strategies, like HRM strategies, flow from the business strategy.

☐ Personnel management, like HRM, recognises that line

managers are responsible for managing people. The personnel function provides the necessary advice and support services to enable managers to carry out their responsibilities.

☐ The values of personnel management and at least the 'soft' version of HRM are identical with regard to 'respect for the individual', balancing organisational and individual needs, and developing people to achieve their maximum level of competence both for their own satisfaction and to facilitate the achievement of organisational objectives.

☐ Both personnel management and HRM recognise that one of their most essential processes matches people to ever-changing organisational requirements – placing and developing the right people in and for the right jobs.

☐ The same range of selection, competence analysis, performance management, training, management development and reward management techniques are used in both HRM and personnel management.

☐ The 'soft' version of HRM, like personnel management, attaches importance to the processes of communication and participation within an employee relations system.

Differences

The differences between personnel management and human resource management can be seen as a matter of emphasis and approach rather than of substance. Or, as Hendry and Pettigrew (1990) put it, HRM can be perceived as a 'perspective on personnel management and not personnel management itself'.

From her review of the literature, Legge (1989) has identified three features that would seem to distinguish HRM and personnel management:

☐ Personnel management is an activity aimed primarily at non-managers, whereas HRM is less clearly focused but is certainly more concerned with managerial staff.

☐ HRM is much more of an integrated line management activity, whereas personnel management seeks to influence line management.

□ HRM emphasises the importance of senior management's being involved in the managing of culture, whereas personnel management has always been rather suspicious of organisational development and related unitarist social-psychology-orientated ideas.

The strategic nature of HRM is another difference commented on by a number of people who in effect dismiss the idea that traditional personnel management was ever really involved in the strategic areas of business. Hendry and Pettigrew (1990), for example, believe that the strategic character of HRM is distinctive.

Perhaps the most significant difference is that the concept of HRM is based on a management- and business-orientated philosophy. It is claimed to be a central senior-management-driven strategic activity developed, owned and delivered by management as a whole to promote the interests of the organisation it serves. It purports to be a holistic approach concerned with the total interests of the organisation – the interests of the members of the organisation are recognised but subordinated to those of the enterprise. Hence the importance attached to strategic integration and strong cultures, which flow from top management's vision and leadership, and which require people who will be committed to the strategy, who will be fully engaged in delivering it, who will be adaptable to change, and who will fit the culture. By implication, as Guest (1991) says, 'HRM is too important to be left to personnel managers.'

HRM could be described as an approach to, rather than as an alternative to, traditional personnel management. When comparing HRM and personnel management, more similarities emerge than differences. However, concepts such as strategic integration, culture management, commitment, total quality, and investing in human capital, together with a unitary philosophy (in which the interests of management and employees coincide), are essential parts of the HRM model. And this model fits the way in which organisations have to do business and manage their resources in the environments in which they now exist. In spite of the reservations expressed about the concept by academics, the term 'human resource management' is therefore being used increasingly in businesses as an alternative to personnel management. This is because more and more people feel that it is in tune with the realities of organisational life.

Reactions to HRM from employees

Much of the hostility to HRM expressed by a number of academics centres on the belief that it is hostile to the interests of workers – ie that it is 'managerialist'. Research conducted by Guest and Conway (1997) covering a stratified random sample of 1,000 workers established that a notably high level of HRM was already in place. This contradicted the view that management has tended to 'talk up' the adoption of HRM practices. The HRM characteristics covered by the survey included the opportunity to express grievances and raise personal concerns on such matters as opportunities for training and development, communications about business issues, single status, effective systems for dealing with bullying and harassment at work, making jobs interesting and varied, promotion from within, involvement programmes, no compulsory redundancies, performance-related pay, profit sharing, and the use of attitude surveys. The reports of workers on outcomes showed that a higher number of HR practices was associated with higher ratings of fairness, trust and management's delivery of their promises. Those experiencing more HR activities also felt more secure in and more satisfied with their jobs. Motivation was significantly higher for those working in organisations where more HR practices were in place. In summary, as commented by Guest (1999), it appears that workers like their experience of HRM. These findings appear to contradict the 'radical critique' view produced by academics such as Mabey *et al* (1998) that HRM has been ineffectual, pernicious, managerialist, or all three. Some of those who adopt this stance tend to dismiss favourable reports from workers about HRM because they have, in effect, been brainwashed by management. But there is no evidence to support this view.

Yet Gratton *et al* (1999) are convinced on the basis of their research that there is 'a disjunction between rhetoric and reality in the area of human resource management between HRM theory and HRM practice, between what the HR function says it is doing and that practice as perceived by employers, and between what senior management believes to be the role of the HR function, and the role it actually plays'. In their conclusions they refer to the 'hyperbole and rhetoric of human resource management'. The incessant use of the word 'rhetoric' by these and other academics suggests that there is a deeply held and cynical belief amongst them that managements never mean what they say – or if they do mean it, do not do anything about it.

The assimilation of HRM

Personnel managers are increasingly being called human resource managers. This may often mean that it is only the name that has changed, but by a process of osmosis much of the philosophy of HRM seems to be spreading into the day-to-day thinking and practice of personnel professionals. The debate that raged during the second phase of development referred to above no longer seems relevant to these practitioners. They simply get on with doing it; often imperfectly because of organisational constraints, but based on the observations made by the writers of this book in research carried out over the last few years in over 100 British organisations, many are trying hard.

Conclusions

Human resource management has been described as 'high-concept person management' (Armstrong, 2001). Some commentators (Legge, 1989 and 1995; Keenoy, 1990b; Sisson, 1990; Storey, 1993; Hope-Hailey *et al*, 1998) have highlighted the revolutionary nature of HRM. The latter mention the 'rhetoric' of HR practitioners, but should more accurately have referred to the rhetoric of the HR academics who have been debating what HRM means, how different it is from other forms of people management, and whether or not it is a good thing – indeed, whether or not it exists – endlessly and unproductively. Practitioners have pressed on regardless, in the justified belief that what the academics were writing about had little relevance to their day-to-day lives as they wrestled with the realities of organisational life. They did not suddenly see the light in the 1980s and change their ways, for better or for worse. The true personnel or HR professionals just kept on doing what they had always done but tried to do it better. They took note of the much wider range of publications about personnel practices and the information on so-called 'best practice' provided by management consultants and conference organisers, and they learned from the case studies emanating from the research conducted by the burgeoning academic institutions. They also recognised that to succeed in an increasingly competitive world they had to become more professional, and they were encouraged to do so by bodies such as the then Institute of Personnel Management.

Personnel practitioners became more interested in business strategy and the development of HR strategies not because an academic treatise on HRM said that this was what they ought to be doing but because they appreciated that they could survive at the top of an organisation only if they did get involved in strategic decisions as business partners. They took account of new ideas and implemented new practices because they appreciated that they were appropriate, not because they fitted into any sort of HRM philosophy. As Armstrong (2000a) pointed out:

> HRM cannot be blamed or given credit for changes that were taking place anyway. For example, it is often alleged to have inspired a move from pluralism to unitarism in industrial relations. But newspaper production was moved from Fleet Street to Wapping by Murdoch not because he had read a book about HRM but as a means of breaking the print unions' control.

2 THE CONCEPT OF STRATEGY

Strategic HRM is based on HRM principles but incorporates the concept of strategy. This chapter examines what strategy means and thus represents an introduction to the examination of the notion of strategic HRM featured in Chapter 3.

The origins and development of the concept of strategy

'Strategy' derives as a military term, and for that reason is primarily defined in the *Oxford English Dictionary* as:

> the art of a commander-in-chief; the art of projecting and directing the larger military movements and operations of a campaign.

This may not seem to bear much relevance to strategy in business, public sector or voluntary organisations, but at least it conveys the message that strategy is an art, and that the ultimate responsibility for it lies with the head of the organisation.

It was Drucker who as long ago as in 1955 in *The Practice of Management* pointed out the importance of strategic decisions, which he defined as 'all decisions on business objectives and on the means to reach them'.

However, the concept of business strategy was not fully realised until the pioneers Alfred Chandler (1962), Kenneth Andrews (1965), Igor Ansoff (1965) and Michael Porter (1980) – the 'shapers and movers' as described by Moore (1992) – developed what could be regarded as the classical approach. This involves the use of formal and systematic design techniques, is quantified and externally focused, concentrates on long-term plans without being much concerned with implementation, and more or less ignores the human element. Later writers, especially Henry Mintzberg (1994), emphasised the process and qualitative aspects of strategy, seeing it as evolutionary and as a pattern of activities rather than a formal design. Prahalad and Hamel (1990), Barney (1991, 1995) and others developed the concepts of distinctive competences and resource-based strategy, and more recently, academics such as Purcell (2001) have stressed that strategy is about implementation as well as planning.

This shift in thinking about strategy has been described by Ghoshal and Bartlett (1999) as moving 'from strategy, structure and systems, to purpose, process and people'. It is the later developments represented by this shift that have provided much of the theoretical underpinning for strategic HRM.

Strategy defined

Strategy was defined by one of the pioneering writers on this subject as the 'determination of the basic long-term goals and objectives of an enterprise, and the adoption of courses of action and the allocation of resources necessary for carrying out these goals' (Chandler, 1962). More recently strategy has been defined as being concerned with 'the direction and scope of an organisation over the longer term ideally, which matches its resources to its changing environment, and in particular, to its markets, customers and clients to meet stakeholder expectations' (Johnson and Scholes, 1993).

These definitions refer to the external (market) orientation of strategy. But strategy is also concerned with internal resources, an aspect addressed by the concept of resource-based strategy examined later in this chapter. As cited by Purcell (2001), a useful definition of strategy that combines external focus with internal resources is provided by Quinn (1990):

> A strategy is a pattern or plan that integrates an organisation's major goals, policies and action sequences into a cohesive whole. A well-formulated strategy helps marshal and allocate an organisation's resources into a unique and viable posture based on its relative internal competencies and shortcomings, anticipated changes in

the environment, and contingent moves by intelligent opponents.

Business or corporate strategies consist of statements of what the organisation wants to become, where it wants to go, and, broadly, how it means to get there. In its crudest form, strategy in a commercial enterprise answers the questions 'What business are we in?' and 'Over the longer term, how are we going to make money out of it?' In a public sector or not-for-profit organisation, these questions might be phrased as 'What is the purpose of this organisation, and over the longer term how are we going to achieve that purpose?'

Strategy in a business context determines the direction in which the enterprise is going in relation to its environment in order to achieve sustainable competitive advantage. The emphasis is on focused actions that differentiate the firm from its competitors (Purcell, 1999). It is a declaration of intent that defines means to achieve ends, and is concerned with the long-term allocation of significant company resources and with matching those resources and capabilities to the external environment. Strategy is a perspective on the way in which critical issues or success factors can be addressed, and strategic decisions aim to make a major and long-term impact on the behaviour and success of the organisation.

The concept of strategy is not a straightforward one. There are many different theories about what it is and how it works. Mintzberg *et al* (1998) suggest that 'strategy' can have a number of meanings:

- *a plan*, or something equivalent – a direction, a guide, a course of action
- *a pattern* – that is, consistency in behaviour over time
- *a perspective* – an organisation's fundamental way of doing things
- *a ploy* – a specific 'manoeuvre' intended to outwit an opponent or a competitor.

The fundamentals of strategy

Fundamentally, strategy is concerned with achieving *competitive advantage*. Formulating a strategy to do so requires defining intentions (*strategic intent*) and allocating or matching resources to opportunities (*resource-based strategy*) thus achieving *strategic fit* between them. The effective development and implementation of strategy depends on the *strategic capability* of the organisation, which will include the ability not only to determine strategic goals but also to develop and implement strategic plans through the process of *strategic management*.

Competitive advantage

The concept of competitive advantage as formulated by Michael Porter (1980, 1985) plays an important part in the theory of strategy. Competitive advantage arises when a firm creates value for its customers. To achieve it, firms select markets in which they can excel and present a moving target in front of their competitors by continually improving their position.

Porter emphasised the importance of:

□ *differentiation*, which consists of offering a product or service 'that is perceived industry-wise as being unique'
□ *focus* – seeing a particular buyer group or product market 'more effectively or efficiently than competitors who compete more broadly'.

He then developed his well-known framework of three generic strategies that organisations can use to gain competitive advantage:

□ *innovation* – being the unique producer
□ *quality* – delivering high-quality goods and services to customers
□ *cost leadership* – the planned result of policies aimed at 'managing away expense'.

Porter belongs to what Purcell (2001) describes as the 'positioning school' for whom strategy formulation is an analytical process and the focus is on how the firm positions itself in relation to the outside market in order to achieve competitive advantage. Internal matters, including HR, are given little or no attention.

A distinction has been made by Barney (1991) between the competitive advantage that a firm presently enjoys but others are able to copy, and sustained competitive advantage, which competitors cannot emulate. This leads to the important concept of distinctive capabilities, as examined later in this section.

Strategic intent

Hamel and Prahalad (1989) coined the term 'strategic intent', which can be described as an expression of purpose – what the organisation intends to do and how, as Wickens (1987) put it, it means to 'get from here to there'. Hamel and Prahalad explained that strategic intent refers to the expression of the leadership position the organisation wants to attain, and establishes a clear criterion by which progress towards its achievement is to be measured. The notion suggests that in its simplest form strategic intent could be a very broad statement of vision or mission – and/or it could more specifically spell out the goals and objectives to be attained over the longer term, and the ways in which those goals are to be attained.

The 'strategic intent sequence' is defined by Miller and Dess (1996) as:

1   a broad *vision* of what the organisation should be
2   the organisation's *mission*
3   specific *goals*, which are operationalised as
4   strategic *objectives*.

Strategic fit

The concept of strategic fit implies that to maximise competitive advantage a firm must match its capabilities and resources to the opportunities available in the external environment. Hofer and Schendel (1986) conclude that:

A critical aspect of top management's work today involves matching organisational competences (internal resources and skills) with the opportunities and risks created by environmental change in ways that will be both effective and efficient over the time such resources will be deployed.

This notion of strategic fit examines what the organisation as a whole must do. In the field of strategic HRM as outlined in Chapter 3, it has been extended to embrace the need for fit between HR and business strategy, and the concept has been further developed to cover the needs for both vertical integration in this sense, and for horizontal integration between the different components of HR strategy.

Resource-based strategy

The resource-based view of strategy is that the strategic capability of a firm depends on its resource capability, especially its distinctive resources. The resource-based view of the firm emphasises, in the words of Cappelli and Crocker-Hefter (1996), that 'Distinctive human resource practices help to create unique competences that differentiate products and services and, in turn, drive competitiveness.'

Resource-based strategy theorists such as Barney (1991) argue that sustained competitive advantage stems from the acquisition and effective use of bundles of distinctive resources that competitors cannot imitate. As Kay (1999) comments: 'The opportunities for companies to sustain competitive advantage are determined by their capabilities.' A distinctive capability or competence can be described as an important feature which in Quinn's (1980) phrase 'confers superiority on the organisation'. Kay (1999) extends this definition by emphasising that there is a difference between distinctive capabilities and reproducible capabilities. Distinctive capabilities are those characteristics that cannot be replicated by competitors, or can be imitated only with great difficulty. Reproducible capabilities can be bought or created by any company with reasonable management skills, diligence and financial resources. Most technical capabilities are reproducible. As Boxall (1996) comments: 'Competitive success does not come simply from making choices in the present; it stems from building up distinctive capabilities over significant periods of time.' Teece *et al* (1997) define 'dynamic capabilities' as 'the capacity of a firm to renew, augment and adapt its core competencies over time'.

Distinctive capabilities or core competences describe what the organisation is specially or uniquely capable of doing.

They are what the company does particularly well in comparison with its competitors. Key capabilities can exist in such areas as technology, innovation, marketing, delivering quality, and making good use of human and financial resources. If a company is aware of what its distinctive capabilities are, it can concentrate on using and developing them without diverting effort into less rewarding activities.

Four criteria have been proposed by Barney (1991) for deciding whether a resource can be regarded as a distinctive capability:

☐ value creation for the customer
☐ rarity, compared to the competition
☐ non-imitability
☐ non-substitutability.

Prahalad and Hamel (1990) argue that competitive advantage stems in the long term when a firm builds 'core competences' that are superior to its rivals', and when it learns faster and applies its learning more effectively than its competitors. The latter point provides the rationale for the concept of knowledge management.

Indeed, the whole theory of resource-based strategy, with its focus on distinctive capabilities, underpins the concept of strategic HRM by emphasising that the unique and non-imitable resources that create competitive advantage are the human resources of the organisation.

Strategic capability

Strategic capability is a concept that refers to the ability of an organisation to develop and implement strategies that will achieve sustained competitive advantage. It is therefore about the capacity to select the most appropriate vision, to define realistic intentions, to match resources to opportunities, and to prepare and implement strategic plans.

Strategic capability has been defined by Harrison (1997) as:

a capability that is based on a profound understanding of the competitive environment, the resource base and potential of the organisation, and the values that engender commitment from stakeholders to organisational goals. It provides the strategic vision, the rich and sustained knowledge development, the integrity of common purpose, and the durable coherent direction and scope to the activities of the firm that are needed to secure long-term survival and advancement.

The formulation of strategy

The formulation of corporate strategy can be defined as a process for developing and defining a sense of direction. It has often been described as a logical step-by-step affair, the outcome of which is a formal written statement that provides a definitive guide to the organisation's long-term intentions. Many people still believe and act as if this were the case – but it is a misrepresentation of reality. This is not to dismiss completely the ideal of adopting a systematic approach as described below. It has its uses as a means of providing an analytical framework for strategic decision-making and a reference-point for monitoring the implementation of strategy. But in practice, and for reasons also explained below, the formulation of strategy can never be as rational and linear a process as some writers describe it or as some managers attempt to make it.

The systematic approach to formulating strategy

In theory, the process of formulating strategy consists of the following steps:

1 Define the mission.
2 Set objectives.
3 Conduct internal and external environmental scans to assess internal strengths and weaknesses and external opportunities and threats (a SWOT analysis) and to analyse political, economic, social, technological, legal and environmental factors (a PESTLE analysis).
4 Analyse existing strategies to determine their relevance in the light of the internal and external appraisal. This may include gap analysis, which will establish the extent to which environmental factors might lead to gaps between what could be achieved if no changes were made

and what needs to be achieved. The analysis would also cover resource capability, answering the question 'Have we sufficient human or financial resources available now, or which can readily be made available in the future, to enable us to achieve our objectives?'

5 Define in the light of this analysis the distinctive capabilities of the organisation.

6 Define the key strategic issues emerging from the previous analysis. These will focus on such matters as product-market scope, enhancing shareholder value, and resource capability.

7 Determine corporate and functional strategies for achieving goals and competitive advantage, taking into account the key strategic issues. These may include business strategies for growth or diversification, or broad generic strategies for innovation, quality or cost leadership; or they could take the form of specific corporate/functional strategies concerned with product-market scope, technological development or human resource development.

8 Prepare integrated strategic plans for implementing strategies.

9 Implement the strategies.

10 Monitor implementation and revise existing strategies or develop new strategies as necessary.

This model of the process of strategy formulation allows scope for continuous evolution and feedback, and the activities incorporated in the model are all appropriate in any process of strategy formulation. But the model is essentially linear and deterministic – each step logically follows the previous one and is conditioned entirely by the preceding sequence of events. . .which is not what happens in real life.

The reality of strategy formulation – the process view

It has been said (Bower, 1982) that 'strategy is everything not well defined or understood'. This may be going too far, but strategy formulation can be described as 'problem-solving in unstructured situations' (Digman, 1990), and strategies are generally developed under conditions of partial ignorance. It is important to understand the processes by which strategies are formed, which may not be so deliberate as the classical school of strategy theorists would have us believe. The traditional approach to strategy largely ignored the process issues of implementation and attached insufficient importance to the resource implications of developing strategies or putting them into effect.

The difficulty is that strategies are often based on the questionable assumption that the future will resemble the past. Many years ago, Robert Heller (1972) had a go at the cult of long-range planning: 'What goes wrong', he wrote, 'is that sensible anticipation gets converted into foolish numbers – and their validity always hinges on large, loose assumptions.'

More recently, Faulkner and Johnson (1992) have said of long-term planning that it:

> was inclined to take a definitive view of the future, and to extrapolate trend lines for the key business variables in order to arrive at this view. Economic turbulence was insufficiently considered, and the reality that much strategy is formulated and implemented in the act of managing the enterprise was ignored. Precise forecasts ending with derived financial projections were constructed, the only weakness of which was that the future almost invariably turned out differently.

Mintzberg (1987) believes that strategy formulation is not necessarily a rational and continuous process. Rather than being consciously and systematically developed, strategy reorientation happens in what he calls brief 'quantum loops'. A strategy, according to Mintzberg, can be deliberate: it can realise the intentions of senior management – for example, to attack and conquer a new market. But this is not always the case. In theory, he says, strategy is a systematic process. First we think, then we act; we formulate, then we implement. But we also 'act in order to think'. In practice, 'a realised strategy can emerge in response to an evolving situation', and the strategic planner is often 'a pattern organiser, a learner, if you like, who manages a process in which strategies and visions can emerge as well as be deliberately conceived'.

Mintzberg was even more scathing about the weaknesses of strategic planning in his 1994 article in the *Harvard Business Review* on 'The rise and fall of strategic planning'. He contends that 'the failure of systematic planning is the failure of systems to do better than, or nearly as well as, human beings'. He went on to say that 'Far from providing strategies, planning could not proceed without their prior existence...Real strategists get their hands dirty digging for ideas, and real strategies are built from the nuggets they discover.' And 'Sometimes strategies must be left as broad visions, not precisely articulated, to adapt to a changing environment.'

Other writers have joined in this chorus of disapproval – Pettigrew and Whipp (1991), for example, wrote:

> Business strategy, far from being a straightforward, rational phenomenon, is in fact interpreted by managers according to their own frame of reference, their particular motivations and information.

Quinn (1980) offers further criticism:

> Although excellent for some purposes, the formal planning approach emphasises 'measurable quantitative forces' at the expense of the 'qualitative, organisational and power-behavioural factors that so often determine strategic success'. Large organisations typically construct their strategies with processes which are 'fragmented, evolutionary, and largely intuitive'.

Digman (1990) adds:

> The most effective decision-makers are usually creative, intuitive people 'employing an adaptive, flexible process'. Moreover, since most strategic decisions are event-driven rather than pre-programmed, they are unplanned.

Goold and Campbell (1986) also emphasise the variety and ambiguity of influences that shape strategy:

> Informed understandings work alongside more formal processes and analyses. The headquarters agenda

becomes entwined with the business unit agenda, and both are interpreted in the light of personal interests. The sequence of events from decision to action can often be reversed, so that 'decisions' get made retrospectively to justify actions that have already taken place.

Mintzberg (1978, 1987, 1994) summarises the non-deterministic view of strategy admirably. He perceives strategy as a 'pattern in a stream of activities' and highlights the importance of the interactive process between key players. He has emphasised the concept of 'emergent strategies', in which a key aspect is the production of something new to the organisation even if it is not developed as logically as the traditional corporate planners believed to be appropriate.

Kay (1999) also refers to the evolutionary nature of strategy. He comments that there is often little 'intentionality' in firms, and that it was frequently the market rather than the visionary executive which chose the strategic match that was most effective. Quinn (1980) produced the concept of 'logical incrementalism' which suggests that strategy evolves in several steps rather than being conceived as a whole.

Types of strategy

A fourfold typology of strategy has been formulated by Whittington (1993):

☐ *classical* – strategy formulation as a rational process of deliberate calculation: the process of strategy formulation is perceived as being separate from the process of implementation

☐ *evolutionary* – strategy formulation as an evolutionary process that is a product of market forces in which the most efficient and productive organisations win through

☐ *'processual'* – strategy formulation as an incremental process which evolves through discussion and disagreement. It may be impossible to specify what the strategy is until after the event (this is in line with the Mintzberg view)

☐ *systemic* – strategy is shaped by the social system in which it is embedded. Choices are constrained by the cultural and institutional interests of a broader society rather than by the limitations of those attempting to formulate corporate strategy.

As Legge (1995) comments, the Whittington 'processual' perspective inverts many of the assumptions of the classical perspective: 'Rather than strategy cascading down and driving the organisation, it is recognised as a way in which managers try to simplify and order a world too complex and chaotic for them to understand.'

Strategic management

The concepts of strategy and its main characteristics are operationalised by strategic management. This can be regarded as a continuing process which in theory consists of a sequence of activities – strategy formulation, strategic planning, implementation, review, and updating – but in practice, as noted above, is seldom applied so logically. Strategic management has been defined as:

> The set of decisions and actions resulting in the formulation and implementation of strategies designed to achieve the objectives of an organisation. (Pearce and Robinson, 1988)

> Concerned with policy decisions affecting the entire organisation, the overall objective being to position the organisation to deal effectively with its environment. (Gunnigle and Moore, 1994)

Strategic management means that managers are looking ahead at what they need to achieve in the middle or relatively distant future. They are concerned with the broader issues facing the organisation and the general directions in which they must go to deal with these issues and achieve longer-term objectives. They do not take a narrow or restricted view.

Strategic management deals with both ends and means. As its ends it describes a vision of what things should look like in a few years' time. As a means, it shows how it is expected that that vision will be realised. Strategic management is therefore visionary management, concerned with creating and conceptualising ideas of where the organisation should be going. But it is also empirical management which decides how in practice it is going to get there, bearing in mind that organisations exist in a constant state of change.

The focus is on identifying the organisation's mission and strategies – but attention has to be paid also to the resource base required to make it succeed. It is necessary always to remember that strategy is the means to create value. Managers who think strategically will have a broad and long-term view of where they are going. But they will also be aware that they are responsible firstly for planning how to allocate resources to opportunities that contribute to the implementation of strategy, and secondly for managing these opportunities in ways that will significantly add value to the results achieved by the firm.

Strategic management has been described by Burns (1992) as being primarily concerned with:

☐ the full scope of an organisation's activities, including corporate objectives and organisational boundaries

☐ matching the activities of an organisation to the environment in which it operates

☐ ensuring that the internal structures, practices and procedures enable the organisation to achieve its objectives

☐ matching the activities of an organisation to its resource capability, assessing the extent to which sufficient resources can be provided to take advantage of opportunities or to avoid threats in the organisation's environment

☐ the acquisition, divestment and reallocation of resources

☐ translating the complex and dynamic set of external and internal variables which an organisation faces into a structured set of clear future objectives that can then be implemented on a day-to-day basis.

The purpose of strategic management has been expressed by Rosabeth Moss Kanter (1984) as being to 'elicit the present actions for the future' in such a way that those involved become 'action vehicles – integrating and institutionalising mechanisms for change'. She goes on to say that:

Strong leaders articulate direction and save the organisation from change by drift...They see a vision of the future that allows them to see more clearly what steps to take, building on present capacities and strengths.

But beyond this rhetoric lies the reality of managers' attempting to behave strategically in conditions of uncertainty, change, and turbulence, even chaos. Strategic management is as much, if not more, about managing change during the process of implementation as it is about producing long-term corporate plans – a point emphasised by Purcell (1999), who suggested that 'We should be much more sensitive to processes of organisational change and avoid being trapped in the logic of rational choice.' He quotes with approval Johnson and Scholes (1997):

> Organisations which successfully manage change are those which have integrated their human resource management policies with their strategies and the strategic change process...Training, employee relations, compensation packages and so on are not merely operational issues for the personnel department – they are crucially concerned with the way in which employees relate to the nature and direction of the firm, and as such they can both block strategic change and be significant facilitators of strategic change.

This underlines the importance of the human resource element in achieving change. But it can be concluded from the analysis of strategic management in this chapter that it is as difficult as it is desirable, and this has to be borne in mind at all times when considering strategic HRM.

3 THE CONCEPT OF STRATEGIC HRM

The initial sections of this chapter contain definitions of strategic HRM and its aims, rationale and meaning. The chapter then deals at length with perhaps its most important feature – the concept of strategic fit, or integration between the various people management and development activities which go towards making up people management strategy. Finally, there is an examination of resource-based strategic HRM, which can be used as a basis for the development of strategies to manage people more effectively.

The role of intellectual capital in the development of strategic HRM and the various academic models of strategic HRM and approaches to formulating HR strategies are dealt with in the subsequent three chapters.

Strategic HRM

What is strategic HRM?

Strategic human resource management has been defined as:

> All those activities affecting the behaviour of individuals in their efforts to formulate and implement the strategic needs of the business. (Schuler, 1992)

> The pattern of planned human resource deployments and activities intended to enable the firm to achieve its goals. (Wright and McMahan, 1992)

Strategic HRM can be regarded as a general approach to the strategic management of human resources in accordance with the intentions of the organisation on the future direction it wants to take. It is concerned with longer-term people issues as part of the strategic management processes of the business. What emerges from this process is a stream of decisions over time which form the pattern adopted by the organisation for managing its human resources and define the areas in which specific HR strategies should be developed. Strategic HRM deals with macro-concerns about structure, values, culture, quality, commitment, matching resources to future needs, performance, competence, knowledge management and human resource development, and creating a positive climate of employee relations.

The aims of strategic HRM

The fundamental aim of strategic HRM is to generate strategic capability by ensuring that the organisation has the skilled, committed and well-motivated employees it needs to achieve sustained competitive advantage. Its narrower objective is to provide a sense of direction in an often turbulent environment so that the business needs of the organisation, and the individual and collective needs of its employees, can be met by the development and implementation of coherent and practical HR policies and programmes. As Dyer and Holder (1988) remark, strategic HRM should provide 'unifying frameworks which are at once broad, contingency-based and integrative'.

The rationale for strategic HRM

The rationale for strategic HRM rests on the perceived advantage of having an agreed and understood basis for developing approaches to managing people in the longer term. It has also been suggested by Lengnick-Hall and Lengnick-Hall (1990) that underlying this rationale in a business is the concept of achieving competitive advantage through HRM:

> Competitive advantage is the essence of competitive strategy. It encompasses those capabilities, resources, relationships and decisions which permit an organisation to capitalise on opportunities in the marketplace and to avoid threats to its desired position.

Increasingly, they claim, it is being acknowledged that the management of people is one of the key links in generating a competitive edge.

This rationale accepts the fact that the degree to which the concept of strategic HRM can be applied within organisations, and its form and content, will vary widely. It is understood that organisations may be so preoccupied with survival and managing the here-and-now that – perhaps unwisely – they do not have an articulated corporate or business strategy. In these circumstances, which are typical of many organisations in the UK where 'short-termism' has prevailed, strategic HRM cannot happen. A strategic approach to HR issues manifests itself only in an environment in which there is a strategic approach to corporate or business issues. In many, the HR function fulfils a primarily administrative and service role and is not at all concerned with strategic matters.

The meaning of strategic HRM

According to Hendry and Pettigrew (1986), strategic HRM has four implications:

- the use of planning
- a coherent approach to the design and management of personnel systems based on an employment policy and manpower strategy, and often underpinned by a 'philosophy'
- HRM activities and policies matched to some explicit business strategy
- the people of the organisation perceived as a 'strategic resource' for the achievement of 'competitive advantage'.

The main features of strategic HRM as defined by Dyer and Holder (1988) are:

- *organisational level* – Because strategies involve decisions about key goals, major policies and the allocation of resources, they tend to be formulated at the top
- *focus* – Strategies are business-driven and focus on organisational effectiveness; in this perspective people are thus viewed primarily as resources to be managed toward the achievement of strategic business goals
- *framework* – Strategies by their very nature provide unifying frameworks that are at once broad, contingency-based and integrative. They incorporate a full complement of HR goals and activities designed specifically to fit extant environments and to be mutually reinforcing or synergistic.

Strategic fit

The notion of strategic fit or integration, sometimes described as the matching model, is central to the concept of strategic HRM. The HR strategy should be aligned to the business strategy (vertical fit). Better still, HR strategy should be an integral part of the business strategy, contributing to the business planning process as it happens. Strategic integration is necessary to provide congruence between business and human resource strategy so that the latter supports the accomplishment of the former, and, indeed, helps to define it. This point was originally made by Fombrun *et al* (1984), who stated that:

> Just as firms will be faced with inefficiencies when they try to implement new strategies with outmoded structures, so they will also face problems of implementation when they attempt to effect new strategies with inappropriate HR systems. The critical management task is to align the formal structure and the HR systems so that they drive the strategic objectives of the organisation.

Horizontal integration or fit is required between the different elements of the people strategy. The aim is to achieve a coherent approach to managing people in which the various practices are mutually supportive.

Guest (1989b) has suggested that strategic human resource management is largely about integration. One of his key policy goals, as listed in Chapter 1, is to ensure that HRM 'is fully integrated into strategic planning so that HRM policies cohere both across policy areas and across hierarchies, and HRM practices are used by line managers as part of their everyday work'.

Walker (1992) has pointed out that HR strategies are functional strategies like financial, marketing, production or IT strategies. In many organisations long-range functional planning is a mandated element of the long-range business planning process.

HR strategies are different, however, in the sense that they are intertwined with all other strategies. The management of people is not a distinct function but the means by which all business strategies are implemented. HR planning should be an integral part of all other strategy formulations. Where it is treated separately, it needs nonetheless to be closely aligned.

Five types of fit have been identified by Guest (1997):

☐ fit as strategic interaction – linking HR practices to the external context

☐ fit as contingency – approaches which ensure that internal practices should respond to particular external factors such as the nature of the market

☐ fit as an ideal set of practices – the view that there are 'best practices' that all firms can adopt, to their advantage

☐ fit as Gestalt – an approach that emphasises the importance of finding an appropriate combination of practices

☐ fit as 'bundles' – the search for distinct configurations or 'bundles' of complementary practices in order to determine which is likely to be most effective.

Fit as an ideal set of practices (the 'best practice' approach), fit to the circumstances of the firm (the 'best fit' approach) and fit as bundles (the 'configurational' approach) are three possible approaches to strategic HRM. However, most discussions on the concept of fit or matching concentrate on vertical and horizontal fit, which are further described below.

Vertical fit

Vertical fit occurs where HR strategies are congruent with business strategies, match the firm's stage of development, take account of organisational dynamics, and are in line with the characteristics of the organisation. These can be classified as contingency models (Marchington and Wilkinson, 1996).

Congruence with business strategies

The whole concept of strategic HRM is predicated on the belief that HR strategies should be integrated with corporate or business strategies. Miller (1989) believes that for this state of affairs to exist it is necessary to ensure that management initiatives in the field of HRM are *consistent* – consistent with those decisions taken in other functional areas of the business, and consistent with an analysis of the product-market situation. The key is to make operational the concept of 'fit' – the fit of human resource management with the strategic thrust of the organisation. The development of operational links is an important characteristic of strategic HRM. Tyson and Witcher (1994) consider that 'human resource strategies can only be studied in the context of corporate and business strategies'.

Congruence with business strategies may mean aligning HR strategies to the strategic orientation of the firm. Different orientations establish the need for different types of people and require changes in approaches to investing in the firm's human capital. The most familiar classification of strategic orientation is that of Porter (1980), who distinguished three generic approaches: innovation, quality, and cost leadership.

Matching life-cycle stages

Matching the stage of the firm's development means aligning HR strategy to the business strategies appropriate at each stage of the life cycle of the business – start-up, maturity, decline or degeneration, re-generation or transformation. Clearly, the business strategies and therefore the HR strategies will differ, say, between a firm opening up on a greenfield site and one forced to embark on a comprehensive transformation programme.

Dynamics

The dynamics of organisational change exert a marked influence on HR strategies. A transformational programme in any part of the life cycle will indicate what specific organisational development and culture management strategies the organisation should adopt. Managing the transition between the present state and a future state will mean the development of change strategies and, possibly, new strategic approaches to the employment relationship. HR strategies may have to be developed to support business initiatives in such areas as total quality, customer care, organisational re-structuring, process re-engineering, product/market development, and require the introduction of new technology or production systems – eg computer-integrated manufacturing or just-in-time production.

Organisational characteristics

An alternative way of determining HR strategy requirements is to relate them to the overall characteristics of the organisation. The most familiar classification is that produced by Miles and Snow (1978), who distinguish between:

☐ 'defenders' who seek stability and believe in strict control

☐ 'prospectors' who seek new opportunities, focus on continuous development and believe in flexibility

☐ 'analysers' who seek to incorporate the benefits of both defenders and prospectors.

Problems in achieving vertical integration

Vertical integration (strategic fit between business and HR strategies) may be desirable but for a number of reasons it is not easy to achieve. Such reasons include:

☐ the diversity of strategic processes, levels and styles

☐ the complexity of the strategy formulation process

☐ the evolutionary nature of the business strategy

☐ the absence of articulated business strategies

☐ the qualitative nature of HR issues

☐ differing definitions of what there is to integrate with.

The diversity of strategic processes, levels and styles

The different levels at which strategy is formulated and the different styles adopted by organisations may make it difficult to develop a coherent view of what sort of HR strategies will fit the overall strategies and what type of HR contributions are required during the process of formulation.

It has been argued by Miller (1987) that to achieve competitive advantage, each business unit in a diversified corporation should tailor its HRM policy to its own product-market conditions, irrespective of the HRM policies being pursued elsewhere in the corporation. If this is the case, there may be coherence within a unit but not across the whole organisation, and it may be difficult to focus HR strategies on corporate needs. In a 'financial control' type of corporation, as defined by Goold and Campbell (1986) – ie one in which the centre is mainly concerned with financial results monitored against targets – there may be no pressure for the creation of a corporate culture and HR strategies to support it at the centre. But need this matter? The centre could exercise financial control while the strategic business units (SBUs) are allowed to go their own way, so far as strategic HRM is concerned – as long as they deliver the financial results expected of them. And there is no reason why the SBUs should not decide independently that the best way to achieve those results is to pursue their own version of strategic HRM.

The only time a serious problem is likely to emerge is when units have to be merged. Admittedly, synergy may have to be sacrificed and the organisation might not reap the benefits of a corporate management development and career planning strategy. But the choice on that has been made by those who are in organisational command, and if it is their loss, it is only they who can do anything about it.

The complexity of the strategy formulation process

As Hendry and Pettigrew (1986) maintain, strategy formulation and implementation is a complex interactive process heavily influenced by a variety of contextual and historical factors. In these circumstances, as David Guest (1991) has asked, how can there be a straightforward flow from the business strategy to the HR strategy? It has been pointed out by Truss (1999) that an assumption in some matching models of strategic HRM is that there is a simple linear relationship between business strategy and human resource strategy. But this assumption 'fails to acknowledge the complexities both between and within notions of strategy and human resource management...and is based on a rational model of organisations and individuals which takes no account of the significance of power, politics and culture'.

The evolutionary nature of business strategy

This phenomenon, and the incremental nature of strategy-making, may make it difficult to pin down the HR issues likely to be relevant. Hendry and Pettigrew (1990) suggest that there are limits to the extent to which rational HR strategies can be drawn up if the process of business strategic planning is itself irrational. Mintzberg's (1978) description of strategy as a *pattern* in a stream of decisions over time implies that it may be difficult to 'fit' HR strategy into the process in any well-defined way. HR strategies may well therefore be equally evolutionary and just as difficult to pin down to a set of definitive statements. If this is the case, why bother to seek the Holy Grail of strategic fit, which presupposes a certain rigidity that is not in keeping with the realities of organisational life and the chaotic conditions in which organisations have to subsist?

The absence of articulated business strategies

If, because of its evolutionary nature, the business strategy has not been clearly articulated, this would add to the problems of clarifying the business strategic issues that human resource strategies should address. But it should be noted that 'clearly articulated' in this context means that the business strategies are fully understood by those concerned. It does *not* mean that they have to be written down, although that may help to create understanding.

The qualitative nature of HR issues

Business strategies tend, or at least aim, to be expressed in the common currency of figures and hard data on portfolio management, growth, competitive position, market share, profitability, etc. HR strategies may deal with quantifiable issues such as resourcing and skill acquisition but are equally likely to refer to qualitative factors such as commitment, motivation, good employee relations and high employment standards. The relationship between the pursuit of policies in these areas and individual and organisational performance may be difficult to establish.

Integration with what?

The concept of strategic HRM implies that HR strategies must be totally integrated with corporate/business strategies in the sense that they both flow from and contribute to such strategies. But as Brewster (1993) argues, HR strategy may be subjected to considerable environmental pressure – for example, in Europe, by legislation over involvement. Pressures of this type may mean that HR strategies cannot be entirely governed by the corporate/business strategy.

The question has also to be asked 'To what extent should HR strategy take into account the interests of all the stakeholders in the organisation, employees in general as well as owners and management?'

In Storey's (1989) terms 'soft strategic HRM' places greater emphasis on the human relations aspect of people management, stressing security of employment, continuous development, communication, involvement and the quality of working life. 'Hard strategic HRM', on the other hand, emphasises the yield to be obtained by investing in human resources in the interests of the business. As Lengnick-Hall and Lengnick-Hall (1990) comment:

> There is now a growing realization that the overriding concern should be the yield from employees. Yield concentrates on the intricate web of costs and benefits that result from investing in and focusing human resource activities toward a certain set of activities and away from other behaviours and attitudes. Yield recognises both trade-offs and choices. Yield depends on shared responsibilities and collaboration across functional units and hierarchical levels.

Ideally, strategic integration should attempt to achieve a proper balance between the hard and soft elements. The emphasis may be on achieving corporate or business objectives, but it should be a process of planning with people in mind (Quinn Mills, 1983), taking into account the needs and aspirations of all the members of the organisation.

Whereas finding the Holy Grail of strategic fit may be desirable, it is still essential to appreciate how resource-based and intellectual capital theories inform approaches to the development of integrated HR strategies by providing a conceptual framework within which HR strategies that achieve strategic fit can be developed.

Resource-based strategic HRM

The concept of resource-based strategic HRM strategy is derived from the resource-based theory of business strategy as described in Chapter 2. The concept is founded on the belief that competitive advantage is obtained if a firm can obtain and develop human resources that enable it to learn faster and apply its learning more effectively than its rivals (Hamel and Prahalad, 1989).

Barney (1995) defines such human resources: 'Human resources include all the experience, knowledge, judgement, risk-taking propensity and wisdom of individuals associated with the firm.' While Kamoche (1996) suggests that 'In the resource-based view, the firm is seen as a bundle of tangible and intangible resources and capabilities required for product/market competition.'

The aim of a resource-based approach is to improve resource capability – achieving strategic fit between resources and opportunities and obtaining added value from the effective deployment of resources. Resource-based theory provides a rationale for strategic HRM but does not attempt to prescribe solutions as do the models described in Chapter 4.

In line with intellectual capital theory, resource-based theory emphasises that investment in people adds to their value to the firm. Resource-based HR strategy, as Barney (1991) indicates, can develop strategic capability. The strategic goal will be to 'create firms which are more intelligent and flexible than their competitors' (Boxall, 1996) by hiring and developing more talented staff and by extending their skills base. Resource-based strategic HRM is therefore concerned with the enhancement of the intellectual capital of the firm. As Ulrich (1998) comments:

> Knowledge has become a direct competitive advantage for companies selling ideas and relationships. The challenge to organisations is to ensure that they have the capability to find, assimilate, compensate and retain the talented individuals they need.

A convincing rationale for resource-based strategy has been produced by Grant (1991):

When the external environment is in a state of flux, the firm's own resources and capabilities may be a much more stable basis on which to define its identity. Hence, a definition of a business in terms of what it is capable of doing may offer a more durable basis for strategy than a definition based upon the needs (eg markets) which the business seeks to satisfy.

Unique talents among employees, including superior performance, productivity, flexibility, innovation, and the ability to deliver high levels of personal customer service are ways in which people provide a critical ingredient in developing an organisation's competitive position. People also provide the key to managing the pivotal interdependencies across functional activities and the important external relationships. It can be argued that one of the clear benefits arising from competitive advantage based on the effective management of people is that such an advantage is hard to imitate. An organisation's HR strategies, policies and practices are a unique blend of processes, procedures, personalities, styles, capabilities and organisational culture. One of the keys to competitive advantage is the ability to differentiate what the business supplies to its customers from what could be supplied to them by its competitors. Such differentiation can be achieved by having HR strategies which ensure that the firm has higher-quality people than its competitors, by developing and nurturing the intellectual capital possessed by the business, and by focusing on organisational learning.

A resource-based approach addresses methods of increasing the firm's strategic capability through the development of managers and other staff who can think and plan strategically, and who understand the key strategic issues. As Harrison (1997) notes:

> It is strategic capability that significantly determines the extent to which the organisation achieves the best possible fit between the unique tangible and intangible assets that it possesses and the competitive position it occupies in its environment. It involves selecting resources, and combinations of resources, most likely to generate the new strategic assets of the business.

The enhancement of strategic capability is an important part of the process of formulating a human resource management strategy, as described in Chapter 6.

Conclusions

Resource-based strategy can provide a strong base for strategic HRM. As Purcell (2001a) points out, 'It is to do with internal implementation and performance strategies.' He also suggests that change is especially important in HRM strategies 'since their concern is with the future, the unknown, thinking of and learning how to do things differently, undoing the ways things have been done in the past, and managing its implementation'.

This supports the argument that the processes of formulating and implementing HR strategies, as discussed in Chapter 6, are mainly about making decisions on what needs to be changed and managing those changes. It is, however, worth bearing in mind that HRM is concerned with the delivery of effective people management services as well as innovating new policies and practices. HR strategies could, therefore, focus on how those services can be maintained at the right level as well as on what changes should be made to them.

4 INTELLECTUAL CAPITAL: THE THEORY AND ITS PRACTICAL IMPLICATIONS

The concept of intellectual capital has climbed up the management agenda in recent years. Plant, machinery and other forms of capital are now recognised to account for only a fraction of an organisation's wealth. The rest of that wealth is bound up in the knowledge, skills, abilities and intellect of the people of the organisation, and their willingness and ability to apply them in the pursuit of organisational goals.

The theory of intellectual capital is closely related to much of what strategic HRM attempts to achieve in terms of building and maintaining the human capital resources required by the firm. It also encompasses the development of structure to ensure that people work effectively together, and that they exchange relevant information and ideas and make the best use of the resources of knowledge possessed by the organisation

Intellectual capital defined

Intellectual capital consists of the stocks and flows of knowledge, ability, skill and competence available to an organisation. These can be regarded as intangible resources which, together with tangible resources (money and physical assets), comprise the market or total value of a business. Bontis (1996, 1998) defines intangible resources as the factors other than financial and physical assets that contribute to the value-generating processes of a firm and are under its control. As described by Edvinson and Malone (1997), these incorporate the value of all relationships inside and outside the organisation including those with customers and suppliers. They also cover the values attached to such intangibles as goodwill, corporate image and brands.

The three elements of intellectual capital are:

□ *human capital* – defined in numerous ways by the various writers in the field. However, most have agreed that at the micro-level the term refers to the knowledge, skills and abilities of the employees in an organisation and can be 'made' by developing existing staff through training and development or 'bought' by attracting new staff with the skills and knowledge required

□ *social capital* – the stocks and flows of knowledge derived from networks of relationships within and outside the organisation. Social capital may also refer to the structure within which human capital is most effectively deployed, and includes the use of communication, involvement and other initiatives to facilitate the exchange of knowledge

□ *organisational capital* – defined by Youndt (2000) as the institutionalised knowledge possessed by an organisation that is stored in databases, manuals, etc. It is alternatively called *structural capital* (Edvinson and Malone, 1997), but the term 'organisational capital' is preferred by Youndt because, he argues, it conveys more clearly that this is the knowledge that the organisation actually *owns*. Organisational capital is most likely to be the object of knowledge management systems as organisations strive to find better ways to capture, store and use knowledge effectively.

The significance of intellectual capital

This threefold concept of intellectual capital indicates that while it is individuals who generate, retain and use knowledge (human capital), this knowledge is enhanced by the interactions between them (social capital) to generate the institutionalised knowledge possessed by an organisation (organisational capital). Clearly, it is the knowledge, skills and abilities of individuals that create value, which is why the focus has to be on means of attracting, retaining, developing and maintaining the human capital they represent.

But organisational effectiveness also depends upon making good use of their knowledge, which has to be developed, captured and exchanged (knowledge management) in order to create organisational capital. In relation to adding value in this way it should be remembered that, as stated by Daft and Weick (1984): 'Individuals come and go, but organisations preserve knowledge over time.' Or, as expressed more colourfully by Fitz-enj (2000): 'Organisational capital [knowledge] stays behind when the employee leaves; human capital is the intellectual asset that goes home every night with the employee.'

However, many companies are still naïve about the process of gathering, storing and using organisational capital, with the result that the departure of an individual often results in the loss of valuable organisational as well as human capital that is both difficult and expensive to replace. It is therefore imperative to capture individual knowledge through knowledge management processes as described in Chapter 10, but it is also important to take into account social capital considerations – that is, the way in which knowledge is developed through interaction between people and the way in which organisations can encourage individuals to share and apply their knowledge towards the achieving of business goals.

Bontis *et al* (1999) point out that it is flows as well as stocks that matter. Intellectual capital develops and changes over time, and a significant part is played in these processes by people acting together.

Vital intellectual capital is often lost to organisations simply because they fail to recognise it as an important strategic asset. Even those organisations that do recognise intellectual capital often fail to measure it effectively. The result is that they make hasty decisions that prove immensely costly in the long term. Strategies for managing human resources must therefore include tools to identify sources of intellectual capital and methods of measuring the contribution of human capital to achieving business goals and objectives. Only then can a realistic set of data be assembled on which to base business decisions about the resource needs of the organisation. However, in doing so, businesses developing HR strategies should recognise the difference between human capital and the associated concepts of social and organisational capital. If they do not, they risk losing vital knowledge and expertise that could make a real difference to their financial performance.

Human capital

Bontis *et al* (1999) give a definition of human capital:

> Human capital represents the human factor in the organ-
> isation; the combined intelligence, skills and expertise
> that gives the organisation its distinctive character. The
> human elements of the organisation are those that are
> capable of learning, changing, innovating and providing
> the creative thrust which if properly motivated can
> ensure the long-term survival of the organisation.

The term 'human capital' was coined by Schulz (1961), who
elaborated on the concept in 1981:

> Consider all human abilities to be either innate or
> acquired. Attributes...which are valuable and can be
> augmented by appropriate investment will be human
> capital.

But the idea of investing in human capital was first developed
by Adam Smith, who in *An Inquiry into the Nature and
Causes of the Wealth of Nations* (1776) contended that differences between the ways of individuals with different levels of
education and training reflected differences in the returns
necessary to defray the costs of acquiring those skills. The
return on investment in skills can therefore be compared to
the returns from investing in physical capital. But this comparison has its limitations. Firms own physical capital but
not their workers (except in a slave society).

Nevertheless, an accountancy approach to human capital
emphasising investment-and-return is taken by a number of
theorists. Davenport (1999) offers this model:

TOTAL HUMAN CAPITAL INVESTMENT =
(ABILITY + BEHAVIOUR) × EFFORT × TIME

However, he tempers this rather mechanical approach by
recognising the human element of human capital, and goes on
to comment:

> People possess innate abilities, behaviours and personal
> energy and these elements make up the human capital
> they bring to their work. And it is they, not their

employers, who own this capital and decide when, how and where they will contribute it. In other words, they can make choices. Work is a two-way exchange of value, not a one-way exploitation of an asset by its owner.

The point emphasised by Davenport – that workers as well as employers invest in human capital – is in accord with the economic theory of human capital. As expressed by Ehrenberg and Smith (1994), human capital theory 'conceptualises workers as embodying a set of skills which can be "rented out" to employers'.

For the worker, the expected returns on human capital investments are a higher level of earnings, greater job satisfaction, better career prospects, and, more secure employment. In today's conditions, investments by workers in developing transferable skills can be attractive as a means of increasing employability. The costs of such investments, as spelled out by Elliott (1991), take a psychological, social and monetary form. Psychological costs are those borne by individuals, perhaps the less able, who may find learning difficult. Social costs take the form of missed market opportunities (ie opportunity costs – the time devoted to investing in human capital that could have been spent on other activities). Monetary costs include both direct financial outlays and missed market opportunities. As suggested by Elliott, the decision to acquire skills is an investment decision. Individuals will invest in human capital if they believe that the benefits to them will exceed the costs they will incur. These benefits consist of the net addition to life-long earnings that results from selling skilled rather than unskilled labour.

Other definitions take a more humanist approach to human capital. For example, Fitz-enj (2000) comments:

> The value is not found in the initial output *per se*, but rather in the effect it has on enhancing the outputs of its operating-unit customers. As staff groups utilise human capital more effectively, they increase their contribution to the goals of the enterprise.

For the employer, the returns on investment in human capital is expected to be improvements in performance, productivity and flexibility, and the capacity to innovate that should result from enlarging the skills base and increasing levels of knowledge and competence. Schuller (2000) suggests that 'The general message is persuasive: skills, knowledge and competences are key factors in determining whether organisations and nations will prosper.'

Workers as assets

The added value that people can contribute to an organisation is emphasised by human capital theory. It regards people as assets and stresses that investment by organisations in people will generate worthwhile returns. The theory therefore underpins the philosophy of human resource management which, as developed in the 1980s, stated that employees should be treated as assets rather than costs.

Recent research by Youndt (2000) provides support for the idea that HR systems are fundamental in the development of intellectual capital. He found that investment in strategies to attract or develop talent were positively related to the stock of intellectual capital available.

But as Davenport (1999) maintains, the concept is limited – indeed, questionable – because

Workers should not be treated as passive assets to be bought, sold, and replaced at the whim of their 'owners' – increasingly, they actively control their own working lives.

The notion that companies own human assets as they own machines is unacceptable in principle and inapplicable in practice; it short-changes people by placing them in the same category as plant and equipment.

No system of 'human asset accounting' has succeeded in producing a convincing method of attaching financial values to human resources; in any case, this demeans the more intangible added value that can be delivered to organisations by people.

Employers must remember that workers, especially knowledge workers, may regard themselves as free agents who can choose how and where they invest their talents, time and energy. In recent years workers have become less loyal to the organisations that employ them. Many highly skilled employees see their knowledge as a bargaining chip not to be shared easily unless there are significant gains to be had. They expect employers to take an active role in the development of their skills, and as well as monetary reward they expect to be stimulated and challenged by their work, to have the flexibility to manage their lives positively, and to be managed effectively. As a result, people management practices should be given significant prominence in any strategy to get, retain and maximise the investment in human capital.

Measuring human capital

As yet there are few sophisticated tools to effectively measure human capital and its contribution to business goals and objectives. However, the Chartered Institute of Personnel and Development and other bodies recognise that this is an issue that urgently needs addressing. More and more companies have come to appreciate that human capital represents the means of securing competitive advantage, which has led to a greater interest in its measurement. Motives behind the quest for measurement tools include:

- Human capital constitutes a key element of the market worth of a company, and its value should therefore be included in the accounts as an indication to investors or those contemplating a merger or acquisition of the total value of a business, including its intangible as well as its tangible assets.
- The process of identifying measures and collecting and analysing information relating to them will focus the attention of the organisation on what needs to be done to find, keep, develop and make the best use of its human capital.
- Measurements of the value of human capital can provide the basis for resource-based HR strategies that are concerned with the development of the organisation's core competencies.
- Measurements can be used to monitor progress in

achieving strategic HR goals and generally to evaluate the effectiveness of HR practices.

The first, and to a certain extent the second, of these arguments were advanced in a pioneering study by Hermanson (1964). His views were popularised by Likert (1961), and in the 1960s and 1970s efforts were made to get the notion accepted by investors and businesses. To no avail. Members of the accountancy profession have, in the past, been dismissive of ideas because they believe that the figures would almost certainly be based on crude assumptions.

However, financial analysts and accountants are now actively seeking reliable measures of human capital because of the growing recognition of its significance to the overall value of organisations. Most practitioners in both the HR and financial fields accept that it is not possible to present one definitive value statement summarising the value of human capital but recognise that there are instead a number of indicators to be taken into account. The difficulty occurs in deciding what these indicators should be. An authoritative report by the OECD (1998) states that 'Measures of human capital have been strongly guided by what it is possible to measure, rather than by what it is desirable to measure.' Certainly, whereas some organisations have highly sophisticated models for measuring human capital, others rely on secondary quantitative data such as absence or staff turnover, and fail to fully develop methods of quantifying such abstract concepts as commitment, motivation or willingness to apply discretionary effort.

The result is that we are embedded in a situation in which human capital as cost is relatively easy to measure using hard metrics such as wages, cost of absenteeism, benefits, cost of training, etc. And yet the return on investment in human capital or its worth as an asset is much harder to measure because this value is rooted in things that can only be expressed using softer measures not always translatable into financial terms.

David Guest *et al* (2000b) found that despite the wealth of evidence that people management makes a significant difference to business performance, and despite the fact that no fewer than 70 per cent of CEOs believed it, only 10 per cent were willing to act upon it. One explanation for this is that the difficulties in measuring the contribution of human capital prevents business leaders from taking that contribution seriously.

There are, however, some models available that can prove helpful in the measurement of human capital and its contribution. LeBlanc *et al* (2000) assert that 'Human capital is optimised when there is significant *knowledge, motivation* and *opportunity* to perform.'

As 'knowledge' they are referring to investments in growing the base of talent through recruitment or development. 'Motivation' includes investment in reward, both financial and non-financial. And 'opportunity' is about investment in job content, making work meaningful and giving support, tools and enough job autonomy to add value.

Andrew Mayo (1999) believes that the secret of measuring human capital is in developing measures that are meaningful in terms of everyday business realities. It may not, therefore, be helpful to look for absolute measures but more useful to develop a set of indicators that measure change over time. He states:

> We need strategic and useful indicators of such [people] assets, in order to understand how value is changing. By definition, all measures of intellectual capital are predicting future success and they need the credibility to stand side by side with the so-called 'bottom-line' measures that track current performance.

Ernst and Young's *Measures that Matter* survey found that more than a third of the data used to justify business analysts' decisions were non-financial, and that when non-financial factors were taken into account better investment decisions were made, reducing the risk to investors. Their top ten list of the non-financial measures most valued by investors include eight human capital factors (see Table 2).

Table 2

NON-FINANCIAL METRICS MOST VALUED BY INVESTORS

METRIC	QUESTIONS TO WHICH MEASURABLE ANSWERS ARE REQUIRED
1 Strategy execution	How well does management leverage its skills and experience? Gain employee commitment? Stay aligned with shareholder interests?
2 Management credibility	What is management's behaviour and forthrightness in dealing with issues?
3 Quality of strategy	Does management have a vision for the future? Can it make tough decisions and quickly seize opportunities? How well does it allocate resources?
4 Innovativeness	Is the company a trendsetter or a follower? What's in the R&D pipeline? How readily does the company adapt to changing technologies and markets?
5 Ability to attract talented people	Is the company able to hire and retain the very best people? Does it reward them? Is it training the talent it will need tomorrow?
6 Market share	Is the company capturing the value of the current market? Is it well positioned to expand that value in the future?
7 Management experience	What is the management's staff history and background in the field, and their track record of performance?
8 Quality of executive compensation	Is executive pay tied to strategic goals? How well is it linked to the creation of shareholder value?
9 Quality of major processes	Does the organisation reduce risk – and enhance return – through the deft execution of its current operations? Is the transition seamless in changing conditions?
10 Research leadership	How well does management understand the link between creating knowledge and using it?

(Human capital factors are highlighted in bold.)
Based on Ernst and Young, *Measures that Matter*, Ernst and Young Center for Business Innovation Report, March 1997

Human asset accounting

Human asset accounting was a process which, in the words of Sackmann *et al* (1989), aimed to 'quantify the economic value of people to the organisation' in order to provide input for managerial and financial decisions.

Bontis *et al* (1999) refer to three types of human resource accounting models:

☐ cost models, which consider the historical, acquisition, replacement or opportunity cost of human assets

□ HR value models, which combine non-monetary behavioural with monetary economic value models

□ monetary models, which calculate discounted estimates of future earnings.

In their basic form, as indicated by Bontis *et al*, human resource or human asset accounting models attempt to calculate the contributions that human assets make to firms by capitalising pay expenditures. A discounted cash flow of total pay is included in the asset section of the balance sheet rather than classifying it as an expense.

The problem with human resource or asset accounting is that, as Bontis *et al* point out, 'All of the models suffer from subjectivity and uncertainty, and lack reliability in that the measures cannot be audited with any assurance.' It is for this reason that the notion of human resource accounting is not generally accepted by accountants or financial analysts. It can also be argued that it is morally unacceptable to treat people as financial assets, and that in any case, people are not 'owned' by the company.

But people in organisations do add value, and there is a case for assessing this value to provide a basis for HR planning and for monitoring the effectiveness and impact of HR policies and practices. This approach involves the assessment of the value or contribution to business success of HR practices generally rather than simply measuring the value of human capital. The aims are to measure how efficiently organisations are using their human capital, and, in the words of Mayo (1999), to assess 'the value of future earnings opportunities'.

Human capital and other aspects of intellectual capital theory

Important though human capital theory may be, interest in it should not divert attention from the other aspects of intellectual capital – social and organisational capital – which are concerned with developing and embedding the knowledge possessed by the human capital of an organisation. Schuller (2000) contends that

The focus on human capital as an individual attribute may lead – arguably, has already led – to a very unbalanced emphasis on the acquisition by individuals of skills and competences which ignores the way in which such knowledge is embedded in a complex web of social relationships.

Social capital

The term social capital has been in use since the 1960s when it was applied in community studies to emphasise the need for strong personal networks to stimulate effective community action. According to Nahpiet and Ghoshal (1998):

> The central proposition of social capital theory is that networks of relationships constitute a valuable resource for the conduct of social affairs. . .Much of this capital is embedded within networks of mutual acquaintance and recognition.

The concept of social capital has been defined by Putnam (1996) as 'the features of social life – networks, norms and trust – that enable participants to act together more effectively to pursue shared objectives'. The World Bank (2000) offers another definition on its website:

> Social capital refers to the institutions, relationships and norms that shape the quality and quantity of a society's social interactions. . .Social capital is not just the sum of the institutions which underpin a society – it is the glue that holds them together.

The World Bank also notes that social capital can be perceived as a set of *horizontal associations* between people, consisting of social networks and associated norms that have an effect on community, productivity and well-being. This brings us closer to the meaning and significance of the concept of social capital as an element of intellectual capital.

Coleman (1990) identified two characteristics of social capital: first, it is an aspect of the social structure; and second, it facilitates the actions of individuals within the structure

Social capital is knowledge tied up and developed by relationships among employees, partners, customers and suppliers. It is built by the exchange of such knowledge, and this requires a collaborative organisational environment in which knowledge and information can flow freely (Bontis, 1996; Coleman, 1990). Such an environment is more likely to exist in a 'boundary-less' organisation where the emphasis is on lateral processes, teams and taskforces that can leverage knowledge across the business. Social capital, as Schuller (2000) puts it, 'enables human capital to realise its potential'.

In summary, social capital defines the environment and structure in which human capital can flourish and be applied effectively to maximise the benefit to the organisation. Strategies for managing human resources would therefore be well advised to take account of social capital factors because they are likely to be important facilitators – or, if disregarded, barriers – to the effective utilisation of intellectual capital.

Organisational capital

Organisational or structural capital consists of the knowledge owned by the organisation rather than by individual employees. It can be described as *embedded* or *institutionalised* knowledge which may be retained with the help of information technology on readily accessible and easily extended databases. It can include explicit knowledge that has been recorded on a database or in manuals and standard operating procedures, or tacit knowledge that has been captured, exchanged and, as far as possible, codified. Yet it is individuals, not organisations, who own human capital. So, as Youndt (2000) claims, because employees are free, within limits, to leave their firm, there is a significant risk that organisations may incur an intellectual capital loss 'unless individual knowledge is transferred, shared, transformed and institutionalised'.

Any process or procedure in an organisation is constructed from the knowledge of individuals. As Davenport and Prusak (1998) comment:

> In theory this embedded knowledge is independent of those who developed it – and therefore has some organisational stability – an individual expert can disappear without bringing the process to a halt or reducing the company's stock of embedded knowledge.

Organisational capital is created by people (human capital) but is also the outcome of social capital interactions. It belongs to the firm and can be developed by knowledge management processes – as described in Chapter 9 – which aim to obtain and record explicit and tacit knowledge.

The management of knowledge and hence the development of organisational capital is often seen as an information management activity rather than an HR activity. However, the close relationship between organisational capital and its main input, human capital, strongly suggests that the development of organisational capital should be a central issue for strategic HRM.

Conclusions

The concept of intellectual capital and, in particular, the definition and measurement of human capital is fundamental to strategic HRM. However, as yet there are few widely recognised, effective measures of human capital. Although some organisations have highly-developed models of human capital, most tend to rely on what is measurable rather than seek what information is required to make effective decisions. At the time of writing, a CIPD-funded project is attempting to identify more robust indicators of the value of human capital, and address some of the problems of measurement discussed above.

If strategic HRM is to be effective, it must take at least some account of the need to recognise, retain and measure the contribution of intellectual capital.

5 MODELS OF STRATEGIC HRM

There are a number of models which, within the framework of the concept of strategic HRM, describe various approaches to its development and implementation. The models fall into two types. First there are those that refer to general approaches to strategic HRM as defined by Delery and Doty (1996) and Richardson and Thompson (1999). And second, there are those that prescribe particular approaches to the practice of strategic HRM – namely, resource capability, high-performance management (high-performance working), high-commitment management, and high-involvement management. These general and prescriptive models are examined in this chapter.

General models

The three main approaches to the development of HR strategies were described by Delery and Doty (1996) as the 'universalistic', the 'contingency' and the 'configurational'. Richardson and Thompson (1999) renamed the first two approaches as 'best practice' and 'best fit', but retained the description 'configurational', meaning the use of 'bundles', as the third approach. Guest (1997) refers to fit as an ideal set of practices – fit as contingency, and fit as 'bundles'.

The best-practice approach

This approach is based on the belief that there is a set of best HRM practices and that adopting them will lead to superior organisational performance. It is often associated with the high-performance model. Perhaps the best known set is Pfeffer's (1994) list of the seven HR practices of successful organisations:

1   *employment security* – This means that employees are not quickly made redundant in the face of such things as economic downturns or the strategic mistakes of senior management over which they have no control. It is fundamental to the implementation of such high-performance management practices as selective hiring, extensive training, information-sharing and delegation. Companies are unlikely to invest resources in the careful screening and training of new people if they are not expected to stay long enough with the firm for it to recoup its investment. And if the policy is to avoid lay-offs, the company will hire sparingly.

2   *selective hiring* – This requires the organisation to be clear about the critical skills and attributes it needs in order for it to make a choice on the basis of those attributes that are difficult or impossible to change and to train people in those behaviours and skills that are easily learned. It looks for people with the right attitudes, values and cultural fit – attributes that are harder to train or change and that predict performance and likelihood to remain with the company.

3   *self-managed teams* – These are a critical component of high-performance management systems. They (a) substitute peer-based control for hierarchical control of work, (b) by such substitution allow the removal of layers of hierarchy, and (c) permit employees to pool their ideas in order to produce better and more creative solutions to work problems.

4   *high compensation contingent on performance* – This also figures in most high-performance work systems. Such compensation can be contingent on organisational performance – eg gainsharing or profit sharing – or it can be related to individual or team performance or individual skill.

5   *training* – Virtually all descriptions of high-performance work practices emphasise the importance of training to provide a skilled and motivated workforce that has the knowledge and capability to perform the requisite tasks.

6   *reduction of status differentials* – The fundamental premise of high-performance work systems is that

organisations perform at a higher level if they are able to tap into the ideas, skill and effort of all their people. But this will not happen if status differentials send signals that people are not both valuable and valued. This is not the message that is delivered if status differences exist.

7   *sharing information* – This is an essential component of high-performance work systems for two reasons. First, the sharing of information on the firm's financial performance and business strategies conveys to employees the fact that they are trusted. Second, even motivated and trained people cannot contribute to enhancing organisational performance if they do not have information on important dimensions of performance and, in addition, training in how to interpret and use that information.

The 'best practice' rubric has been attacked by a number of commentators. Cappelli and Crocker-Hefter (1996) comment that the notion of a single set of best practices has been overstated:

> There are examples in virtually every industry of firms that have very distinctive management practices. . . Distinctive human resource practices shape the core competencies that determine how firms compete.

Purcell (1999) has also criticised the best-practice or universalist view by pointing out the inconsistency between a belief in best practice and the resource-based view which focuses on the intangible assets, including HR, that allow a firm to do better than its competitors. He asks, how can 'the universalism of best practice be squared with the view that only some resources and routines are important and valuable by being rare and imperfectly imitable?' The danger, as Legge (1995) points out, is that of 'mechanically matching strategy with HRM policies and practices'.

In accordance with contingency theory, it is difficult to accept that there is any such thing as universal best practice. What works well in one organisation will not necessarily work well in another because it may not fit its strategy, culture, management style, technology or working practices. As Becker *et al* (1997) remark: 'Organisational high-performance work systems are highly idiosyncratic and must be tailored carefully to each firm's individual situation to achieve optimum results.' But a knowledge of best practice as long as it is understood *why* it is best practice can inform decisions on what practices are most likely to fit the needs of the organisation. And Becker and Gerhart (1996) argue that the idea of best practice might be more appropriate for identifying the principles underlying the choice of practices, as opposed to the practices themselves

Best fit

For the reasons given above, it is accepted by most commentators that 'best fit' is more important than 'best practice'. There can be no universal prescriptions for HRM policies and practices. It all depends. This is not to say that 'good practice' or 'leading-edge practice' – ie practice that does well in one successful environment – should be ignored. Benchmarking has its uses as a means of identifying areas for innovation or development that are practised to good effect elsewhere by leading companies. But having learned about what works and, ideally, what does not work in comparable organisations, it is up to the firm to decide what may be relevant in general terms and what lessons can be learned that can be adapted to fit its own particular strategic and operational requirements. The starting-point should be an analysis of the business needs of the firm within its context (culture, structure, technology and processes). This may indicate clearly what has to be done. Thereafter, it may be useful to pick and mix various 'best practice' ingredients, and develop an approach which applies those that are appropriate in a way that is aligned to the identified business needs.

But there are problems with the best-fit approach, as stated by Purcell (1999) who, having rubbished the concept of best practice, proceeded to do the same for the notion of best fit:

> Meanwhile, the search for a contingency or matching model of HRM is also limited by the impossibility of modelling all the contingent variables, the difficulty of showing their interconnection, and the way in which changes in one variable have an impact on others.

In Purcell's view, organisations should be less concerned with best fit and best practice, and much more sensitive to processes of organisational change so that they can 'avoid being trapped in the logic of rational choice'.

The configurational approach

As Richardson and Thompson (1999) comment, 'A strategy's success turns on combining "vertical" or external fit and "horizontal" or internal fit.' They conclude that a firm with bundles of HR practices should have a higher level of performance, provided it also achieves high levels of fit with its competitive strategy.

This has emphasised the importance of 'bundling' – the development and implementation of several HR practices together so that they are interrelated and therefore complement and reinforce each other. The process is sometimes referred to as the use of 'complementarities' (MacDuffie, 1995) or as the adoption of a 'configurational mode' (Delery and Doty, 1996).

MacDuffie (1995) explained the concept of bundling:

> Implicit in the notion of a 'bundle' is the idea that practices within bundles are interrelated and internally consistent, and that 'more is better' with respect to the impact on performance, because of the overlapping and mutually reinforcing effect of multiple practices.

Dyer and Reeves (1995) note that 'The logic in favour of bundling is straightforward. . .Since employee performance is a function of both ability and motivation, it makes sense to have practices aimed at enhancing both.' There are thus several ways in which employees can acquire needed skills (such as careful selection and training) and multiple incentives to enhance motivation (different forms of financial and non-financial rewards). A study by Dyer and Reeves (1995) of various models listing HR practices which create a link between HRM and business performance found that the activities appearing in most of the models were involvement, careful selection, extensive training, and contingent compensation.

On the basis of his research in flexible production manufacturing plants in the United States, MacDuffie (1995) noted that flexible production gives employees a much more central role in the production system. They have to resolve problems as they appear on the line, and this means that they have to possess both a conceptual grasp of the production process and the analytical skills to identify the root cause of problems. But the multiple skills and conceptual knowledge developed by the workforce in flexible production firms are of little use unless workers are motivated to contribute mental as well as physical effort. Such discretionary effort on problem-solving will only be contributed if workers 'believe that their individual interests are aligned with those of the company, and that the company will make a reciprocal investment in their well-being'. This means that flexible production techniques have to be supported by bundles of high-commitment human resource practices such as employment security, pay that is partly contingent on performance and a reduction of status barriers between managers and workers. Company investment in building worker skills also contributes to this 'psychological contract of reciprocal commitment'. The research indicated that plants using flexible production systems which bundle human resource practices into a system integrated with production/business strategy outperform plants using more traditional mass-production systems in both productivity and quality.

Following research in 43 automobile processing plants in the USA, Pil and MacDuffie (1996) established that when a high-involvement work practice is introduced in the presence of complementary HR practices, not only does the new work practice produce an incremental improvement in performance but so do the complementary practices.

The aim of bundling is to achieve coherence, which is one of the four 'meanings' (implications) of strategic HRM defined by Hendry and Pettigrew (1986). Coherence exists when a mutually reinforcing set of HR policies and practices have been developed which jointly contribute to the attainment of the organisation's strategies for matching resources to organisational needs, improving performance and quality and, in commercial enterprises, achieving competitive advantage.

In one sense, strategic HRM is holistic – it is concerned with the organisation as a total entity and addresses what needs to be done across the organisation as a whole in order to enable it to achieve its corporate strategic objectives. It is not interested in isolated programmes and techniques, or in the *ad hoc* development of HR programmes.

In their discussion of the four policy areas of HRM (employee influence, human resource management flow, reward systems, and work systems) Beer *et al* (1984) suggested that this framework can stimulate managers to plan how to accomplish the major HRM tasks 'in a unified, coherent manner rather than in a disjointed approach based on some combination of past practice, accident and *ad hoc* response to outside pressures'.

David Guest (1989b) includes in his set of propositions for HRM the point that strategic integration is about, *inter alia*, the ability of the organisation to ensure that the various aspects of HRM cohere. One way of looking at the concept is to say that some measure of coherence will be achieved if there is an overriding strategic imperative or driving force such as customer service, quality, performance or the need to develop skills and competences, and this initiates various processes and policies designed to link together and operate in concert to deliver certain specific results. For example, if the driving force were to improve performance, competence profiling techniques could be used to specify recruitment standards, identify learning and development needs, and indicate the standards of behaviour or performance required. The competence frameworks could be used as the basis for human resource planning and in development centres. They could also be incorporated into performance management processes in which the aims are primarily developmental and in which competencies are used as criteria for reviewing behaviour and assessing learning and development needs. Job evaluation could be based on levels of competence, and competence-based pay systems could be introduced. This ideal would be difficult to achieve as a 'grand design' that could be put into immediate effect, and might have to be developed progressively.

The major problem with the bundling approach is that of deciding which is the best way to relate different practices together. There is no evidence that one bundle is generally better than another, although the use of performance management practices and competence frameworks are two ways typically adopted to provide for coherence across a range of HR activities. *Pace* the findings of MacDuffie, there is no conclusive proof that in the UK bundling has actually improved performance.

The high-performance working model

High-performance working involves the development of a number of interrelated approaches which together make an impact on the performance of the firm through its people in such areas as productivity, quality, levels of customer service, growth, profits, and, ultimately, the delivery of increased shareholder value. This is achieved by 'enhancing the skills and engaging the enthusiasm of employees' (Stevens, 1998). According to Stevens, the starting-point is leadership, vision and benchmarking to create a sense of momentum and direction, measuring progress constantly. He suggests that the main drivers, support systems and culture are:

- decentralised, devolved decision-making undertaken by those closest to the customer – so as constantly to renew and improve the offer to customers
- development of people capacities through learning at all levels, with particular emphasis on self-management and team capabilities – to enable and support performance improvement and organisational potential
- performance, operational and people management processes aligned to organisational objectives – to build trust, enthusiasm and commitment to the direction taken by the organisation
- fair treatment for those who leave the organisation as it changes, and engagement with the needs of the community outside the organisation – this is an important component of trust and commitment-based relationships both within and outside the organisation.

High-performance management practices include rigorous recruitment and selection procedures, extensive and relevant training and management development activities, incentive pay systems and performance management processes.

In the United States this approach is described as the use of high-performance work systems or practices. The characteristics of a high-performance work system were defined by the US Department of Labor (1993) as:

- careful and extensive systems for recruitment, selection and training
- formal systems for sharing information with the individuals who work in the organisation
- clear job design
- high-level participation processes
- monitoring of attitudes
- performance appraisals
- properly functioning grievance procedures
- promotion and compensation schemes that provide for the recognition and financial rewarding of the high-performing members of the workforce.

High-performance working may involve the adoption of high-performance design methods as described by Buchanan (1987). These require certain steps:

- Management clearly defines what it needs in the form of new methods of working and the results expected following their introduction.
- Management sets goals and standards for success.
- Multiskilling is encouraged – that is, job demarcation lines are eliminated as far as possible and encouragement and training are provided for employees to acquire new skills.
- Equipment is selected that can be used flexibly and is laid out to allow freedom of movement and vision.
- Self-managed teams or autonomous working groups are established.
- Managers and team leaders adopt a supportive rather than an autocratic style (this is the most difficult part of the system to introduce).
- Support systems are provided that help the teams to function effectively as operating units.

□ The new system is introduced with great care by means of involvement and communication programmes.

□ Thorough training is carried out on the basis of an assessment of training needs.

□ The payment system is specially designed with employee participation to fit their needs as well as those of management.

□ Payment may be related to team performance (team pay) but with skill-based pay for individuals.

□ In some cases, a 'peer performance review' process may be used which involves team members assessing one another's performance as well as the performance of the team as a whole.

The high-commitment management model

One of the defining characteristics of HRM is its emphasis on the importance of enhancing mutual commitment (Walton, 1985). High-commitment management has been described by Wood (1996) as:

> a form of management which is aimed at eliciting a commitment so that behaviour is primarily self-regulated rather than controlled by sanctions and pressures external to the individual, and relations within the organisation are based on high levels of trust.

Ways to achieve high commitment as described by Beer *et al* (1984) and Walton (1985) are:

□ the development of career ladders and an emphasis on trainability and commitment as highly valued characteristics of employees at all levels in the organisation

□ a high level of functional flexibility, with the abandonment of potentially rigid job descriptions

□ the reduction of hierarchies and the ending of status differentials

□ a heavy reliance on team structure for disseminating information (team briefing), structuring work (teamworking) and problem-solving (quality circles).

Wood and Albanese (1995) added to this list:

☐ job design as something management consciously does in order to provide jobs that have a level of considerable intrinsic satisfaction

☐ a policy of no compulsory lay-offs or redundancies and permanent employment guarantees, with the possible use of temporary workers to cushion fluctuations in the demand for labour

☐ new forms of assessment and payment systems and, more specifically, merit pay and profit sharing

☐ a high involvement of employees in the management of quality.

The high-involvement management model

This approach involves treating employees as partners in the enterprise whose interests are respected and who have a voice on matters that concern them. Focused on communication and participation, the aim is to create a climate in which a continuing dialogue between managers and the members of their teams takes place in order to define expectations and share information on the organisation's mission, values and objectives. This establishes full mutual understanding of what is desired, and a framework for managing and developing people to ensure that it is achieved.

Five key high-involvement work practices have been identified by Pil and MacDuffie (1999):

☐ 'on-line' work teams

☐ 'off-line' employee involvement activities and problem-solving groups

☐ job rotation

☐ suggestion programmes

☐ decentralisation of quality efforts.

From their research in the US motorcar industry, they concluded that there was clear evidence that high-involvement work practices result in superior performance, although they acknowledged that there is tremendous variance in such practices' use and implementation. They referred to a review by the US Department of Labor (1993) which established that of 29 studies focusing on the links between high-involvement work practices and performance, the majority found significant positive effects, and only two found negative effects. They also quoted the conclusions of Ichniowski and Kochan (1995) that high-involvement work practices have a clear and demonstrated effect on productivity, and such effects 'are large enough to be economically important to the businesses that adopted the new practices'.

Conclusions

The general models describing the best practice, best-fit and configurational approaches to strategic HRM provide a useful conceptual framework which can help in the analysis and development of HR strategies. The other models in this chapter, however, are prescriptive and should be treated with some caution. They describe best practice under various headings. This may interest and be helpful to practitioners who are looking for a starting-point in the development of a people management and development strategy, but for the reasons given earlier, the 'best practice' approach has severe limitations. Best fit is perhaps more helpful and allows for the influence of distinctive business drivers such as specific sector, market or economic forces.

Any one or combination of these approaches may prove helpful in the development of strategy although, as noted by the CIPD (2001b), 'an emerging consensus favours what has become known as the "high-performance management approach"'. But it will still be necessary to consider how such an approach or any other model is likely to be most appropriate in particular organisational circumstances.

6 THE DEVELOPMENT AND DELIVERY OF HR STRATEGIES

Within the sections listed below, this chapter provides a conceptual framework for the practical issues explored in later parts of this book – especially the final chapter, which deals with the formulation and implementation of HR strategies. The sections comprise and deal with:

- □ an introductory summary of propositions relating to the formulation of HR strategy
- □ the process issues affecting the formulation of strategy
- □ the key concepts and issues affecting the nature of HR strategy
- □ the agenda for HR strategies
- □ the development process
- □ the implementation process.

Strategy formulation propositions

Boxall (1993) has drawn up a number of useful propositions concerning the formulation of HR strategy:

- □ There is typically no single HR strategy in a firm.
- □ Business strategy may be an important influence on HR strategy, but it is only one of several factors and the relationship is not unilinear.
- □ Implicit (if not explicit) in the mix of factors that influence the shape of HR strategies is a set of historical compromises and trade-offs from stakeholders.
- □ Management may seek to shift the historical pattern of HR strategy significantly in response to major contextual change, but not all managements will respond in the same way or equally effectively.

- ☐ The strategy formation process is complex, and excessively rationalistic models that advocate formalised links between strategic planning and HR planning are not particularly helpful to our understanding of it.
- ☐ Descriptions of the dimensions that underpin HR strategies are critical to the development of useful typologies but remain controversial, in that no one set of constructs has established an intellectual superiority over the others.

Process issues

There are a number of process issues that affect the ways in which strategy is formulated. These are concerned with the problematical nature of strategic HRM, the overall complexity of the process, and the existence of different approaches to the development of strategy.

The problematical nature of HR strategy

It is not too difficult to conceptualise strategic HRM. It is much harder to assess what factors organisations should take into account and what processes they can use when developing and implementing strategies. Account has also to be taken of the problematical nature of HR strategy as a formal, well-articulated and linear process that flows logically from the business strategy. Tyson (1997) points out that:

> The process by which strategies come to be realised is not only through formal HR policies or written directions: strategy realisation can also come from actions by managers and others. Since actions provoke reactions (acceptance, confrontation, negotiation, etc), these reactions are also part of the strategy process.

He suggests that:

- ☐ Strategy has always been emergent and flexible – it is always 'about to be', it never exists at the present time.
- ☐ Strategy is not only realised by formal statements but comes about also by actions and reactions.
- ☐ Strategy corresponds to a description of a future-orientated action intended to lead to change.

□ The management process itself conditions the strategies that emerge.

When considering approaches to the formulation of HR strategy, the interactive (not unilinear) relationship between business strategy and HRM should be emphasised, as Hendry and Pettigrew (1990) have done. They pointedly note the limits of excessively rationalistic models of strategic and HR planning. Purcell (2001a) believes that:

> Big strategies in HRM are most unlikely to come, *ex cathedra*, from the board as a fully-formed written strategy or planning paper. Strategy is much more intuitive and often only 'visible' after the event seen as 'emerging patterns of action'. This is especially the case where much of the strategy, as in HRM, is to do with internal implementation and performance strategies, not exclusively to do with external market ploys.

The complexity of the process

Many different routes may be followed when formulating HR strategies. On the basis of their research in 30 well-known companies, Tyson and Witcher (1994) commented that 'The different approaches to strategy form[ul]ation reflect different ways to manage change and different ways to bring the people part of the business into line with business goals.'

In strategic HRM, process may be as important as content. Tyson and Witcher (1994) also noted from their research that:

> The process of formulating HR strategy was often as important as the content of the strategy ultimately agreed. It was argued that by working through strategic issues and highlighting points of tension, new ideas emerged and a consensus over goals was found.

The research conducted by Armstrong and Long (1994) and our more recent research has indicated that many approaches can be adopted to the formulation of HR strategy – there is no one right way.

Concepts of strategy development

Purcell (2001a) has identified three main schools of strategy development: the design school, the process school, and the configuration school.

The design school is deliberate, and is 'based on the assumption of economic rationality'. It uses quantitative rather than qualitative tools of analysis and focuses on market opportunities and threats. What happens inside the company is 'mere administration or operations'.

The process school adopts a variety of approaches and is concerned with how strategies are made and what influences strategy formulation: 'It is much more a study of what actually happens, with explanations coming from experience rather than deductive theory.' As Purcell suggests, the implication of the design concept is that 'everything is possible' while that of the process school is that 'little can be done except swim with the tide of events'. The rationalist approach adopted by Purcell's design school broadly corresponds with the classical approach to strategy, and Porter is a typical representative of it. Purcell's process school is the post-modern version of strategy of which Mintzberg is the most notable exponent. Nonetheless, as Grant (1998) cited by Purcell (2001a) has indicated, the rationalist approach may indeed be over-formalised and rely too much on quantitative data, but the Mintzberg approach – which downplays the role of systematic analysis and emphasises the role of intuition and vision – fails to provide a clear basis for reasoned choices.

Additionally, Purcell (2001a) refers to what he calls the 'configuration' school (confusingly, the term 'configurational' is also used by Delery and Doty (1996) to describe 'bundling', as mentioned in Chapter 3). Purcell's notion of a configuration school draws attention to three beliefs: first, that strategies vary according to the life cycle of the organisation; second, that they will be contingent to the sector of the organisation; and third, that they will be about change and transformation. The focus is on implementation strategies, which is where Purcell thinks HR can play a major role.

Key concepts and issues

There are a number of concepts and issues that affect the nature of strategy and its development. These comprise the overarching concept of resource capability, and the issues that centre on the relationship between HR and business strategies (vertical fit) and the achievement of horizontal fit.

Resource capability

The fundamental notion of resource-based strategy as described in Chapter 2 provides the inspiration for the concept of resource capability. This regards the firm as a bundle of tangible and intangible resources and capabilities required for product/market competition (Kamoche, 1996). Human resources are perceived as a major source of competitive advantage.

As expressed by Kamoche, the basis of this approach to HR strategy is the acknowledgement of the 'stock of know-how' in the firm. The capability-based framework is concerned with the actions, processes and related behavioural efforts required to attain a competitive position. Schuler and Jackson (1999) note that 'Within this framework, firms attempt to gain competitive advantage using human resources through developing distinctive capabilities (competencies) that arise from the nature of the firm's relationships with its suppliers, customers and employees.'

Kamoche (1996) describes the resource-capability view of the firm as one that 'builds on and provides a unifying framework for the field of strategic human resource management'.

A resource-capability approach is concerned with the acquisition, development and retention of human capital. It focuses on how added value can be obtained by treating people as strategic assets in the sense that they perform activities which create advantage in particular markets. It emphasises the importance of knowledge management to enhance the intellectual capital of the organisation. It is concerned with developing reward strategies that drive desired behaviours. This is in accord with the fundamental principle of economics that wealth is created when assets are moved from lower-value to higher-value uses.

Alignment to business strategy

The formulation of HR strategies is conceived as a process that is closely aligned to the formulation of business strategies. Schuler (1992) stated that 'It is the linking of HR policies and practices to the firm's business objectives and plans that defines strategic human resource management and differentiates it from the older practice of personnel management.'

People management strategy will influence as well as be influenced by business strategy. This does not mean that product, market and financial considerations are not important, but rather that decisions in these areas will be informed by detailed knowledge of the capability of the organisation in terms of its intellectual capital. For example, knowledge that certain skills exist in the organisation may prompt a decision to diversify in a particular direction.

This contribution may be more significant if strategy formulation is an emergent or evolutionary process such that the organisation builds upon its knowledge of the capability of its people or capitalises on improvements in skills and abilities. A forward-thinking people management strategy may cause the organisation to pursue more ambitious business aims that require a greater level of knowledge, ability or innovative capacity from the people of the organisation.

A distinction is made by Purcell (1989) and Purcell and Ahlstrand (1994) between:

☐ *'upstream' first-order decisions*, which are concerned with the long-term direction of the enterprise or the scope of its activities

☐ *'downstream' second-order decisions*, which are concerned with internal operating procedures and how the firm is organised to achieve its goals

☐ *'downstream' third-order decisions*, which are concerned with choices on human resource structures and approaches and are strategic in the sense that they establish the basic parameters of employee relations management in the firm.

It can, indeed, be argued that HR strategies – like other functional strategies such as those for product development, manufacturing and the introduction of new technology – will be developed within the context of the overall business strategy, but this need not imply that HR strategies come third in the pecking order. Observations made by Armstrong and Long (1994) during research into the strategy formulation processes of ten large UK organisations suggested that there were only two levels of strategy formulation:

□ the corporate strategy relating to the vision and mission of the organisation but often expressed in terms of marketing and financial objectives

□ the specific strategies within the corporate strategy concerning product/market development, mergers and acquisitions, divestments, human resources, finance, new technology, and such overall aspects of management as quality productivity, innovation and cost reduction.

When considering how to integrate business and HR strategies it should be remembered that business and HR issues influence each other and in turn influence corporate and business unit strategies. Note also that in establishing these links, account must be taken of the fact that strategies for change have additionally to be integrated with changes in the external and internal environments. Fit may exist at one point in time, but when circumstances change, there may no longer be fit. An excessive pursuit of 'fit' with the *status quo* will inhibit the flexibility of approach essential in turbulent conditions. This is the 'temporal' factor in achieving fit identified by Gratton *et al* (1999). A further factor which makes the achievement of good vertical fit difficult is that the business strategy may not be clearly defined – it could be in an emergent or evolutionary state. This would mean that there could be nothing with which to make the HR strategy fit.

Achieving horizontal fit

Horizontal fit is achieved when the various HR strategies cohere and are mutually supporting. This can be attained by the process of 'bundling' – ie the use of complementary HR practices, also known as 'configuration'.

Bundling implies the adoption of a holistic approach to the development of HR strategies and practices. No single aspect of HR strategy should be considered in isolation. Links between one area and other complementary areas must be established so that the ways in which they can provide mutual support to the achievement of the overall strategy can be ascertained. The synergy that can result from this process means that the impact of the whole bundle on organisational effectiveness can be greater than the sum of its parts. A job family pay structure can thus be associated with competence frameworks and profiles and the definition of career paths as a basis for identifying and meeting development needs. The message provided by the pay structure that rewards follow from career progression is much more powerful if it is linked to processes that enable people to develop their capabilities and potential.

The strategic agenda

The strategic agenda for HR is affected by the key business issues, together with the contextual factors related to the external and internal environment of the organisation. Preparing the agenda involves considering what HR policies and practices should be developed, bearing in mind the need to achieve vertical and horizontal fit or alignment.

Key business issues

The key business issues that may impact on HR strategies include:

- intentions concerning growth or retrenchment, acquisitions, mergers, divestments, diversification, product/market development
- the implications of globalisation and international operations and the impact of worldwide recessions
- proposals on increasing competitive advantage through innovation leading to product/service differentiation, productivity gains, improved quality/customer service, cost reduction (downsizing)
- a perceived need to develop a more positive, performance- or customer-orientated culture
- any other culture management imperatives associated

with changes in the philosophies of the organisation in such areas as gaining commitment, developing what the Hay Group (2001) call 'engaged performance', mutuality, communications, involvement, devolution and teamworking.

Business strategies in these areas may well be influenced by HR factors, but crucially these strategies will be difficult to implement without a well-thought-through and integrated people management strategy that includes an analysis of the HR opportunities and constraints.

Contextual factors

The contextual factors include the external business, social and economic environment and the internal environment of the organisation. The latter consists of its culture and core values, its social system (the ways in which work groups are organised, and the processes of interaction that take place), and its technical system (the ways in which the work is organised and carried out to deliver products or services to customers). The internal environment is also increasingly being shaped by the use of technology.

As Ulrich (1998) emphasises, environmental and contextual changes present a number of competitive challenges to organisations which mean that the HR strategic agenda has to focus on helping to build new capabilities. He concludes that the main issues are:

□ *globalisation* – which requires organisations to move people, ideas, products and information around the world to meet local needs. New and important ingredients must be added to the mix when making strategy: volatile political situations, contentious global trade issues, fluctuating exchange rates and unfamiliar cultures.

□ *profitability through growth* – The drive for revenue growth means that companies must be creative and innovative, and this in turn means encouraging the free flow of information and shared learning among employees.

□ *technology* – The challenge is to make technology a viable, productive part of the work setting.

□ *intellectual capital* – Knowledge has become a direct competitive advantage for companies selling ideas and relationships. The challenge to organisations is to ensure that they have the capability to find, assimilate, compensate and retain the talented individuals they need who can drive a global organisation that is both responsive to its customers and 'the burgeoning opportunities of technology'.

□ *change, change and more change* – The greatest challenge companies face is adjusting to – indeed, embracing – non-stop change. They must be able to 'learn rapidly and continuously, and take on new strategic imperatives faster and more comfortably'.

Components of the strategic HR agenda

The components of the strategic people management agenda consist of strategies that address overall organisational issues and strategies for particular areas of HR policy and practice.

Organisational strategies

Organisational strategies are concerned with:

□ organisational development – planned and coherent approaches to improving organisational effectiveness

□ culture management – the management of corporate culture change

□ change management – strategies for organisational transformation

□ developing high-performance, high-commitment and high-involvement management approaches

□ the employment relationship – strategies for developing a positive psychological contract and creating a climate of trust

□ knowledge management – strategies for 'systematically and actively managing and leveraging the stores of knowledge in an organisation' (Tan, 2000).

Strategies for key areas of HR policy and practice

The key areas of HR policy and practice for which specific HR strategies are most likely to be developed are:

- resourcing
- human resource development
- performance management
- the development and use of competency frameworks
- reward
- employee relations
- health and safety
- equal opportunities and the management of diversity
- the provision of effective HR services including the use of information technology.

Although it is possible to identify specific items on the strategic agenda for the management of people, this does not mean that these strategies should be developed or exist in isolation. If strategies are developed piecemeal, there will be a greater risk of a lack of fit between them, and in extreme cases we might even find strategies working against one another.

The development process
Overall approach

Gratton (2000) proposes the following six-step approach:

1 *building the guiding coalition* – Involve people from all parts of the business.

2 *imaging the future* – Create a shared vision of areas of strategic importance.

3 *understanding current capabilities and identifying the gap* – Understand 'where the organisation is now and the gap between aspirations for the future and the reality of the present'.

4 *creating a map of the system* – Ensure 'that the parts can be built into a meaningful whole'.

5 *modelling the dynamics of the vision* – Ensure that the dynamic nature of the future is taken into account.

6 *bridging into action* – 'There is no great strategy, only great execution':

  - agree the broad themes for action and the specific issues related to those themes

□ develop guiding principles

□ build the guiding coalition by involving line managers

□ create 'issue-based' cross-functional teams to define what has to be done, identify targets and stretch goals, and establish performance indicators.

Types of processes

Walker (1992) suggests that the following three types of process are used in developing HR strategy:

□ *the integrated process* – In this approach, HR strategy is an integral part of the business strategy, along with all the other functional strategies. In strategy review discussions, HR issues are addressed as well as financial, product-market and operational ones. However, the focus is not on 'downstream' matters such as staffing, individual performance or development but rather on people-related business issues, resource allocation, the implications of internal and external change and the associated goals, strategies and action plans.

□ *the aligned process* – In this approach, HR strategy is developed together with the business strategy. They may be presented and discussed together but they are distinct outcomes of parallel processes. By developing and considering them together 'there is some likelihood that they will influence each other and be adopted as a cohesive, or at least an adhesive, whole'.

□ *the separate process* – In this approach, a distinct HR plan is developed. It is both prepared and considered separately from the overall business plan. It may be formulated concurrently with strategic planning before (and an input to) or following (to examine its implications). The environmental assessment is wholly independent. It focuses on human resource issues and, so far as possible, looks for the 'business-relatedness' of the information obtained. Because the assessment is outside the strategic planning process, consideration of business strategy depends on a review of the current and past business strategies. The value of the HR strategy is therefore governed by the sufficiency (or insufficiency) of the business-related data. This approach perpetuates the notion of HR as a staff-driven, functionally specialist concern.

Strategic options and choice

It has been noted by Cappelli (1999) that 'The choice of practices that an employer pursues is heavily contingent on a number of factors at the organisational level, including [the] business and production strategies, support [for] HR policies, and co-operative labour relations.' The process of developing HR strategies involves the adoption of a contingent approach in generating strategic HRM options and then making appropriate strategic choices. There is seldom, if ever, one right way forward.

Approaches to the development of HR strategies

In most situations strategy formulation is an evolutionary process, and strategies have not only to inform change management but have also to be capable of rapid adjustment to meet changing circumstances. It would be unrealistic to suggest that in the modern fast-changing world strategies could ever be static or endure without change for any length of time.

At the least, a deliberate attempt to define the strategic intent of an organisation provides a sense of purpose and direction. The logical conclusion of a slavish belief in the impossibility of deliberately and systematically defining strategies is that the business will simply be allowed to drift or, as expressed graphically by Grant (1998), it will 'move into a world of New-Age mysticism in which there is no basis for reasoned choices and in which disorder threatens the progressive accumulation of knowledge'.

This section therefore sets out how strategies can be developed in a deliberate fashion, while bearing in mind that there will always be limitations to the extent to which definitive, long-lasting and fully integrated strategies can be formulated.

Essential questions

Essentially, the formulation of HR strategy requires answers to just three questions:

- ☐ Where are we now?
- ☐ Where do we want to be in one, two, or three years' time?
- ☐ How are we going to get there?

But these questions have to be posed and answered within the framework of an understanding of the business strategy imperatives, or at least the key business needs, in the context of the organisation (its internal and external environment). It is also necessary to appreciate the approaches that are available to meet those needs by reference to leading edge (without slavishly following it), the need to achieve internal fit and coherence, and the obligation to focus on managing change.

Methods of developing HR strategies differ according to the extent to which there are formally expressed business strategies. There are a variety of approaches. The first of those described below – the classical sequential approach – is based on the assumption that there are formal and well-articulated business strategies and there is a logical flow from the defined mission of the organisation to the delivery of programmes for implementation. The second – the empirical-needs-based approach – takes into account the more common situation in which such strategies may or may not exist in the minds of those concerned, but if they do, have not been formalised. Attention is directed to linking HR plans to assessments of the realities of the organisation's requirements in terms of its business needs.

The classical sequential approach

An approach based on the neat sequential model illustrated in Figure 3 could be regarded as 'classical' in that it conforms to the beliefs of the design strategy formulation school. It is certainly neat and logical and incorporates all the actions that ideally should take place *if* there is a formally expressed mission and business strategy.

If the information is there and the mission and business strategies have been articulated, a systematic approach to formulating HR strategies which considers all the relevant business and environmental issues has much to commend it. A methodology for this purpose was developed by Dyer and Holder (1988):

Figure 3
A SEQUENTIAL STRATEGIC HRM MODEL

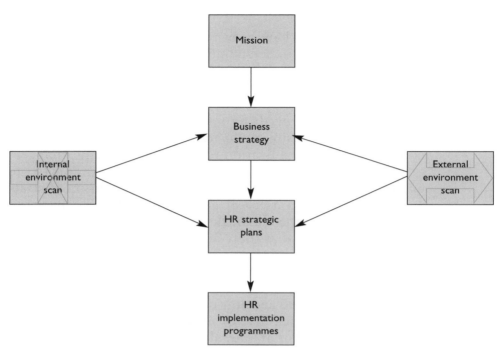

1   *Assess feasibility* – From an HR point of view, feasibility depends on whether the numbers and types of key people required to make the proposal succeed can be obtained on a timely basis and at a reasonable cost, and whether the behavioural expectations assumed by the strategy are realistic (eg retention rates and productivity levels).

2   *Determine desirability* – Examine the implications of strategy in terms of sacrosanct HR policies (eg a strategy of rapid retrenchment would have to be called into question by a company with a no-redundancy policy).

3   *Determine goals* – These indicate the main issues to be worked on, and they derive primarily from the content of the business strategy. For example, a strategy to become a lower-cost producer would require the reduction of labour costs. This in turn translates into two types of HR

goals: higher performance standards (contribution) and reduced headcounts (composition).

4   *Decide the means of achieving goals* – The general rule is that the closer the external and internal fit, the better the strategy, consistent with the need to adapt flexibly to change. External fit refers to the degree of consistency between HR goals on the one hand and the exigencies of the underlying business strategy and relevant environmental conditions on the other. Internal fit measures the extent to which HR means follow from the HR goals and other relevant environmental conditions, as well as the degree of coherency or synergy among the various HR means.

In addition, Dyer and Holder recommend that the HR strategist should take pains to understand the levels at which business strategies are formed and the style adopted by the company in creating strategies and monitoring their implementation. It will then be easier to focus on those corporate or business unit issues likely to have HR implications.

The empirical-needs-based approach

Although systematic approaches such as those described above appear to be desirable, it should be remembered that strategic HRM could be regarded as an empirical approach based on an understanding of the realities of organisational life – as an attitude of mind rather than as a step-by-step process that glides smoothly with inexorable logic from a mission statement to implementation.

Strategic HR planning is usually a much less orderly affair than the models suggest. This is entirely understandable in the light of the fact that strategic HRM is as much about the management of change in conditions of uncertainty as about the rigorous development and implementation of a logical plan.

Perhaps the best way to look at the reality of strategic HRM is to remember Mintzberg *et al*'s (1988) statement that strategy formulation is about 'preferences, choices, and matches' rather than an exercise 'in applied logic'. It is also desirable to follow Mintzberg's analysis and treat HR strategy as a perspective rather than a rigorous procedure for mapping the future. Moore (1992) has suggested that Mintzberg has looked inside the organisation – indeed, inside the heads of the collective strategists – and come to the conclusion that relative to the organisation, strategy is analogous to the personality of an individual. As Mintzberg sees them, all strategies exist in the minds of those people they make an impact upon. What is important is that people in the organisation share the same perspective 'through their intentions and/or by their actions'. This is what Mintzberg calls the 'collective mind', and reading that mind is essential if we are 'to understand how intentions...become shared, and how action comes to be exercised on a collective yet consistent basis'.

No one else has made this point so well as Mintzberg, and what the research conducted by Armstrong and Long (1994) and the more recent research carried out by the writers of this book has revealed is that in the organisations they visited strategic HRM *is* being practised in the Mintzbergian sense. In other words *intentions* are shared amongst the top team, and this leads to actions being exercised on a *collective yet consistent basis.* In each case the shared intentions emerged as a result of strong leadership from the chief executive with the other members of the top team, including the HR director, acting *jointly* in pursuit of well-defined goals. These goals indicated quite clearly the critical success factors of competence, commitment, performance, contribution, customer service and quality which drive the HR strategy.

However, at least an attempt can be made to understand the direction in which the organisation is going, even if this is not expressed in a formal strategic plan. Most businesses have strategies in the sense of intentions, although these may be ill-formed, short-term and subject to change. The ideal of achieving a link in rigorous terms may be difficult to attain, but an attempt to connect what should be done in the shape of HR policies and practices with what the organisation is doing is worth making.

The essence of the empirical approach

The empirical approach to formulating HR strategies is therefore a matter of tuning in to the processes of business decision-making at the top, identifying the key business issues and needs, and thus being able to describe in broad and possibly informal terms the strategic intentions of the business. These form the basis for establishing the implications of those issues, needs and intentions, and the associated organisational development implications. It is then possible in conjunction with the stakeholders – line managers and employees generally – to determine the options, make strategic choices and plan implementation programmes. But this is an interactive and continuously evolutionary process, not a linear decision-making one. And it has to take account of the need for considerations of strategic fit and flexibility.

Strategic fit considerations

Up for consideration is not only what policies and practices are appropriate to realise the strategic intent and meet the business needs, but also how vertical and horizontal integration (strategic fit) are to be achieved.. As suggested by Wright and Snell (1998), seeking fit requires:

☐ knowledge of the skills and behaviours necessary to implement the strategy

☐ knowledge of the HRM practices necessary to elicit those skills and behaviours

☐ the ability quickly to implement the desired system of HRM practices.

Flexibility considerations

Fit is concerned with aligning business and HR strategy, whereas strategic flexibility is about the ability of a firm to respond and adapt to changes in its environment. It has been argued that these concepts of flexibility and fit are incompatible. 'Fit' implies a fixed relationship between the HR strategy and business strategy, but the business strategy cannot but be flexible, so how can good fit be maintained? Wright and Snell (1998) have nonetheless suggested that the concepts of fit and flexibility are complementary – fit exists at a point in time whereas flexibility has to exist over a period of time.

Environmental differences affect a fit/flexibility strategy. As indicated by Wright and Snell, in a stable predictable environment the strategy could be to develop people with a narrow range of skills (or not to develop multiskilled people) and to elicit a narrow range of behaviour (eg tight job descriptions). However, in the more likely surroundings of a dynamic and unpredictable environment, organisations might develop evolutionary HR systems that produce a human capital pool which contains people who possess a wide range of skills and who can engage in a wide diversity of behaviours. The need is to achieve resource flexibility by developing a variety of 'behavioural scripts', and to encourage employees to apply them in different situations, bearing in mind the increased amount of discretionary behaviour that may be appropriate in roles. The main components of the flexibility strategy could be to:

- develop HR systems that can be adapted flexibly
- develop a human capital pool with a broad range of skills
- select people who have the ability to train and adapt
- promote behavioural flexibility by, for example, training to extend 'behavioural repertoire'
- use performance management and reward processes that encourage flexible behaviour
- bundle these with participative work systems that give employees opportunities to contribute their discretionary behaviours.

A model of the empirical approach to strategic HRM

A model of the empirical approach to strategic HRM is shown in Figure 4. This pictures the formulation process as interactive and continuously evolving.

Implementing HR strategies: a systematic approach

Coherent and integrated HR strategies are likely to be developed only if the top team understands and acts upon the strategic imperatives associated with the employment, development and motivation of people. This will be achieved more effectively if there is an HR director playing an active and respected role as a business partner. A further important consideration is that the effective implementation of HR

Figure 4
AN EMPIRICAL STRATEGIC HRM MODEL

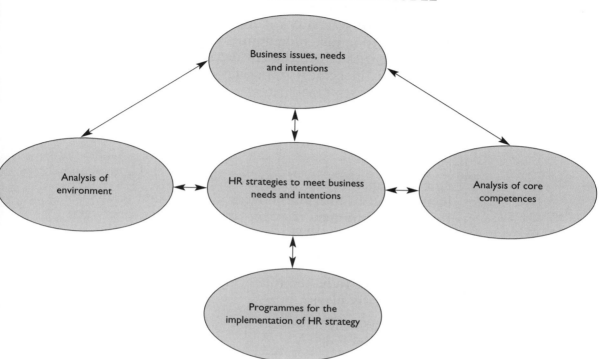

strategies depends on the involvement, commitment and co-operation of line managers and staff generally. There is often a wide gap between what strategic HRM sets out to do and what actually happens, as Gratton *et al* (1999) emphasise. Good intentions can too easily be subverted by the harsh realities of organisational life. For example, strategic objectives such as improving commitment by providing more security and offering training to augment employability may have to be abandoned or at least modified because of the short-term demands made on the business to increase shareholder value.

Because strategies tend to be expressed as abstractions, they must be translated into programmes with clearly stated objectives and deliverables. But turning strategies into positive action is not easy. The term 'strategic HRM' has been devalued in some quarters – sometimes to include no more than a few generalised ideas about HR policies, at other times to describe a short-term plan (for example, to increase the retention rate of graduates). It must be emphasised that HR strategies are not just programmes, policies, or plans concerning HR issues which the HR department happens to feel are important. Piecemeal initiatives do not constitute strategy.

The problem with strategic HRM, as noted by Gratton *et al* (1999), is that too often there is a gap between the rhetoric of the strategy and the reality of what happens to it. As they put it:

> One principal strand that has run through this entire book is the disjunction between rhetoric and reality in the area of human resource management – between HRM theory and HRM practice, between what the HR function says it is doing and how that practice is perceived by employees, and between what senior management believes to be the role of the HR function and the role it actually plays.

The factors identified by Gratton *et al* that contribute to creating this gap include:

□ the tendency of employees in diverse organisations only to accept initiatives they perceive to be relevant to their own areas

□ the tendency of long-serving employees to cling to the *status quo*

□ that complex or ambiguous initiatives may not be understood by employees or may be perceived differently by them, especially in large, diverse organisations

□ that it is more difficult to gain acceptance of non-routine initiatives

□ that employees will be hostile to initiatives if those initiatives are believed to conflict with the organisation's identity – eg downsizing in a culture of 'jobs-for-life'

□ that the initiative is seen as a threat

□ inconsistencies between corporate strategies and values

- the extent to which senior management is trusted
- the perceived fairness of the initiative
- the extent to which existing processes could help to embed the initiative
- a bureaucratic culture that tends towards inertia.

Barriers to the implementation of HR strategies

Each of the factors listed by Gratton *et al* can create barriers to the successful implementation of HR strategies. Other major barriers that can be encountered by HR strategists when attempting to implement strategic initiatives include:

- failure to understand the strategic needs of the business, with the result that HR strategic initiatives are seen as irrelevant, even counter-productive
- inadequate assessment of the environmental and cultural factors that affect the content of the strategies
- the development of ill-conceived and irrelevant initiatives, possibly because they are current fads or because there has been a badly-digested analysis of best practice which does not fit the organisation's requirements – the questions 'Why is it considered best practice?' and 'Why should it be relevant to our business needs?' have not been answered properly
- the selection of one initiative in isolation without considering its implications on other areas of HR practice or trying to ensure that a coherent, holistic approach is adopted
- failure to appreciate the practical problems of getting the initiative accepted by all concerned and of embedding it as part of the normal routines of the organisation
- inability to persuade top management actively to support the initiative
- inability to achieve ownership among line managers
- inability to gain the understanding and acceptance of employees
- failure to take into account the need to have established supporting processes for the initiative (for example, performance management to support performance pay)

- ☐ failure to recognise that the initiative will make new demands on the commitment and skills of the line managers who may have to play a major part in implementing it (for example, skills in setting objectives, in providing feedback, in coaching, and in helping to prepare and implement personal development plans in performance management processes)
- ☐ failure to ensure that the resources (finance, people and time) required to implement the initiative will be available; these include the HR resources needed to provide support for line managers, to conduct training programmes and to communicate with and involve employees
- ☐ failure to monitor and evaluate the implementation of the strategy and to take swift remedial action if things are not going according to plan
- ☐ and finally and importantly, failure to appreciate that the implementation involves major changes to existing policies and practices which have to be managed.

This is a formidable list – no one should underestimate the challenge not only of articulating HR strategies but also of putting them into effect. Issues to be addressed in developing and implementing HR strategies that make a significant impact on performance are examined in Chapter 12.

PART II

THE IMPACT OF
STRATEGIC HRM

7 THE IMPACT OF HRM ON PERFORMANCE

The Holy Grail sought by many commentators on human resource management is to establish a clear positive link between HRM practices and organisational performance. There has been considerable research over the last decade or so which has attempted to answer two basic questions: 'Do HR practices make a positive impact on organisational performance?' and 'If so, how is the impact achieved?' The second question is the more important one. It is not enough to justify HRM by proving that it is a good thing. What counts is what can be done to *ensure* that it is a good thing. This is the 'black box' mentioned by Purcell *et al* (2000) and the CIPD (2001b) which lies between intentions and outcomes. However, the research conducted by Guest *et al* (2000b) as summarised below has provided a preliminary answer to the 'black box problem', and the research currently being undertaken by John Purcell and his colleagues is designed to provide further insights to the nature of the 'connecting rods'. This research, as reported by Purcell *et al* (2000) and by Purcell (2001b), has so far identified three factors: first, there is a 'big idea' or a guiding vision that is clearly understood and accepted by all; second, organisations try to put the big idea into practice by the integration of different functional specialisms; and third, the enhancement of individual and team-based skills 'to encourage employee contributions to knowledge, skill and organisational success'.

Guest *et al* (2000a) have confirmed the findings of a large number of studies and produced additional evidence from their own large-scale multi-sector survey for a positive relationship between HRM and performance. But on the basis of their research they also commented that 'senior executives have yet to be convinced, for reasons of scepticism, ignorance

or prioritisation', and that 'there is no agreement on a definitive set of "best" practices that will give improved performance'.

In this chapter the factors affecting the link between HRM
and performance are considered first. The findings of a
number of studies conducted in the United States and the
United Kingdom aiming to establish the existence of a positive relationship are then analysed. The chapter is completed
with an examination of the means by which HR performance
can be measured.

The link between HRM and performance

According to Guest (1997), performance outcomes can be
understood in terms of internal outcomes – such as employee
relations indicators, including labour turnover and absence,
productivity, and quality of products and services – and external performance outcomes, including in particular financial
performance. There is also a range of background variables
that may influence the relationship between HR practices
and outcomes, such as size, sector, ownership, business strategy and union membership.

In Guest *et al* (2000a) the relationship between HRM and
performance is modelled as shown in Figure 5.

In essence, this model indicates that HR practices influence HR outcomes, which in turn leads to lower absence and

Figure 5
MODEL OF THE LINK BETWEEN HRM AND PERFORMANCE

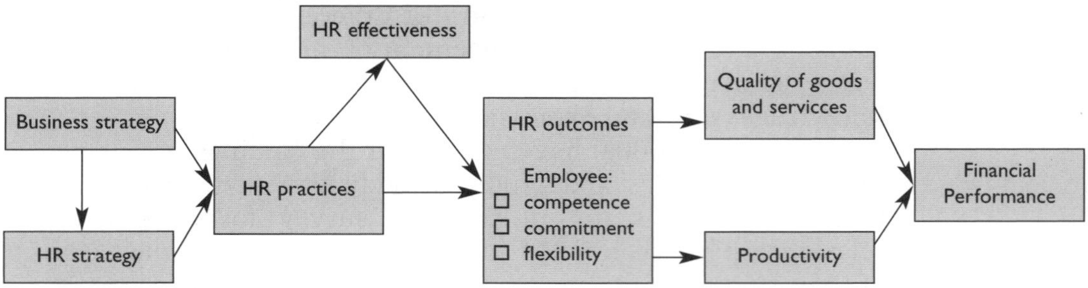

Source: Guest *et al*, *Effective People Management*, CIPD, 2000

labour turnover and increased productivity and quality – and these in turn should lead to an increase in sales and profitability.

The outcomes of key research projects on HRM and firm performance are summarised below, starting with US contributions and then dealing with the British ones.

Research on HRM and performance outcomes – American contributions

Arthur (1990, 1992, 1994 and 1999)

The research conducted by Arthur is based on data collected from 30 US steel mini-mills. He investigated the impact on labour efficiency and scrap rate of either a control strategy (enforced employee compliance through rules and procedures, little employee participation, little general training, low wages, high proportion of employees on bonus schemes) or a commitment strategy (shaping employee behaviours by creating psychological links between organisational and employee goals, moderate employee participation, moderate general training, high wages, fewer employees on bonus or incentives). Arthur found that mills conforming to a commitment strategy had significantly higher levels of productivity and quality and lower scrap rates. The average employee turnover rate in high-commitment mills was less than half that in firms with a low-commitment strategy.

Arthur also examined the performance effects associated with a fit between business and HR strategy. He defined fit as occurring when a cost-based business strategy was combined with a control-orientated HR strategy and when a differentiating-based business strategy was combined with a commitment-type HR strategy. The results were not statistically significant, but he did find that those mills practising a differentiation-based strategy with fit had 25 per cent higher productivity than those without fit. They thus provided some modest support for the contingency hypothesis. He noted (Arthur, 1999) that the HR systems used in the newer mini-mills share many general characteristics of the best practices described in the literature. 'The companies, however, have chosen very different means for implementing these concepts. These differences are integrally tied to the different competitive strategies being pursued in these firms.'

Huselid (1995)

Huselid conducted research into the impact of human resource management practices on company performance by analysing the responses of 968 US firms to a questionnaire. In general, he found that if firms increase their high-performance work practices, there are significant reductions in employee turnover and significant increases in productivity and profits. The three hypotheses he tested were that diminished employee turnover and increased productivity and corporate financial performance would result from:

☐ The use of systems of high performance work practices.

☐ The development of complementarities or synergies among high performance work practices.

☐ The alignment of a firm's system of high performance work practices with its competitive strategy.

The 13 questions he asked firms were:

1 What is the proportion of the workforce who are included in a formal information programme?

2 What is the proportion of the total workforce whose job has been subjected to a formal job analysis?

3 What proportion of non-entry jobs have been filled from within in recent years?

4 What is the proportion of the workforce who are administered attitude surveys on a regular basis?

5 What is the proportion of the workforce who participate in Quality of Work Life programs, quality circles and/or labour-management participation teams?

6 What is the proportion of the workforce who have access to company incentive plans, profit-sharing plans and/or gain-sharing plans?

7 What is the average number of hours' training received by a typical employee over the last 12 months?

8 What is the proportion of the workforce who have access to a formal grievance procedure and/or complaint resolution system?

9 What proportion of the workforce is administered an employment test prior to hiring?

10 What is the proportion of the workforce whose performance appraisals are used to determine their compensation?

11 What proportion of the workforce receive formal appraisals?

12 Which of the following promotion decision rules do you use most often? (a) merit or performance rating alone; (b) seniority among employees who meet a minimum merit requirement; (c) seniority.

13 For the five positions that your firm hires most frequently, how many qualified applicants do you have per position (on average)?

The dependent variables were the average annual rate of employee turnover, sales per employee, and corporate financial performance as measured by economic profits (the net cash flow that accrues to shareholders) and accounting profits (the profit figures as published in company accounts). The main findings were that:

□ Turnover is determined by employee skills and organisational structures; motivation has an insignificant effect.

□ Productivity is determined by employee motivation.

□ Financial performance is determined by employee skills, motivation and organisation structure.

□ One standard deviation in the use of the practices reduces turnover by 7.05 per cent.

□ One standard deviation increase in the use of the practices raises sales by an average of $27,044 per employee.

□ One standard deviation increase in the use of the practices produces an increase in profit of $18,641 per employee.

As Huselid comments, the impact of high-performance work practices on corporate financial performance 'is in part due to their influence on employee turnover and productivity'. However, his research produced little or no evidence that internal or external fit increases firm performance, and he concludes that the simple adoption of high-performance work practices is more important than efforts to ensure that these are internally consistent or aligned with firm competitive strategy. But he does believe that 'the theoretical arguments for internal and external fit remain compelling'.

Huselid and Becker (1995)

Huselid and Becker created an index of the HRM systems in 740 firms reflecting the degree to which each firm adopted a high-performance work system (HPWS). They found that firms with higher values on this index, other things being equal, have economically and statistically significant higher levels of firm performance. They further estimated that significant changes in the quality of a firm's HPWS are associated with changes in market value of $15,000 to $60,000 per employee. It is suggested that a properly designed and deployed HRM system represents a significant economic asset for an organisation, although the research has not identified precisely *how* such a system creates that value.

Becker, Huselid, Pickus and Spratt (1997)

These writers summarised the outcomes of a number of research projects they conducted into the relationship

Figure 6
A MODEL OF THE HR-SHAREHOLDER VALUE RELATIONSHIP

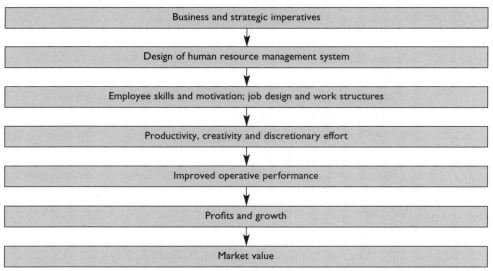

Source: Becker, B. E., Huselid, M. A., Pickus, P. S. and Spratt, M. F. from *Human Resource Management*, 1997. Reprinted by permission of John Wiley and Sons, Inc.

between HRM and company performance in relation to organisations with which they were associated. The focus was on the strategic impact on shareholder value of high-performance work systems. Their model of the relationship is shown in Figure 6.

But Becker *et al* did point out that:

> HRM systems only have a systematic impact on the bottom line when they are embedded in the management infrastructure and help the firm achieve important business priorities such as shortening product development cycle times, increasing customer service, lowering turnover among high-quality employees, etc.

Research on HRM and performance outcomes – British contributions

Patterson, West, Lawthom and Nickell (1997)

Extensive research has been conducted by the Institute of Work Psychology at Sheffield University over the last ten years looking at productivity and profitability in a number of single-site manufacturing operations. Results from this study (Patterson *et al*, 1997), published by the then Institute of Personnel and Development (IPD), addressed the question of what factors most influence business performance. The study looked at the impact of a number of activities including employee attitudes, organisational culture and human resource management practices. An assessment was made of the extent to which each of these factors predicted company performance as gauged by independent measures of productivity and profits per employee.

The results were expressed in terms of the percentage variation in performance attributable to a particular factor:

☐ Job satisfaction explained 5 per cent of the variation between companies in profitability and 16 per cent of the variation in productivity.

☐ Organisational culture explained 10 per cent of the variation in profitability and 29 per cent of the variation in productivity.

□ Human resource management practices explained 19 per cent of the variation in profitability and 18 per cent of the variation in productivity.

These analyses revealed very strong relationships between employee attitudes, organisational culture, HRM practices and company performance. This was particularly convincing in the case of the link between HRM practices and performance.

The analysis of the links between managerial practices and performance showed that the impact on performance was much lower – between 1 and 3 per cent for strategy, technology and quality, and 6 per cent for the link between R&D and productivity, and 8 per cent for the link between R&D and profitability. These figures are not statistically significant.

As the report on the research states:

> Overall these results very clearly indicate the importance of people management practices in predicting company performance...The results suggest that if managers wish to influence the performance of their companies, the most important area they should emphasise is the management of people.

The conclusion reached by the IPD on this research was that employee commitment and a positive psychological contract are fundamental to improving performance. Two HR practices were identified as being particularly significant:

□ acquisition and development of employee skills (including selection, induction and the use of appraisals)

□ job design (including skill flexibility, job responsibility, variety, and the use of formal teams).

The 1998 Workplace Employee Relations Survey

This survey sampled some 2,000 workplaces and also obtained the views of about 28,000 employees. The results as analysed by Guest et al (2000b) indicated that HR practices are not well established in the majority of workplaces. They confirmed, however, that a strong association exists between human resource management and both employee attitudes and workplace performance in the private sector. The results are summarised in Figure 7.

Figure 7
RELATIONSHIPS BETWEEN HR PRACTICES AND PERFORMANCE

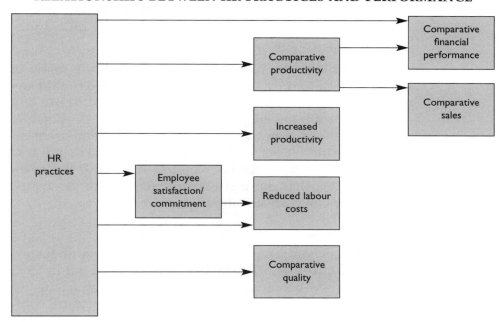

Source: WERS reported in Guest et al, 2000b

Future of Work Survey

The Future of Work Survey (Guest *et al*, 2000a) covered 835 private sector organisations and included interviews with 610 HR professionals and 462 CEOs. Its initial findings were that a greater use of HR practices is associated with higher levels of employee commitment and contribution and greater flexibility. Employee commitment and contribution is in turn linked to higher levels of reported productivity and quality of goods and services compared with major competitors. Employee flexibility is also associated with higher productivity. Finally, productivity and quality of goods and services are linked to higher estimates of comparative financial performance.

Guest *et al* concluded that this initial set of findings is a strong endorsement of the model linking HRM and performance shown in Figure 5. However, they added a specific proviso:

It should be noted that that HR practices have no direct link to performance. Instead, it is an indirect link through their apparent impact on employee commitment, quality and flexibility. These in turn are linked to performance outcomes.

The conclusion of the researchers was that 'While many of the results of this study are encouraging, we failed to find any "bundles" of HR practices and therefore resorted to use of a count of the number of practices in place. It is therefore unclear which practices are having an effect and whether there is a distinctive set of "best" practices.' But they found that there was a widespread perception from both HR managers and CEOs that more effective practices are associated with superior company economic performance

Marc Thompson Study in the UK Aerospace Sector M

The findings (Thompson, 1998b) are based on two industry-wide surveys covering 623 establishments carried out in 1997 and 1999. It was concluded that the adoption of a range of high-performance HR practices is crucial to the future competitiveness of the industry. The list of high-performance HR practices referred to by Thompson included practices covering teamworking, appraisal, job rotation, broad grading structures, and sharing of business information. Thompson found that firms increasing their use of high-performance HR practices between 1997 and 1999 recorded increases in value added per employee ranging from 20 to 34 per cent.

Thompson established that it is both the number of HR practices and the proportion of the workforce covered that appears to be the key differentiating factor between more and less successful firms. However, he also found that only 20 per cent of establishments were using high-performance HR practices to any significant degree.

When he compared the value added per employee by quartiles, he found that although there were significant gains to be made from moving into the lower two quartiles, the performance improvement gains for the upper two quartiles were much lower. In other words, when organisations move from doing very little in terms of high-performance HR practices to

doing just a little more, they see significant leaps in performance but as they go on to do more and more, the gains made
from implementing new practices diminish. Thompson
showed that in firms moving from the first to the second
quartile, or from using fewer than five high-performance HR
practices to using more than six experiences, a typical gain of
34 per cent in value added per employee was achieved. Just
making a start and implementing up to five high-performance
HR practices brings an extra 20 per cent value added per
employee.

Hence Thompson concludes:

> These findings indicate that modest reforms in work-
> place HR policies and practices can deliver considerable
> business benefits in the early stages of transition to a
> high-performance work system. In other words, invest-
> ing in HR pays.

Conclusions from the research

A convincing case has been made as a result of both the US
and the British research that there is a positive relationship
between HRM and performance, although how this relationship is established has not been convincingly explained. It has
something to do with the number of HR practices and the
effectiveness with which these practices are implemented,
which includes how many people they cover. But there is no
proof that any particular bundle of practices is better than
another.

Legge (2001) asserts that much of the research on HR practices and performance is 'at best confused, and at worst con-
ceptually and methodologically deeply flawed'. She draws
attention to the wide range of potentially intervening variables that lead to 'unmanageable complexity' and make the
establishment of a clear link difficult to prove. But she notes
that many of the researchers – including, for example, David
Guest – recognise the problem.

Guest has written (1997) that 'At present the studies report
a promising association between HRM and outcomes, but we
are not yet in a position to assert cause and effect.' However,
he suggests that the expectancy theory of motivation provides

a possible basis for developing a more coherent rationale about the link between HRM practices and performance. He cites remarks by MacDuffie (1995) as indicating an approach close to expectancy theory:

> Innovative human resource practices are likely to contribute to improved economic performance only when three conditions are met: when employees possess knowledge and skills that managers lack; when employees are motivated to apply this skill and knowledge through discretionary effort; and when the firm's business or production strategy can only be achieved when employees contribute such discretionary effort.

Guest (1997) comments that expectancy theory proposes that high performance at the individual level depends on high motivation plus the necessary skills and abilities and an appropriate role and understanding of that role. He suggests that 'it is a short step to specify the HRM practices that encourage high skills and abilities' and argues that HRM practices can improve company performance by:

□ increasing employees' skills and abilities

□ promoting positive attitudes that result in a committed and motivated workforce

□ providing expanded responsibilities that allow employees to make full use of their skills and abilities.

If it is accepted that these are reasonable propositions – and they have considerable face value – then we should explore the role of HR in making the impact through them and other means. And we do so in the next chapter. But it is also necessary to consider methods of measuring performance as a means of evaluating the impact of people management policies and practices with a view to providing the information that will enable them to be focused on meeting the needs of the business for performance improvement.

Measuring HR performance

This is the most difficult area to get to grips with, and yet measurement is vital as a means of establishing the impact of

Table 3

CRITERIA FOR HR EFFECTIVENESS

HRM area	Measurement dimensions
Selection and recruitment	Sophistication of processes (eg use of psychometric tests, clear criteria for selection, structured interviews)
Induction	Sophistication in running and evaluating induction programmes for new employees
Training	Sophistication and coverage of training
Performance management	Coherence and coverage of performance management processes
Skill flexibility	Flexibility of work skills
Job variety	Variety in jobs (eg job rotation)
Job responsibility	Level of responsibility in jobs for various tasks and problem-solving
Teamworking	Use of formal teams
Communication	Frequency and comprehensiveness of communication to workforce (eg newsletter, briefing groups, meetings between top management and workforce)
Involvement and participation	Extent to which people in the organisation are involved and participate in decision-making processes on matters that affect them
Partnership	The existence of a partnership agreement with trade unions in which both parties undertake to work together to their mutual advantage
Quality improvement teams	Use of quality improvement teams
Harmonisation	Extent of harmonised terms and conditions
Comparative pay	Extent to which levels of pay are higher or lower than the competition's
Contingent pay	Use of various forms of contingent pay (eg performance-related pay, competence-related pay, skills-based pay, team pay, gain-sharing)

people management practices. Unfortunately, it is the area most lacking in research material.

It is possible, however, to start to evaluate the effectiveness of progressive HR practices by using the measurement dimensions set out in Table 3, which are adapted from those adopted by Patterson *et al* (1997).

Carter and Robinson (2000) conclude that it is not necessary to measure everything. 'Instead, a focus on key measures linked to key objectives is recommended.' They also argue that key measures should be underpinned by comparative measures such as headcount, wastage rates, and absence.

What literature there is available on measurement concludes that organisations need to achieve a balance in their measurement activity. Too heavy an emphasis on financial measures can force a cost-led strategy, which may not be in the long-term interest of the business. Too heavy an emphasis on soft measures may cause financial imperatives to be lost from view and so leave an organisation ripe for takeover. HR measures should be part of that portfolio, but as a minimum it should be possible to measure the effectiveness of HR processes, the service delivery levels achieved by HR, the cost of HR, and the extent to which people and development strategies are implemented. The measurements could be based on performance metrics, employee behaviour criteria and HR function service level criteria. This has caused some organisations to take a 'balanced scorecard' approach using a range of measures and metrics to assess the impact of HRM. Some measures that might be used in this approach are outlined below.

Performance metrics

Tyson (1985) suggested that a good reason for using quantified measures or metrics was that:

> The business objectives become 'sold' as part of the personnel policies. The discipline of sitting down to look at training objectives, for example, in terms of sales value or added value, brings out what can be assessed and raises the useful question of why we are proposing this programme if we are unable to relate it to the business.

Quantitative criteria can include:

☐ added value per employee

☐ added value per £ of employment costs

☐ profit per employee

☐ sales turnover per employee

☐ costs per employee.

Thompson (1998b) in his research in the aerospace industry on HR performance used value added per employee as the main measure. This was calculated by subtracting the value of bought-in goods from the total turnover and dividing this by the number of employees. Alternatively, added value per £ of employment costs has the advantage of bringing together both benefits (added value) and costs (of employment).

Employee behaviour criteria

Employee behaviour criteria can include:

- employee retention and turnover rates
- absence rates
- frequency/severity rates of accidents
- improvements in productivity as a direct result of training
- improvements in organisational performance as a direct result of pay for performance or performance management schemes.

The last two are more difficult to measure, being less firmly rooted in quantifiable metrics.

HR function service level criteria

These can include:

- average time to fill vacancies
- time to respond to applicants
- time to respond to requests for help or guidance
- cost of providing recruitment, training and other services
- ratio of HR costs to total costs
- ratio of HR staff to employees.

Examples of approaches to measuring performance adopted by organisations

Service industry case studies

Marc Thompson (2000) made the following comments on approaches to measuring effectiveness in his overview of the case studies generated by the CIPD-sponsored research.

> In almost all the cases, the importance of attitudinal and behavioural change shaped the performance metrics used. Consequently, there was widescale use of attitude surveys either locally developed or centrally managed. In one public sector case the attitude survey had been

revamped to include a broader range of measures that could be used to chart progress on the organisational change journey and the goal of becoming a more customer-focused business. This organisation had also allocated time and resources to developing a suite of performance metrics against which it could evaluate its change programme, and these were built into its HR strategy document.

Across most of the cases standard HR metrics were being used (absence, turnover, paybill costs). In one hotel, the high levels of labour turnover were seen as being partly due to a highly competitive local labour market, but the tight control over wage levels (rather than salary bill) exercised by the head office made it difficult to adjust pay to these conditions. The HR manager was therefore using a turnover costing model to demonstrate how an increase in wages would lower overall HR management costs. This illustrates how the collection of performance metrics can not only help prove the impact of HR strategies but can also be used in a strategic way to influence future policy development.

Overall, the various cases demonstrated an active involvement in the measurement of HR impact on the business. In a service environment more weight was being given to attitudinal and behavioural modelling, as one might expect, from both an employee and a customer satisfaction perspective. It was interesting that none of the businesses had gone one step further and explored the links between attitudes and business performance, and this may reflect the complexity of undertaking such a process.

Civil Service College

As Ewart Wooldridge, chief executive of the Civil Service College, commented:

> The measures [we use] generally relate to targets that are set for us by the Cabinet Office and the Treasury. We have all the conventional measures and controls and we conduct an annual attitude survey. Our targets may be

quantitative ones about cost control and contribution, and non-financial ones about customer satisfaction. We have measures in terms of our student population. We also use the EFQM model, and we have just completed our second review, which brought out a whole series of issues relating to leadership and business processes. A change programme is flowing from our use of the model.

Corporation of London

Garry Annels, HR director, pointed out that 'It is not just looking at one thing, it is looking at a range of things – the management of people and the use of human resources as well as money. At the end of the day, however, there is still this financial imperative to meet your targets.'

Great Ormond Street NHS Trust

Sarah Bonham, HR director, told us that:

If we don't do the work that we have got funding for, it puts the service at risk for future funding. We have service agreements, and the performance management framework looks at the issues such as recruitment, sickness, and turnover. We have to stay on target for service delivery and keep within budget. These are hard measures and we are required to report to the Trust Board on a monthly basis.

Lloyds TSB

Paul Turner, Group HR business director, said that quantified measures can be used in some areas and that the return on training had been calculated. He thought that others were less easy. However, he informed us that by using academic research 'we can make coherent arguments that, for example, employee satisfaction is related to customer satisfaction, and that therefore having better satisfied employees is likely to lead to higher customer satisfaction, etc.' He also remarked that:

Metrics are more likely to get the HR professional into the picture. The question for HR people should be 'How can I get into the dialogue about the business?' The answer is that they have to be able to argue the return on investment from their initiatives and actions. It is no good going to the board and asking for £2 million to spend on a new employee communication system. You must be able to say, 'If you give me this money, this is what I will be able to give you in return.'

New Forest District Council

Keith Ireland, director of HR, told us that:

The first measure is the extent to which people achieve their objectives for their work programmes. Secondly, we report to members on the objectives they have set – have we achieved them, or haven't we achieved them? Each of the business units has to send members a performance measurement report. They will be looking at the Best Value performance indicators, both internal and external. We also benchmark using the Saratoga database and the South East Employers Benchmark Group. We use benchmarking as one indicator amongst many. We won the Saratoga award for excellence in personnel in 1999.

Peabody Trust

When asked what kind of measures he would seek that would convince him to spend money on a new employee communication system, Richard McCarthy, chief executive, replied that:

I would have to be convinced that people would be better informed, and that the information would be of value to them so that they were more effective at the end of the day. There are ways in which you can test that, even though it might be hard to set specific targets. For example, you can check through the appraisal process, you can ask people to report back through the team-briefing system, and you might expect more questions coming to the management team because people are better informed and more able to challenge. I would be breaking the proposal down to find where the added value was and how the director of HR was going to achieve that added value.

Conclusions

Measuring HR performance is important as a guide to the action required by the HR function to ensure that people management practices make an impact on the firm's performance. How the function can carry out that role is considered in the next chapter.

8 MAKING THE IMPACT: THE ROLE OF HR

The effectiveness of the HR policies and practices developed and implemented through strategic HRM processes is largely dependent on the contribution made by HR. It is vital that there is strong support – indeed, leadership – from the top. It is also important that line managers and employees accept and support the stance taken by HR. But it is the responsibility of people management and development professionals to provide the advice and services which will ensure that an impact is made on the performance of the organisation.

The role of HR

Armstrong (2001) gave a definition of the role of HR:

> The role of the HR function is to enable the organisation to achieve its objectives by taking initiatives, providing guidance and support and delivering effective services on all matters relating to the people who work there. The basic aim is to ensure that the organisation deals properly with everything concerning the employment and development of people and the relationships that exist between management and the workforce. A further key role for the HR function is to play a major part in the creation of an environment which enables people to make the best use of their capacities and to realise their potential to the benefit of both the organisation and themselves.

Research by Guest *et al* (2001) analyses the views of senior managers on the contribution of HR to business performance. They found that on the whole CEOs and non-HR directors were very positive about the contribution of the management of people to the bottom line, most of them accepting that investment in people management should result in superior performance. However, there were mixed opinions about the HR profession's role in maximising this contribution. Many felt that the implementation of HR practices was primarily the responsibility of line managers, and that improving the quality of people management skills among line managers was more important than developing the role of people management professionals. The research also concluded that whereas senior executives value the support and expertise of their board-level HR colleagues, they are often sceptical about HR initiatives, believing that such initiatives will increase bureaucracy, and both they and HR directors themselves have some reservations about the quality of people joining the HR profession.

A new mandate for human resources

Ulrich (1998) said that 'The activities of HR appear to be, and often are, disconnected from the real work of the organisation.' He believes that HR 'should not be defined by what it does but by what it delivers'. According to Ulrich, HR can deliver excellence in four ways:

☐ HR should become a partner with senior and line managers in strategy execution, helping to improve planning from the conference room to the marketplace.

☐ It should become an expert in the way work is organised and executed, delivering administrative efficiency to ensure that costs are reduced while quality is maintained.

☐ It should become a champion for employees, vigorously representing their concerns to senior management and at the same time working to increase employee contribution – that is, employees' commitment to the organisation and their ability to deliver results.

☐ It should become an agent of continuous transformation, shaping processes and a culture that together improve an organisation's capacity for change.

In essence, Ulrich is proposing that HR should have a strategic role, and that the head of HR in particular, but also other members of the function, should act as business partners in exercising that role. But he also stresses that the function has to deliver effective services. It will be judged not simply on the quality of the advice it provides but also on the excellence of the services it provides.

The strategic partner role

To be fully-fledged strategic partners with senior management, Ulrich's (1998) view is that HR executives should 'impel and guide serious discussion of how the company should be organised to carry out its strategy'.

Ulrich (1998) suggests that HR must take stock of its own work and set clear priorities. At any given moment the HR staff might have a dozen initiatives in its sights, such as pay-for-performance, global teamwork, and action-learning development experiences. But to be truly tied to business outcomes, HR needs to join forces with operating managers to systematically assess the impact and importance of each one of these initiatives. Which ones are really aligned with strategy implementation? Which ones should receive immediate attention, and which ones can wait? Which ones, in short, are really linked to business results?

In Ulrich's view, the answers must be obtained to six questions:

1 *shared mind-set* – To what extent does our company have the right culture to achieve our goals?

2 *competence* – To what extent does our company have the required knowledge, skills, and abilities?

3 *consequence* – To what extent does our company have the appropriate measures, rewards and incentives?

4 *governance* – To what extent does our company have the right organisation structure, communication systems and policies?

5 *capacity for change* – To what extent does our company have the ability to improve work processes, to change and to learn?

6 *leadership* – To what extent does our company have the leadership to achieve its goals?

HR practitioners as strategists

As strategists, HR practitioners address major far-reaching issues concerning the management and development of people and the employment relationship. They are guided by the business plans of the organisation but they also contribute to the formulation of the business plans. This is achieved by ensuring that top managers focus on the human resource implications of their strategies. HR strategists persuade top managers that they must develop plans which make the best use of the organisation's human resources in terms of the required core competences. They emphasise, in the words of Hendry and Pettigrew (1986), that people are a strategic resource for the achievement of competitive advantage.

HR as a business partner

HR practitioners as business partners share responsibility with their line management colleagues for the success of the enterprise. As defined by Tyson (1985), they:

☐ integrate their activities closely with top management and ensure that they serve a long-term strategic purpose

☐ have the capacity to identify business opportunities, to see the broad picture, and to see how their HR role can help to achieve the company's business objectives.

Armstrong (2001) points out that HR practitioners in their role as business partners are aware of business strategies and the opportunities and threats that face the organisation. They are capable of analysing organisational strengths and weaknesses and diagnosing the issues confronting the enterprise (PESTLE analysis) and their human resource implications. They are aware of the core competences of the organisation and the critical success factors that will create competitive advantage. They adopt a 'resource-capability' approach, focusing on how added value can be obtained by treating people as strategic assets in the sense that they perform activities which create advantage in particular markets. Importantly, they can draw up a convincing business case for innovations that will add value.

Lengnick-Hall and Lengnick-Hall (1990) have described the 'hard' business partner approach:

☐ The aim of the HR function should be defined as the maximisation of corporate profits through the better use and management of people. This statement focuses attention on corporate-wide objectives and directs activities towards results, not processes.

☐ HR executives should demonstrate a thorough understanding of the competitive climate, product options, cost constraints, marketing characteristics and all other aspects of productivity and profitability that affect the firm.

☐ HR professionals must be expected to understand, predict and be held accountable for the direct and indirect contribution their performance makes to the bottom line.

An analysis by Marc Thompson (2000) of the outcomes of research in a number of service industry organisations produced a pertinent comment about the political role of HR in acting as a business partner:

The political nature of the HR role, in its need to reconcile the demands of various competing interest groups while building broader organisational coalitions of support around specific strategies, would appear to be a highly important differentiator in performance terms. Where HR was seen more as a business partner, more far-reaching and sustainable HR strategies were developed and implemented. This might suggest that the skill sets and personal capabilities of HR leaders could play a crucial part in effective HR.

But Ulrich (1997) cautioned against too narrow a focus on the business partner role by stressing that politics pervades all the four roles of HR as strategic partners, administrative experts, employee champions and change agents.

Caldwell (2001) quotes two HR directors as saying, in one case, 'I am a director first and an HR director second', and in the other, 'I am a business director. I just happen to have an HR background.' But, he asks, 'Do the statements indicate a balanced role, or do they express a misguided desire to over-identify with a strategic "business partner" role at the expense of championing the specialist HR function and role?'

The strategic role of the HR director

As suggested by Armstrong (2000b) HR directors have a key role in strategic HRM, especially if they are – as they should be – on the board. They are there to envision how HR strategies can be integrated with the business strategy, to prepare strategic plans, and to oversee their implementation. They should play a major part in organisational development and in change management and in the achievement of coherence in the different aspects of HR policy.

In his overview of the findings of a number of mini-case-studies in the service industry Marc Thompson (2000) concluded that:

> The development of HR strategies within the businesses, although shaped by a range of both internal and external factors, appeared to hang quite crucially on the competence of HR directors. Central to this were their political skills and influence within the business and their ability to converse with other senior managers on their own terms. Establishing a credible business case for HR strategies and being able to contribute to on-going business discussions were very important in developing HR's strategic role.

HR directors who are most likely to play a full strategic role as business partners are also likely to be:

☐ involved in business planning and the integration of human resource plans with business plans

☐ professionally competent in HR techniques – but their contribution and credibility will depend mainly on their business awareness and skills and their ability to play a full part as members of the top team

☐ able to convince others of the need for change and to act as champions of change and as effective change agents

☐ fully aware of the needs to develop a vision of what the HR function exists to do, to define its mission, to provide leadership and guidance for the members of the function (without getting over-involved in day-to-day HR matters), and to maintain the quality of the support the HR function provides for line managers

□ essentially pragmatists who know about 'best practice' but also know what is right for their organisation and what will work there

□ capable of making a convincing business case for anything they propose should be done.

HR professionals as change agents

A survey by Caldwell (2001) of the roles carried out by 98 HR professionals established that the two most common roles were those of adviser (82 per cent) and change agent (68 per cent). The emphasis on the change agent role is interesting, bearing in mind the contention by Purcell (1999 and 2001a) that change is specially important in HRM strategies and the change-orientated view of HRM expressed by Ulrich (1997). Caldwell (2001) believes that 'HR change champions are those directors or senior executives at the very top of the organisation who can envision, lead or implement strategic HR policy changes of a far-reaching nature.' He categorises HR change agents in four dimensions:

□ *transformational change* – a major change that has a dramatic effect on HR policy and practice across the whole organisation

□ *incremental change* – gradual adjustments of HR policy and practices which affect single activities or multiple functions

□ *HR vision* – a set of values, beliefs and interests that affirm the legitimacy of the HR function as strategic business partner

□ *HR expertise* – the knowledge and skills that define the unique contribution the HR professional can make to effective people management.

Across these dimensions, the change agent roles that Caldwell suggests can be fulfilled by HR professionals are those of change champions, change adapters, change consultants and change synergists. But he cites Ulrich (1997) as arguing that HR professionals are 'not fully comfortable or compatible in the role as change agent', and that their task is therefore 'not to carry out change' but to 'get the change done'.

Getting the fundamentals right

There is more to HRM than developing far-reaching business-orientated strategies. It is necessary also to get the fundamentals right – to deliver effective services that meet business needs. As Geoff Hawkins, HR director of The Children's Society, commented:

> Unless HR delivers high-quality services, new offerings are a waste of time. If people perceive that the contribution of HR is second-rate, those offerings will not be valued, however well designed they are. Our success in HR depends not on what new policies I design with my senior colleagues but on what our personnel and training consultants actually deliver to managers on a day-to-day basis.

Views about the role of HR

Geoff Hawkins

As defined by Geoff Hawkins, the role of the HR function in The Children's Society is:

> The Human Resources Division facilitates the effective and efficient deployment of the people employed by the Society to secure the success of its mission to be a positive force for change in the lives of children and young people whose circumstances make them particularly vulnerable. It does so by providing leadership in people management, by providing services in support of managers, by challenging behaviours, and through development programmes.

The Human Resources Division works with managers and staff of the Society to secure the following outcomes:

☐ the development and continuous improvement of the human resources strategy for the Society

□ the development of the organisation in support of delivering the Corporate Plan and change management leadership

□ the promotion of an employee relations climate which facilitates the aims of The Children's Society to be a force for change in the lives of children and young people

□ the effective use of staff resources within The Children's Society

□ the commissioning of training and development programmes appropriate to business and employee needs.

Judith Evans

Judith Evans, formerly HR director of Homebase, commented that 'I think too many HR people plug away at doing things that are completely irrelevant – doing good things, but not doing the right things.'

John Lee

John Lee, HR director of Halifax plc believes that:

> The role of the HR practitioner is as a business partner. HR directors have got to contribute to the formation of business strategy at the highest level. They must be on the executive management team and capable of contributing to the strategy at both a business and an expert level. What I mean by contributing to the business strategy is, first, that they have got to be accepted by their colleagues as people who can make a valid contribution both to the business strategy and its implementation. Second, they must make certain that people issues are seen as some of the core drivers of the business, are assessed properly, and that a business strategy is not put together in a people issues vacuum.

Barry Hine

Barry Hine formerly HR director of HSBC gave this explanation of his role:

> Because I had a seat on the Executive Committee I was party to the business decisions. I contributed to them, and the HR reaction is instantaneous because I knew

what was going to happen from the start. When we first went into television and Internet banking, I knew right away that we were going to have to create a whole new, different person from those who had grown up in traditional banking; so we were there, and we moved very quickly.

Paul Turner

Paul Turner, Group HR business director at Lloyds TSB, took much the same line:

> If HR people are going to communicate the messages about the long-term benefits of investment in HR successfully, they have to become business-focused. I am a strong supporter of the Ulrich model. You must be a business partner as well as a champion of the workforce. HR people will only get the resources they require if they are able to make a sufficiently strong business case.

Richard McCarthy

A chief executive's view was expressed by Richard McCarthy, Peabody Trust: 'It is necessary to get people to see that we have an HR department – but that they are there to support them, not take away their responsibility.'

Ann Lewis

Ann Lewis, director of HR at the Peabody Trust, believes that:

> HR has a strong strategic role. We are not here just to respond to what managers want us to do. We are here to be very clear about what best practice is, to find out what other organisations are doing, and to look strategically at everything we are trying to do together. We also have to remember that our customers are just as much the Trust tenants as our own people.

Conclusions

Guest and King's (2001) conclusions emerging from their research into the views of chief executives about the HR contribution were that:

HR directors are in a key position of influence and their role should be to help their colleagues with the 'hows' of people management. They also need to work harder at ensuring that their departments are staffed with people who understand the business they work in, who use language that their colleagues can understand, and who devise initiatives that can make a tangible contribution to the organisation.

Our own research into the views of senior HR directors revealed that whether or not they knew about Ulrich, they saw their roles as being business partners and thought they could be effective only if they established their credibility as such with their business colleagues. Credibility could not be achieved in simple ways, and the requirements differed between organisations. But the recurring themes were the needs to understand the business imperatives, to be able to contribute to business decisions, to be politically sensitive, and to be good at innovating, persuading, communicating, networking and managing the delivery of effective services.

PART III

THE COMPONENTS OF STRATEGIC HRM

9 ORGANISATIONAL HR STRATEGIES

Strategic HRM addresses organisation-wide process issues, including organisational development, culture management, knowledge management, and developing a climate of high commitment and trust. This is where a holistic approach is required that provides the basis for integrated HR strategies to address specific issues in the main areas of resourcing, development, reward, and employee relations, all of which are examined in the next chapter.

Organisational development

Strategies for organisational development are concerned with the planning and implementation of programmes designed to enhance the effectiveness with which an organisation functions. They may involve strategies for developing organisational structures, for improving organisational processes or for organisational transformation.

An effective organisation can be defined broadly as one that achieves its purpose by meeting the needs of its stakeholders, by matching its resources to opportunities, by being responsive to the environment in which it operates, and by continuously innovating to remain competitive.

Organisational development strategies are concerned with process as well as structure or systems. They address *how* things are done as well as *what* is done. 'Process' refers to the ways in which people act and interact. It is about the roles they play on a continuing basis to deal with events and with situations involving other people, and to adapt to changing circumstances.

Organisation development (OD) has been defined by French and Bell (1990) as:

a planned systematic process in which applied behavioural science principles and practices are introduced into an on-going organisation towards the goals of effecting organisational improvement, greater organisational competence, and greater organisational effectiveness. The focus is on organisations and their improvement, or, to put it another way, *total systems change.* The orientation is on action – achieving desired results as a result of planned activities.

But belief in traditional approaches to OD has declined. This has been partly caused by disenchantment with the jargon used by consultants and the unfulfilled expectations of significant improvements in organisational effectiveness. There was also a reaction in the hard-nosed 1980s against the perceived softness of the messages preached by the behavioural scientists. Managements in the later 1980s and 1990s wanted more specific strategies that would impact on processes they believed to be important as means of improving performance, such as total quality management, business process re-engineering, and performance management. It is interesting to note that the research conducted by Guest *et al* (2001) revealed that chief executives believed that performance management was the practice that, if implemented effectively, would do most to improve performance. The need to manage change to processes, systems or culture was still recognised, but only if it was results-driven rather than activity-centred.

Team-building activities in the new process-based organisations were also regarded favourably as long as they were directed towards measurable improvements in the shorter term. It was additionally recognised that organisations were often compelled to transform themselves in the face of massive challenges and external pressures, and traditional OD approaches might not make a sufficient or a speedy impact.

Strategies for organisational transformation

Transformation, according to Webster's dictionary, is 'a change in the shape, structure, nature of something'. Organisational transformation strategies are concerned with the development of programmes that will ensure that the company responds strategically to new demands and continues to function effectively in the dynamic environment in which it operates.

Strategic plans for organisational transformation may involve radical changes to the structure, culture and processes of the organisation – the way it looks at the world. This may be in response to competitive pressures, mergers, acquisitions, investments, disinvestments, changes in technology, product lines, markets, cost-reduction exercises and/or decisions to downsize or outsource work. Transformational change may be forced on an organisation by investors or by government decisions. It may be initiated by a new chief executive and top management team with a remit to 'turn the business round'.

Transformational change strategies involve planning and implementing significant and far-reaching developments in corporate structures and organisation-wide processes. The change is neither incremental (bit by bit) nor transactional (concerned solely with systems and procedures). According to Pascale (1990), transactional change is merely concerned with the alteration of ways in which the organisation does business and people interact with one another on a day-to-day basis, and 'is effective when what you want is more of what you've already got'. He advocates a 'discontinuous improvement in capability', and this he describes as transformation.

Four strategies for transformational change have been identified by Beckhard (1989):

□ *a change in what drives the organisation* – for example, a change from being production-driven to being market-driven would be transformational

□ *a fundamental change in the relationships between or among organisational parts* – for example, decentralisation

□ *a major change in the ways of doing work* – for example, the introduction of new technology such as computer-integrated manufacturing

□ *a basic, cultural change in norms, values or research systems* – for example, developing a customer-focused culture.

Transformation programmes are led from the top within the organisation. They do not rely on an external 'change agent' as did many traditional OD interventions, although specialist external advice might be obtained on aspects of the transformation such as strategic planning, reorganisation or developing new HR processes.

The prerequisite for a successful programme is the presence of a transformational leader who, as defined by Burns (1978), motivates others to strive for higher-order goals rather than merely short-term interest. Transformational leaders go beyond dealing with day-to-day management problems. They commit people to action – they focus on the development of new levels of awareness of where the future lies, and on commitment to achieving that future. Burns contrasts transformational leaders with transactional leaders who operate by building up a network of interpersonal transactions in a stable situation, and who evoke compliance rather than commitment through the reward system and the exercise of authority and power. Transactional leaders may be good at dealing with here-and-now problems but they will not provide the vision required to transform the future.

Strategies must be developed for managing the transition from where the organisation is to where the organisation wants to be. This is the critical part of a transformation programme. It is during the transition period of getting from *here* to *there* that change takes place. Transition management starts from a definition of the future state and a diagnosis of the present state. It is then necessary to define what has to be done to achieve the transformation. This means deciding on the new processes, systems, procedures, structures, products and markets to be developed. Having defined these, the work can be programmed and the required resources (people, money, equipment and time) can be defined. The strategic plan for managing the transition should include provisions for involving people in the process and for communicating to them what is happening, why it is happening, and how it will affect them. Clearly, the aims are to get as many people as possible committed to the change.

The eight steps required to transform an organisation are summed up by Kotter (1995) as:

1   Establishing a sense of urgency
     □ examining market and competitive realities
     □ identifying and discussing crises, potential crises, or major opportunities

2 Forming a powerful guiding coalition
   □ assembling a group with enough power to lead the change effort
   □ encouraging the group to work together as a team

3 Creating a vision
   □ creating a vision to help direct the change effort
   □ developing strategies for achieving that vision

4 Communicating the vision
   □ using every vehicle possible to communicate the new vision and strategies
   □ teaching new behaviours by the example of the guiding coalition

5 Empowering others to act on the vision
   □ getting rid of obstacles to change
   □ changing systems or structures that seriously undermine the vision
   □ encouraging risk-taking and non-traditional ideas, activities and actions

6 Planning for and creating short-term wins
   □ planning for visible performance improvements
   □ creating those improvements
   □ recognising and rewarding employees involved in the improvements

7 Consolidating improvements and producing still more change
   □ using increased credibility to change systems, structures, and policies that do not fit the vision
   □ hiring, promoting, and developing employees who can implement the vision
   □ reinvigorating the process with new projects, themes and change agents

8 Institutionalising new approaches
   □ articulating the connections between the new behaviours and corporate success
   □ developing the means to ensure leadership development and succession.

Transformation capability

The development and implementation of transformation strategies require special capabilities. As Gratton (1999) points out:

> Transformation capability depends in part on the ability to create and embed processes which link business strategy to the behaviours and performance of individuals and teams. These clusters of processes link vertically (to create alignment with short-term business needs), horizontally (to create cohesion), and temporally (to transform to meet future business needs).

HR professionals in their capacity as change agents can play a strategic role in developing and implementing organisational transition and transformation strategies. They can provide help and guidance in analysis and diagnosis, highlighting the people issues that will fundamentally affect the success of the strategy. Advice can be given on resourcing programmes and planning and implementing the vital training, reward, communications and involvement aspects of the process. People problems can be anticipated and dealt with before they become serious. If the programme does involve restructuring and downsizing, HR professionals can advise on how it can be done humanely and with the minimum disruption to people's lives.

Strategies for culture change

There are many different definitions and interpretations of organisational culture. Furnham and Gunter (1993) define it as 'the commonly-held beliefs, attitudes and values that exist in an organisation', and most writers on the subject agree that it is about values, customs, norms and objectives. However, there is a distinct difference between culture described as rooted in behaviour and culture rooted in attitude.

Research carried out by the then Institute of Personnel and Development (Baron and Walters, 1994) suggested that it is not enough to manage behaviour. If real culture change is to occur, organisations must in addition foster a positive attitude among their employees. Culture therefore becomes more about how we think about the things we do rather than what we actually do.

Strategies for managing culture change centre on the achievement of longer-term objectives either for changing the culture in specified ways – moving from a present state to a future desired state in order to improve organisational effectiveness – or for preserving and even reinforcing some or as much as possible of the existing culture of an organisation. They could be regarded as a form of organisational development, and because people management is a powerful tool in the management of culture, they are integral to any strategic approach to HR.

Salaman (2001) makes the point that all significant changes to organisational processes, practices and policies 'rely on a change in culture, at least in the sense that they depend on the very circumstances they seek to achieve: a change in the basic attitudes of employees'.

The focus of culture management

Culture management often focuses on the development of shared values and gaining commitment to them. These values are concerned with the sort of behaviour the management believes is appropriate in the interests of the organisation. The core values of a business express the beliefs about what management regards as important with regard to how the organisation functions and how people should behave. The aim is to ensure that these beliefs are also held and acted upon by employees. As Hailey (1999) suggests:

> The business case for inculcating shared values through managing culture is based on the idea that ultimately employees could then be given licence to innovate in the confidence that their adherence to corporate values would prevent them from acting against the interests of the company.

Hailey argues that instead of focusing on values initially (and hoping that behaviour will change), organisations should focus first on behaviours in the hope that positive values and attitudes will emerge. The basis of this approach is that values are abstract and can be espoused but not acted upon.

Behaviour is real – and if it is the right sort of behaviour, it should produce the desired results. It follows, therefore, that culture management strategies should be concerned with analysing what behaviours are appropriate, and then bringing in processes such as performance management and the use of competency frameworks that will encourage the development of those behaviours. If, for example, it is important for people to behave effectively as members of teams, then team performance management processes can be introduced (self-managed teams setting their own standards and monitoring their own performance against those standards) and behaviour conducive to good teamwork rewarded by financial or non-financial means.

However, efforts to change behaviour must be accompanied also by efforts to change attitude – otherwise, the impetus for change will fade once the immediate need appears to have diminished. For example, legislation may change behaviour in relation to equal opportunities, but unless managers actually believe that all groups have equal ability, they will still find ways to justify inequalities – as we have seen happening in the continuing gender pay-gap.

Hailey refers with approval to the approach to culture management adopted by Hewlett Packard, which is based on a values statement 'The HP Way'. This focuses on a 'belief in our people' which incorporates:

> confidence and respect for our people as opposed to depending on extensive rules, procedures and so on; which depends upon people doing their job right (individual freedom) without constant directives.

Hailey comments that the 'two critical issues of managing performance through business planning and "The HP Way" are inextricably connected and account for the success and performance of Hewlett Packard'. Middle managers believe that the culture is 'supportive', 'very, very open', with a 'team ethic'.

Approaches to managing culture

The strategy for managing culture will be based on an analysis of the present culture and the extent that it supports the achievement of business goals. This should identify areas where changes are deemed to be desirable. Those changes can then be specified and plans developed for them to be implemented.

The first step is evidently to analyse the existing culture. This can be done through questionnaires, surveys and discussions in focus groups or workshops. It is often helpful to involve people in analysing the outcome of surveys, getting them to produce a diagnosis of the cultural issues facing the organisation and to participate in the development and implementation of plans and programmes to deal with any issues. This could form part of an organisational development programme.

In analysing the culture, organisations must be careful to identify both what is good about the existing culture as well as the negative points. They might then draw up a culture map, identifying the areas that need attention. Although involvement is highly desirable, there will be situations when management has to carry out the analysis and determine the actions required without the initial participation of employees. But employees should be kept informed and brought into discussions on developments as soon as possible.

Culture change programmes

A comprehensive change programme may be a fundamental part of an organisational transformation exercise as described earlier in this chapter. But culture change programmes can focus on particular aspects of the culture – for example, performance, commitment, quality, customer service, teamwork, organisational learning – according to the analysis of existing culture. In each case the underpinning values have to be defined.

Having identified what needs to be done and the priorities, the next step is to consider what levers for change exist and how they can be used. Such levers might include, as appropriate:

□ *performance* – performance management processes, contribution-related pay schemes; gain-sharing; leadership training, skills development, rewarding the behaviours and attitudes the organisations wants to encourage

- □ *commitment* – communication, participation and involvement programmes; developing a climate of co-operation and trust; clarifying the psychological contract
- □ *quality* – total quality programmes
- □ *customer service* – customer care programmes
- □ *teamwork* – team-building; team performance management; team rewards
- □ *organisational learning* – taking steps to enhance intellectual capital and the organisation's resource-based capability by developing a learning organisation
- □ *values* – gaining understanding, acceptance and commitment through involvement in defining values, performance management processes and employee development interventions, although, as noted above, it is often the case that values are embedded by changing behaviours, not the other way round.

Culture support and reinforcement

Culture support and reinforcement programmes aim to preserve and underpin what is good and functional about the present culture. Schein (1985) has suggested that the most powerful primary mechanisms for culture embedding and reinforcement are:

- □ what leaders pay attention to, measure and control
- □ leaders' reactions to critical incidents and crises
- □ deliberate role modelling, teaching and coaching by leaders
- □ criteria for allocation of rewards and status
- □ criteria for recruitment, selection, promotion and commitment.

Other means of underpinning the culture are:

- □ reaffirming the behaviours believed to be important
- □ providing detailed explanation of the reasons behind the need for these behaviours
- □ encouraging appropriate behaviours by providing financial and non-financial rewards for behaviour that accords with expectations, and by further actions designed, for example, to implement total quality and customer care

programmes, to improve productivity, to promote and reward good teamwork, to develop a learning organisation

□ developing a statement of core values which describe the basis for the desired behaviours using the value set as headings for reviewing individual and team performance, emphasising that people are expected to behave in ways that uphold the values

□ ensuring that induction procedures cover expected behaviours and core values and how people are expected to act upon them

□ reinforcing induction training through further learning processes set up as part of a continuous development programme

□ incorporating competences, behaviours and attitudes expected of employees into the selection process.

Strategies for knowledge management

'Knowledge has become a direct competitive advantage for companies selling ideas and relationships' (Ulrich, 1998). Knowledge management strategies aim to capture an organisation's collective expertise and distribute it to 'wherever it can achieve the biggest payoff' (Blake, 1998). This is in accordance with the resource-based view of the firm which, as argued by Grant (1998), suggests that the source of competitive advantage lies within the firm (ie in its people and their knowledge), not in how it positions itself in the market. Trussler (1998) comments that 'the capability to gather, lever, and use knowledge effectively will become a major source of competitive advantage in many businesses over the next few years.' A successful company is a knowledge-creating company.

The process of knowledge management

Scarbrough *et al* (1999) define knowledge management as 'any process or practice of creating, acquiring, capturing, sharing and using knowledge, wherever it resides, to enhance learning and performance in organisations'. They suggest that it focuses on the development of firm-specific knowledge and skills that are the result of organisational learning processes.

Knowledge management is concerned with both stocks and flows of knowledge. Stocks include expertise and encoded knowledge in computer systems. Flows represent the ways in which knowledge is transferred from people to people or from people to a knowledge database.

The purpose of knowledge management is to transfer knowledge from those who have it to those who need it in order to improve organisational effectiveness. It is concerned with storing and sharing the wisdom and understanding accumulated in an organisation about its processes, techniques and operations. It treats knowledge as a key resource. It can be argued that in the information age, knowledge rather than physical assets or financial resources is the key to competitiveness. In essence, as pointed out by Mecklenberg *et al* (1998), 'Knowledge management allows companies to capture, apply and generate value from their employees' creativity and expertise.'

Knowledge management is as much if not more concerned with people and how they acquire, exchange and disseminate knowledge as it is about information technology. That is why it has become an important strategic HRM area. Scarbrough *et al* (1999) believe that HR specialists should have 'the ability to analyse the different types of knowledge deployed by the organisation...[and] to relate such knowledge to issues of organisational design, career patterns and employment security'.

The concept of knowledge management is closely associated with intellectual capital theory as described in Chapter 4 in that it refers to the notions of human, social and organisational or structural capital. It is also linked to the concepts of organisational learning and the learning organisation as examined in Chapter 10.

Knowledge management involves transforming knowledge resources by identifying relevant information and then disseminating it so that learning can take place. Strategies for knowledge management promote the sharing of knowledge by linking people with people and by linking them to information so that they learn from documented experiences.

Sources and types of knowledge

Knowledge management strategies should be founded on an understanding of the sources and types of knowledge present in organisations. Knowledge can be stored in databanks and found in presentations, reports, libraries, policy documents and manuals. It can be moved around the organisation through information systems and by traditional methods such as meetings, workshops, courses, 'master classes', written publications, videos and tapes. The intranet provides an additional and very effective medium for communicating knowledge.

As argued by Nonaka (1991) and Nonaka and Takeuchi (1995), knowledge is either explicit or tacit. Explicit knowledge can be codified – it is recorded and available and is held in databases, in corporate intranets and intellectual property portfolios. Tacit knowledge exists in people's minds. It is difficult to articulate in writing and is acquired through personal experience. Hansen *et al* (1999) suggest that it includes scientific or technological expertise, operational know-how, insights about an industry, and business judgement. The main challenge in knowledge management is how to turn tacit knowledge into explicit knowledge.

Approaches to the development of knowledge management strategies

Two approaches to knowledge management have been identified by Hansen *et al* (1999):

□ *the codification strategy* – Knowledge is carefully codified and stored in databases where it can be accessed and used easily by anyone in the organisation. Knowledge is explicit and is codified using a 'people-to-document' approach. This strategy is therefore document-driven. Knowledge is extracted from the person who developed it, made independent of that person and re-used for various purposes. It is stored in some form of electronic repository for people to use, which allows many people to search for and retrieve codified knowledge without having to contact the person who originally developed it. This strategy relies largely on information technology to manage databases and also on the use of the intranet.

□ *the personalisation strategy* – Knowledge is closely tied to the person who developed it and is shared mainly through direct person-to-person contacts. It is a person-to-person approach that involves sharing tacit knowledge. The exchange is achieved by creating networks and encouraging face-to-face communication between individuals and teams by means of informal conferences, workshops, brainstorming and one-to-one sessions.

The research conducted by Hansen *et al* established that companies which use knowledge effectively pursue one strategy predominantly and use the second strategy to support the first. Those who try to excel at both strategies risk failing at both.

Strategic knowledge management issues

Various issues have to be addressed in developing knowledge management strategies.

The pace of change

How can the strategy ensure that knowledge management processes keep up with the pace of change and identify what knowledge should be captured and shared?

Relating knowledge management strategy to business strategy

Hansen *et al* (1999) assert that it is not knowledge *per se* but the way it is applied to strategic objectives that is the critical ingredient in competitiveness. They point out that 'competitive strategy must drive knowledge management strategy', and that managements have to answer the question 'How does knowledge that resides in the company add value for customers?' Mecklenberg *et al* (1999) argue that organisations should 'start with the business value of what they gather. If it doesn't generate value, drop it.'

Technology and people

Technology is central to organisations that adopt a codification strategy. But for those following a broader and potentially more productive personalisation strategy, IT assumes more of a supportive role. As Hansen *et al* (1999) comment:

In the codification model, managers need to implement a system that is much like a traditional library – it must contain a large cache of documents and include search engines that allow people to find and use the documents they need. In the personalisation model, it's more important to have a system that allows people to find other people.

Scarbrough *et al* (1999) suggest that 'technology should be viewed more as a means of communication and less as a means of storing knowledge'. Knowledge management is more about people than technology. As research by Davenport (1996) established, managers get two-thirds of their information from face-to-face or telephone conversations. There is a limit to how much tacit knowledge can be codified. In organisations that rely more on tacit than explicit knowledge, a person-to-person approach works best, and IT can only support this process; it cannot replace it.

The significance of process and social capital and culture

A preoccupation with technology may mean that too little attention is paid to the processes (social, technological and organisational) through which knowledge combines and interacts in different ways (Blackler, 1995, cited by Scarbrough *et al*, 1999). The key process is the interactions between people. This constitutes the social capital of an organisation – ie the 'network of relationships [that] constitute a valuable resource for the conduct of social affairs' (Nahpiet and Ghoshal, 1998). Social networks can be particularly important to ensure that knowledge is shared. What is also required is another aspect of social capital – trust. People are not willing to share knowledge with those they do not trust.

The culture of the company may inhibit knowledge-sharing. The norm may be for people to keep knowledge to themselves as much as they can because 'knowledge is power'. An open culture will encourage people to share their ideas and knowledge.

The components of a knowledge management strategy

A knowledge management strategy could be concerned with organisational people management processes which help to develop an open culture in which the values and norms emphasise the importance of sharing knowledge and facilitate it through networks. It might aim to encourage the development of communities of practice (defined by Wenger and Snyder, 2000, as 'groups of people informally bound together by shared expertise and a passion for joint enterprise'). The strategy could refer to methods of motivating people to share knowledge, and rewarding those who do so. The development of processes of organisational and individual learning – including the use of seminars and symposia to generate and assist in disseminating knowledge – could also be part of the strategy.

Commitment strategy

The concept of commitment refers to feelings of attachment and loyalty to the organisation and willingness to contribute to organisational objectives.

The importance of commitment was highlighted by Walton (1985). His theme was that improved performance would result if the organisation moved away from the traditional control-orientated approach to workforce management, which relies upon establishing order, exercising control and 'achieving efficiency in the application of the workforce'. He argued that this approach should be replaced by a commitment strategy. He suggested that workers respond best – and most creatively – not when they are tightly controlled by management, placed in narrowly-defined jobs and treated like an unwelcome necessity, but instead when they are given broader responsibilities, encouraged to contribute and helped to achieve satisfaction in their work. But as Cappelli (2000) comments, the changing employment relationship in many firms has militated against the development of lasting commitment. He suggests that new deals are being made, the central components of which are 'at least an explicit acknowledgement that the employer can no longer offer a long-term relationship, or be responsible for identifying and developing skills'. He also comments that 'In return, the employer will provide employees with the means and opportunity to develop their own skills in ways which will help ensure that they can have career advancement, even if it takes them outside their current employer.'

A commitment strategy will be concerned with the development of communication, education and training programmes, initiatives to increase involvement and 'ownership', and the introduction of performance and reward management processes. Cappelli (2000) sets out his tactics for raising commitment:

□ encouraging employee participation
□ providing employees with greater autonomy
□ indicating that the efforts of employees are respected and valued
□ training employees and making other investments in them to generate a feeling of 'reciprocity', the workers providing increased commitment in return for the employer's investments.

Communication programmes

It seems to be strikingly obvious that commitment will only be gained if people understand what they are expected to commit to. But managements too often fail to pay sufficient attention to delivering the message in terms which recognise that the frame of reference for those who receive it is likely to be quite different from their own. Management's expectations may not necessarily coincide with those of employees. Pluralism prevails. And in delivering the message, the use of different and complementary channels of communication – such as newsletters, briefing groups, videos, the intranet, notice boards, etc – is often neglected.

Education

Education is another form of communication. An educational programme is designed to increase both knowledge and understanding of, for example, total quality management. The aim is to influence behaviour and thereby progressively change attitudes.

Training

Training is designed to change behaviour by developing specific competences. For example, if one of the values to be supported is flexibility, the introduction of multiskilling programmes may be necessary to extend the range of skills possessed by members of work teams. Commitment is enhanced if managers can gain the confidence and respect of their teams, and training to improve the quality of management should form an important part of any programme for increasing commitment. Management training can also be focused on increasing the competence of managers in specific areas of their responsibility for gaining commitment – for example, performance management.

Developing ownership

A sense of belonging is enhanced if there is a feeling of 'ownership' among employees – not just in the literal sense of owning shares (although this can help) but in the sense of believing they are genuinely accepted by management as key stakeholders in the organisation. This concept of 'ownership' extends to participating in decisions on new developments and changes in working practices which affect the individuals concerned. They should be involved in making those decisions and feel that their ideas have been listened to and that they have contributed to the outcome. They will thus be more likely to accept the decision or change because it is owned by them rather than being imposed by management.

Developing job engagement

Job engagement – interest in and commitment to achieving the purpose of the job – can be created when designing jobs by concentrating on intrinsic motivating factors such as responsibility, achievement and recognition, and using these principles to govern the way in which the jobs are designed. Excitement in the job can be evoked by the quality of leadership and the willingness of managers and team leaders to recognise that they will obtain increased motivation and commitment if they pay continuous attention to the ways in which they delegate responsibility and give their staff the scope to use their skills and abilities.

Performance management

Performance management strategies can, as described in Chapter 10, be used to ensure that individuals have a clear understanding of where they fit in in the organisation, what is expected of them, and the skills and abilities they need to carry out their duties effectively.

Strategies for developing a climate of trust

The Institute of Personnel and Development suggested in its statement *People Make the Difference* (1994) that a strategy for building trust is the only basis upon which commitment can be generated. The IPD commented that 'In too many organisations inconsistency between what is said and what is done undermines trust, generates employee cynicism and provides evidence of contradictions in management thinking.'

It has also been suggested by Herriot *et al* (1998) that trust should be regarded as social capital – the fund of goodwill in any social group that enables people within it to collaborate with one another. Thompson (1998a) sees trust as a 'unique human resource capability that helps the organisation fulfil its competitive advantage' – a core competency that leads to high business performance. There is thus a business need to develop a climate of trust, as there is a business need to introduce effective pay-for-contribution processes that are built on trust.

Thompson points out that a number of writers have generally concluded that trust is 'not something that can, or should, be directly managed'. He cites Sako (1994), who wrote that:

> Trust is a cultural norm which can rarely be created intentionally because attempts to create trust in a calculative manner would destroy the effective basis of trust.

It may not be possible to 'manage' trust but, as Thompson comments, trust is an outcome of good management. It is created and maintained by managerial behaviour and by the development of better mutual understanding of expectations – employers of employees, and employees of employers. Herriot *et al* (1998) argue, 'Issues of trust are not in the end to do with managing people or processes, but are more about relationships and mutual support through change.'

Clearly, the sort of behaviour that is most likely to engender trust is exemplified when management is honest with people, keeps its word (delivers the deal) and practises what it preaches. Organisations that espouse core values ('people are our greatest asset') and then proceed to ignore them will be low-trust organisations.

More specifically, trust may be developed if management acts fairly, equitably and consistently, if a policy of transparency is implemented, if intentions and the reasons for proposals or decisions are communicated both to employees generally and to individuals, if there is full involvement in developing reward processes, and if mutual expectations are agreed through performance management.

Herriot *et al* (1998) suggest that if trust is lost, a four-step renewal strategy is required:

1. admission by top management that it has paid insufficient attention in the past to employees' diverse needs

2. a limited process of contracting by which a specific transition to a different way of working for a group of employees is embarked on in a form that takes individual needs into account

3. establishing 'knowledge-based' trust based not on a specific transactional deal but on a developing perception of trustworthiness

4. achieving trust based on identification by which each party empathises with the other's needs and therefore takes them on board themselves (although this final state is seldom reached in practice).

Organisational HR strategies in action
Leadership

The senior HR practitioners we met often referred to the significance of leadership. For example, Sarah Bonham, HR director of Great Ormond Street NHS Trust told us that:

> An important issue is leadership. Apart from structured training for managers we are developing policies,

procedures and processes in order to ensure that they recruit properly, can manage diversity and equality and take active steps to eliminate bullying and harassment of people. We have to demonstrate that all these things are in place because we are professionally and permanently accountable.

Culture management

The study by Marc Thompson (2000) of HR practices in a large hotel highlighted the importance of culture management. As he commented, 'The management of culture was clearly important in installing the centrality of service quality within the minds of both management and staff.' The process initially focused on managerial, and then later on non-managerial, employees, in particular with the introduction of the hotel's 'Statement of Purpose', which all employees were encouraged to see as a guide to individual behaviour. This management of culture has been critical in underpinning the importance and purpose of the HR initiatives subsequently introduced – for example, the purpose and necessity of performance appraisals, or for recruitment to be carried out in a systematic manner – in the minds of both management and employees. The key cultural issues were:

☐ Removal of the blame culture has been essential in encouraging employees to apply their own creativity in problem-solving, together with the development of a 'coaching' rather than a 'controlling' role on the part of managers.

☐ Employees are treated and valued as 'fixed', as opposed to 'variable', assets, given the amount of attitudinal and technical training with which they have been provided. Retention, career development and job security are now viewed by all as extremely important.

☐ The culture at the hotel is based very much on the principle of reciprocity. Management has realised it cannot expect the workforce to be committed to delivering a high-quality professional service and to engage in problem-solving unless a commitment is made back to them in terms of looking after individual needs and staff welfare.

Reward

Other HR directors referred to particular levers they had been using in their organisations to achieve cultural change. Developments to the reward system were often perceived as having the capacity to make a rapid and significant impact.

Developing a performance culture

John Lee, HR director of Halifax plc, explained that company's approach to developing a performance culture:

> Our aim has been to create a performance culture. With the assistance of Towers Perrin, who developed the core model, we can strip this down to four quadrants.

learning	environment
pay	benefits

> We have to be absolutely clear about what the deal is. How are we going to coach and develop them? What do they get out of working for the organisation apart from money? All this is about confidence, self-belief and a self-perception which says that we are good enough to go but also happy to stay. A large part of the last piece is driven by the environment which they are working in. It has got to be open, honest and straightforward and non-hierarchical. People must feel engaged and able to speak their minds. You have to have very clear signals from the top about these standards, and you have got to have managers who follow them. We have to make it very clear that no matter how good you are, if you get your business results by a climate of fear, then we don't want you. If you get there by creating leadership, that is a different thing.

10 FUNCTIONAL HR STRATEGIES

Functional HR strategies deal with the core areas of human resource management – resourcing, development, performance management, pay and conditions, and employee relations. Although treated here as separate entities, they should not be considered in isolation. Each aspect of HR strategy should be perceived as part of the whole strategic HRM process. The links between them, and the way policies and practices in one area can support policies and practices in another area, should be considered and placed in the context of the overall business strategy and any HR strategies that deal with organisational issues. A strategy for developing performance management processes may thus be connected with and reinforce strategies in other areas, such as human resource development and reward. It may also contribute to any overarching strategies – for example, those concerned with culture change. In other words, there is a pre-eminent need to adopt a holistic approach to strategic HRM which may be operationalised by 'bundling' (configuring) mutually reinforcing aspects together.

A comprehensive statement of HR strategy may include some overall goals concerned with organisational issues, but it may also set out priorities in the main areas of HR strategy. For example, the overall thrust of the strategy may be aimed at improving individual performance. This might be achieved by giving priority to the development of reward and performance strategies – which would, however, provide links to resourcing and development strategies, even though detailed development programmes might be scheduled for a later stage.

Resourcing strategy

HRM is fundamentally about matching human resources to the strategic and operational needs of the organisation and ensuring the full utilisation of those resources. It is concerned not only with obtaining and keeping the number and quality of staff required but also with selecting and promoting people who 'fit' the culture and the strategic requirements of the organisation, and then employing them efficiently.

Jean Tomlin, formerly HR director of Egg plc, informed us that 'the resource strategy was explicitly linked to the short- and long-term business goals'. Egg's publicly-stated goal to develop globally required the provision of HR solutions that could be quickly adopted across geographical boundaries. Technological solutions were found to pre-empt these requirements.

The concept that the strategic capability of an organisation depends on its resource capability in the shape of people provides the rationale for resourcing strategy. Iles (2001) in his review of developments in resourcing emphasises its strategic importance: 'Underlying the development of specific products, with their limited life cycles, was seen to be the acquisition and development of strategic skills pools, capabilities and core competences.'

The aim of resourcing strategy is therefore to ensure that a firm achieves competitive advantage by employing more capable people than its rivals. These people will have a wider and deeper range of skills and will behave in ways that maximise their contribution. The organisation attracts such people by being 'the employer of choice'. It retains them by providing better opportunities and rewards than others and by developing a positive psychological contract which increases commitment and creates mutual trust.

The strategic HRM approach to resourcing

HRM places more emphasis than traditional personnel management on finding people whose attitudes and behaviour are likely to be congruent with what management believes to be appropriate and conducive to success. In the words of Townley (1989), organisations are concentrating more on 'the attitudinal and behavioural characteristics of employees'.

The HRM approach to resourcing therefore emphasises that matching resources to organisational requirements does not simply mean maintaining the *status quo* and perpetuating a moribund culture. It can and often does mean radical changes in thinking about the skills and behaviours required in the future to achieve sustainable growth and cultural change.

Integrating business and resourcing strategies

The philosophy behind the strategic HRM approach to resourcing is that it is people who implement the strategic plan. As Quinn Mills (1985) has put it, the process is one of 'planning with people in mind'.

The integration of business and resourcing strategies is based on an understanding of the direction in which the organisation is going and the determination of:

□ the numbers of people required to meet business needs

□ the skills and behaviours required to support the achievement of business strategies

□ the impact of organisational restructuring as a result of rationalisation, decentralisation, delayering, mergers, product or market development, or the introduction of new technology – for example, cellular manufacturing

□ plans for changing the culture of the organisation in such areas as ability to deliver, performance standards, quality, customer service, teamworking and flexibility, which indicate the need for people with different attitudes, beliefs and personal characteristics.

These factors will be strongly influenced by the type of business strategies adopted by the organisation and the sort of business it is in. Resourcing strategies exist to provide the people and skills required to support the business strategy, but they should also contribute to the formulation of that strategy. HR directors have an obligation to point out to their colleagues the human resource opportunities and constraints that will affect the achievement of strategic plans. In mergers or acquisitions, for example, the ability of management within the company to handle the new situation and the quality of management in the new business will be important considerations.

The components of employee resourcing strategy

The components of employee resourcing strategy are:

☐ *human resource planning* – assessing future business needs and deciding on the numbers and types of people required

☐ *resourcing plans* – preparing plans for training programmes to help people from within the organisation to learn new skills. If needs cannot be satisfied from within the organisation, longer-term plans for ensuring that recruitment and selection processes will satisfy them will have to be prepared. These plans may include, as Cappelli (2000) suggests, 'Simply to get better at recruiting'. They may also incorporate policies for making the organisation an 'employer of choice' by providing advantageous terms and conditions, career opportunities, scope for using and developing skills and expertise that are generous or attractive enough to attract employees away from competitors and to keep existing employees from leaving

☐ *retention strategy* – preparing plans for retaining the people the organisation needs. As Cappelli (2000) suggests: 'Perhaps the most promising approach to managing retention relates to how jobs and tasks can be organised – whether it is possible to structure the work process itself so that employees feel more tightly bound to the organisation.' He also proposes that organisations should aim to find workers who are more likely to stay, or simply get better at replacing them when they leave

☐ *flexibility strategy* – planning for increased flexibility in the use of human resources to enable the organisation to make the best use of people and adapt swiftly to changing circumstances.

Strategic human resource development

Strategic human resource development (SHRD) is concerned with the provision of learning, development and training opportunities which (a) ensure that the organisation has the skilled, motivated and committed people it needs now and in the future, and (b) help to improve individual, team and organisational performance. As defined by Harrison (1997), 'Strategic HRD is a development that arises from a powerful vision about the people's abilities and potential, and arises within the overall strategic framework of the business.'

Strategic human resource development takes a broad and long-term view of how HRD strategies can support the achievement of business strategies; they are business-led. HRD strategies flow from business strategies, but they have a positive role in helping to ensure that the business attains its goals. To do this, it is essential to develop the skills base and intellectual capital the organisation requires as well as ensure that the right quality of people is available to meet present and future needs.

Human resource development strategies are business-led in that they are initiated by the strategic plans of the organisation and driven by the human resource plans which define knowledge, skills and competency requirements. They are declarations of intent which state, in effect, that 'we believe a strategy for investing in human capital will pay off, and this is what we are going to do about it'.

Such a strategy addresses issues relating to the development of the capabilities of individuals and teams. It is also concerned with encouraging organisational learning, as outlined below. However, as Argyris (1992) contends:

> Organisations do not perform the actions that produce the learning; it is individual members of the organisations who behave in ways that lead to it, although organisations can create conditions that facilitate such learning.

Human resource development strategies can be aimed at attracting and retaining human capital as well as developing it. This is in accordance with the concept that workers are human capital investors; they will place their investable capital where it can earn the highest return. They want to develop their skills, potential and employability. Employers who undertake to do this and deliver their promises are more likely to get and to keep the sort of human capital they need. This applies to all categories of employees, not just knowledge workers.

The aims of strategic human resource development

Strategic human resource development aims to produce a coherent and comprehensive framework for ensuring that effective organisational and individual learning takes place. Human resource development activities may include traditional training and management development programmes, but the emphasis is much more on developing intellectual capital and promoting organisational, team and individual learning. It is also about planning approaches to the encouragement of self-development (self-managed learning) with appropriate support and guidance from within the organisation.

HRD policies are closely associated with that aspect of HRM which is concerned with investing in people and developing the organisation's intellectual capital. As Keep (1989) says:

> One of the primary objectives of HRM is the creation of conditions whereby the latent potential of employees will be realised and their commitment to the causes of the organisation secured. This latent potential is taken to include not merely the capacity to acquire and utilise new skills and knowledge, but also a hitherto untapped wealth of ideas about how the organisation's operations might be better ordered.

Strategic human resource development deals with the development of individual learning strategies and the development of organisational learning. It may also aspire to the creation of a 'learning organisation'.

Individual learning strategies

The individual learning strategies of an organisation are driven by its human resource requirements, the latter being expressed in terms of the sort of skills and behaviours required to achieve business goals. The starting-point should be the approaches adopted to the provision of learning and development opportunities, bearing in mind the distinction between learning and development made by Pedler *et al* (1989), who see learning as being concerned with an increase in knowledge or a higher degree of an existing skill, whereas development is more towards a different state of being or functioning.

The strategy should cover:

☐ how learning needs will be identified

☐ the role of personal development planning and self-managed learning

☐ the support that should be provided for individual learning in the form of guidance, coaching, provisions for e-learning, learning resource centres, mentoring, external courses designed to meet the particular needs of individuals, internal or external training programmes, and courses designed to meet the needs of groups of employees.

Organisational learning strategies

Organisations can be described (Harrison, 1997) as continuous learning systems. Organisational learning strategy aims to develop a firm's resource-based capability. Pettigrew and Whipp (1991) believe that the focus of organisational learning should be on developing 'organisational capability'. This means paying attention to the intricate and often unnoticed or hidden learning that takes place and influences what occurs within the organisation. 'Hidden learning' is acquired and developed in the normal course of work by people acting as individuals and, importantly, in groups or 'communities of practice' (Wenger and Snyder, 2000).

Organisational learning is concerned with the development of new knowledge or insights that have the potential to influence behaviour (Mabey and Salaman, 1995). It takes place within the wide institutional context of inter-organisational relationships (Geppert, 1996) and 'refers broadly to an organisation's acquisition of understanding, know-how, techniques and practices of any kind and by any means' (Argyris and Schon, 1996). Organisational learning can be characterised as an intricate three-stage process consisting of knowledge acquisition, dissemination, and shared implementation (Dale,

1994). Knowledge may be acquired from direct experience, the experience of others or organisational memory.

Argyris (1982) suggests that organisational learning occurs under two conditions: first when an organisation achieves what is intended, and second when a mismatch between intentions and outcomes is identified and corrected. He distinguishes between single-loop and double-loop learning. These two types of learning have been classified by West (1996) as adaptive and generative learning.

Single-loop or adaptive learning is sequential, incremental and focused on issues and opportunities that are within the scope of the organisation's activities. As described by Argyris (1982), organisations in which single-loop learning is the norm define the 'governing variables' – ie what they expect to achieve in terms of targets and standards – and then monitor and review achievements and take corrective action as necessary, thus completing the loop. Double-loop learning occurs when the monitoring process initiates action to redefine the 'governing variables' to meet the new situation, which may be imposed by the external environment. The organisation has learned something new about what has to be achieved in the light of changed circumstances, and can then decide how this should be effected.

Strategies to enhance organisational learning focus on the processes that are involved. These include the development of a context which encourages individual and team learning but also provides scope for people to reflect on the issues facing the organisation – now and in the longer term – and to decide what has been learned or what needs to be learned in order to make the best use of its business imperatives and opportunities.

Importantly, organisational learning strategies also focus on knowledge management, especially that of tacit or implicit knowledge. Hall (1992) remarks that this type of knowledge will be 'enhanced most effectively by a process of socialisation'. Nonaka (1991) has illustrated through case studies that tacit knowledge is more likely to be distributed if the organisational culture encourages and facilitates teamwork, informal meetings and discussions, exchanges of views and observations of best practice.

The strategy may include the development of procedures to identify and disseminate tacit knowledge, such as interviewing people and teams to release their knowledge, holding seminars in which knowledge is exchanged, or requiring individuals and teams to record 'lessons learned' from projects, assignments, conferences and courses. But it is more important, and more difficult, to develop a culture in which the values and norms of the organisation encourage knowledge-sharing, bearing in mind that knowledge is developed through processes of social interaction. The creation of such a culture can be helped by treating commitment to knowledge-sharing as a factor to be incorporated into performance management processes, and providing financial rewards *and* non-financial rewards (eg recognition) to those who make a worthwhile contribution to the exchange and development of knowledge.

Strategies for developing a learning organisation

The philosophy underpinning the learning organisation concept, as expressed by Garvin (1993), is that learning is an essential ingredient if organisations are to survive; that learning at operational, policy and strategic levels needs to be conscious, continuous and integrated; and that management is responsible for creating a climate in which all their people can learn continuously.

Wick and Leon (1995) have defined a learning organisation as one that 'continually improves by rapidly creating and refining the capabilities required for future success'. Senge (1990) calls the learning organisation 'an organisation that is continually expanding to create its future'. Garvin (1993) defines a learning organisation as one that is 'skilled at creating, acquiring, and transferring knowledge, and at modifying its behaviour to reflect new knowledge and insights'.

A learning organisation strategy is based on the belief that learning is a continuous process rather than a set of discrete training activities (Sloman, 1999). It incorporates strategies for individual and organisational learning and, importantly, for knowledge management. Scarbrough and Carter (2000) suggest that although the concepts of the learning organisation and organisational learning have offered some valuable insights into the way in which knowledge and learning are fostered by management practice, they have been over-shadowed – at least in terms of practitioner interest – by the explosive growth of knowledge management activity. They comment that:

> This may be attributable to the problems of translating their broad, holistic principles into practice. Knowledge management initiatives, by contrast, are often more specifically targeted and can therefore be identified more closely with business needs.

Burgoyne (1999) also believes that the concept of the learning organisation should be integrated with knowledge management initiatives so that different forms of knowledge can be linked, fed by organisational learning and used in adding value to goods and services. This, he states, will replace the 'soft' organisational development tools of the 1970s that were pressed hurriedly into service with the result that 'The learning organisation has not delivered its full potential or lived up to all our aspirations.'

HRD strategies in action

Keith Ireland, former director of HR at New Forest District Council explained that:

> Another big investment has been in our management development programme. It has been a phenomenal success – even if the groups haven't learnt about management, they get to know the other members of their group as their resource to call on if things get tough. I think there has been a general buzz through the whole Council, and people are really looking forward to getting on this year's programme.

A chief executive's point of view was expressed by Richard McCarthy of the Peabody Trust:

> I want people to think more creatively about how they can be developed to contribute to the strategy and to enhance their ability to do more in the Trust. In essence, they need to know that they will be rewarded

by development because it actually enables you to get a different job or to achieve higher responsibility.

Strategies for managing performance

Performance management can be defined as a strategic and integrated approach to delivering sustained success to organisations by improving the performance of the people who work in them and by developing the capabilities of teams and individual contributors.

Performance management is strategic in the sense that it is concerned with the broader issues facing the organisation if it is to function effectively in its environment, and with the general direction in which it intends to go to achieve longer-term goals. It is integrated in four senses:

□ *vertical integration* – linking or aligning business, team and individual objectives

□ *functional integration* – linking functional strategies in different parts of the business

□ *HR integration* – linking different aspects of human resource management, especially organisational development, human resource development and reward, to achieve a coherent approach to the management and development of people

□ *the integration of individual needs with those of the organisation*, as far as is possible.

Aims

Performance management strategy aims to provide the means through which better results can be obtained from the organisation, teams and individuals by understanding and managing performance within an agreed framework of planned goals, standards and competence requirements. It involves the development of processes for establishing shared understanding about what is to be achieved, and an approach to managing and developing people in a way which increases the probability that it *is* achieved in the short and longer term. It is owned and driven by line management.

Performance management is a continuing responsibility for

managers and team leaders. It is not achieved by a once-a-year performance appraisal meeting. Individual employees should also be responsible for managing their own performance, but may need guidance and support in doing so.

When developing performance management strategies it is necessary to recognise that employees increasingly come to possess knowledge and skills that management lacks: 'Employees need to be motivated to apply these skills through discretionary effort. And it is often the case that the firm's business or production strategy can only be achieved when this discretionary effort is contributed' (Purcell, 1999).

Performance management concerns

Performance management strategy is basically concerned with *performance improvement* in order to achieve organisational, team and individual effectiveness. Organisations, as stated by Lawson (1995), have 'to get the right things done successfully'.

Secondly, performance management strategy is concerned with *employee development*. Performance improvement is not achievable unless there are effective processes of continuous development. This addresses the core competences of the organisation and the capabilities of individuals and teams.

Thirdly, performance management strategy is concerned with satisfying the needs and expectations of all the organisation's *stakeholders* – owners, management, employees, customers, suppliers and the general public. In particular, employees are treated as partners in the enterprise whose interests are respected and who have a voice on matters that concern them, whose opinions are sought and listened to. Performance management should respect the needs of individuals and teams as well as those of the organisation, although it must be recognised that those needs will not always coincide.

Finally, performance management strategy is concerned with *communication* and *involvement*. It aims to create a climate in which a continuing dialogue between managers and the members of their teams takes place to define expectations and share information on the organisation's mission, values and objectives. Performance management can contribute to the development of a high-involvement organisation by getting teams and individuals to participate in defining their objectives and the means to achieve them. Performance management strategy aims to provide the means through which better results can be obtained from the organisation, teams and individuals by understanding and managing performance within an agreed framework of planned goals, standards and competence requirements.

Performance management at Coventry Building Society

Julian Atkins, head of human resources at the Coventry Building Society told us that:

> Performance management is integrated with training because much of it is competency-based. Every individual has a role profile which details the competency profile for the job – ie the level of competency we expect people to have to do the job well. Performance management starts with performance planning, followed by a review. Everyone has a personal development plan. This is about any immediate training people require. Development planning looks further. We ask individuals to answer questions about what they want to do, their aspirations, what they think their particular skills are, and where the gaps are. All staff have a development planning interview once a year. This has helped with succession planning.
>
> Competencies have been invaluable to us. They are based on positive behavioural statements. So there is nowhere to hide. You can't achieve anything by doing it in a dysfunctional way – you've got to do it the right way.

Reward strategy

Reward strategy determines the level and mix of financial and non-financial rewards required to attract, retain and encourage individuals with the skills, abilities and competence necessary to deliver performance outcomes that support the achievement of business goals.

It is founded on the proposition that the ultimate source of value is people. This means that reward processes must respond creatively to their needs as well as to those of the organisation. The basis of the strategy is the organisation's requirements for performance in the short and longer term as expressed in its corporate strategy. The strategy relies on an understanding of the behaviours required to achieve high performance and of what can be done to encourage those behaviours by recognising and valuing them. Reward strategy can support change, reinforcing and validating the thrust of the business. But as Murlis (1996) points out, 'Reward strategy will be characterised by diversity and conditioned both by the legacy of the past and the realities of the present.' Essentially, however, 'reward strategies should be business-led, responding to the needs of the business' (Armstrong and Murlis, 1998).

Components of effective reward strategies

Brown (2001) states that it is necessary to recognise that effective reward strategies have three components:

☐ They have to have clearly-defined goals and a well-defined link to business objectives.

☐ There have to be well-designed pay and reward programmes, tailored to the needs of the organisation and its people, and consistent and integrated with one another.

☐ Perhaps most important and most neglected, there must be effective and supportive HR and reward processes in place.

The content of reward strategy

Reward strategies deal with issues concerning pay structures, the use of job evaluation, the approach to keeping pace with market rates, paying for individual performance, competence, contribution or skill, team pay, relating bonuses to organisational performance, and the provision of pensions and benefits, including the use of flexible benefits. They are influenced by the need to adopt a 'total rewards' approach, the objective of which, as defined by WorldatWork (2000):

> is to drive desired behaviours in your workforce, reinforce your overall business strategy and ensure organisational success. The solution is to find the proper mix of

rewards that satisfy the existing and potential needs of your current and potential workforce, given existing business conditions and cost constraints.

WorldatWork defines the concept of total reward as 'all of the available tools that may be used to attract, retain, motivate and satisfy employees'. Three main components are defined by WorldatWork:

- *compensation* – base pay and variable pay
- *benefits* – income and personal protection arrangements
- *work experience* – intrinsic rewards that address the unique individual needs of employees which are less tangible than pay or benefits and include recognition of effort and performance, balance of work–life issues, cultural issues, development opportunities, and environmental factors.

Total reward strategies aim to develop the right balance of those rewards and will pay as much, if not more intention to those relating to the 'work experience' – ie the non-financial rewards that have a more powerful and longer-lasting effect than financial rewards.

Reward strategy in action

The Children's Society

When asked why the development of a reward strategy was a leading-edge part of The Children's Society's HR strategy, Geoff Hawkins, director of HR, replied:

> Partly it was the organisational context. When I joined the Society, one of the concerns of the management team was the limitations of our present reward processes which relied on traditional job evaluation and incremental scales linked to local government pay spines. It was seen as cumbersome and not meeting business needs. We were seeking to be a responsive organisation which values innovation and creativity, but when you analysed the job evaluation scheme factors, the way they were weighted indicated that innovation and creativity featured very low in the list of priorities.

It seemed to me that this provided a vehicle for a number of opportunities for HR. First of all, to ensure that a core process fully reflected the values and the direction the organisation was seeking to go. But secondly, to provide a vehicle for change in managerial behaviour. If, as we intended, managers became more involved in managing the reward of their people, then they would be able to make a greater impact on the way those people were managed than if they simply took a solution from HR, which wasn't a solution at all because it was an administrative process. I saw the development of a reward strategy as an important lever to help HR make a big impact on the managerial culture of the organisation.

A significant cultural change we are introducing in the way we recognise people is the concept of contribution-related pay. This is moving away from strict performance-related pay which is driven by outputs and looking at the competence people bring to their role. It seemed to me that the process had to be capable of evolving so that when it is embedded in the organisation in two or three years' time we could consider adding a performance (output) related element to it. But I was quite happy to make a commitment that we would not introduce performance-related pay in the first instance. This lowered the resistance [discernible] at that time amongst a number of quite important vested interests – the trade union and some senior managers, who felt that they would have to struggle to measure performance as they saw it. Another practical reason for not introducing contribution-related pay is that we also need to review and revise our performance management processes.

The Coventry Building Society

Julian Atkins, head of HR at the Coventry Building Society believes that:

One of the key core values of the organisation [centres on] valuing what people do and recognising what people do. I believe that these are very happily caught up in the concepts of broad-banding and contribution pay as developed in our reward strategy. By having a broader approach you remove a lot of arguments – endless debates to try and fine-tune posts to the nth degree as to whether they should be three increments higher than another post. And we are talking probably about little more than a couple of pounds' difference, but symbolically it was very, very important that those distinctions were made, both to the individual and the manager. So we've got rid of a lot of dross in the process in order to focus on what mattered, which is what people were actually contributing and what recognition they should get for that.

We want to pay people fairly, we want them to share in the success of the business. We introduced salary benchmarking and decided that we wanted to be a market median player but with the ability to reward staff for better performance. Our pay system is underpinned by the competencies an individual has, and that determines where people are in the career-stream structure. How well people achieve their individual objectives and develop their competencies affects their individual pay. We have team-based pay for sales teams, and head office staff are in the corporate bonus scheme.

HSBC

Barry Hine, former head of HR at HSBC, told us that:

The key is reward for performance – no doubt about that. The theme is expressed as 'Let's Reward Success'. It arose as a kind of re-awakening that everyone in the organisation should be able to improve their performance year on year. After all, shareholders require year-on-year improvement. It is geared to the financial strategic plan. And everyone has to fit into that, in branches, call centres, service centres, electronic banking or whatever, and from the top to the bottom. This is linked to a financial reward which has a personal factor according to attainment of objectives, and a corporate factor related to the Bank's performance. It is financially driven, but the reality is that we achieved success by focusing people's attention on five or six main objectives for the year. Everybody's goals are measured in as financial terms as possible, and between that all jobs are definable in terms of customer service – people in support as well as in the front line. We use the term 'managing for value'. All staff know what contribution they are making to team results, but they also know what financial rewards they can expect. People are not necessarily financially-orientated, but they do expect that they are rewarded for the good things they do.

The Peabody Trust

Ann Lewis, director of HR at the Peabody Trust, explained that:

Another important part of the HR strategy was to revise our pay systems so they could serve the organisation better by being more flexible. We wanted to reward people's contribution, what they achieve and the competencies they display in achieving it. We also wanted to take away the mystique. To our staff, we came across as being deliberately obscure – they could not understand how the pay system worked.

Employee relations strategy

Employee relations strategy defines the intentions of the organisation about what needs to be done and what needs to be changed in the ways in which the organisation manages its relationships with employees and their trade unions. Like all other aspects of HR strategy, employee relations strategy should be integrated with the business strategy. For example, if the business strategy is to concentrate on achieving competitive edge through innovation and the delivery of quality to its customers, the employee relations strategy may emphasise processes of involvement and participation, including the implementation of programmes for continuous improvement and total quality management. If, however, the strategy for competitive advantage, or even survival, is cost reduction, the employee relations strategy may concentrate on how this can be achieved by maximising co-operation with the unions and employees and by minimising detrimental effects on employees and disruption to the organisation.

Employee relations strategies should be distinguished from employee relations policies. Strategies are dynamic. They provide a sense of direction, and give an answer to the question 'How are we going to get from here to there?' Employee relations policies are more about the here and now. They express 'the way things are done around here', as far as dealing with unions and employees is concerned. Of course they will evolve, but that may not be as the result of a strategic choice. It is when a deliberate decision is made to change policies that a strategy for achieving this change has to be formulated. So if the policy is to increase commitment, the strategy could consider how this might be achieved by involvement and participation processes.

Concerns of employee relations strategy

Employee relations strategy is concerned with how to:

□ build stable and co-operative relationships with employees which minimise conflict

□ achieve commitment through employee involvement and communications processes

□ develop mutuality – a common interest in achieving the organisation's goals through the development of organisational cultures based on shared values between management and employees.

Strategic directions

The intentions expressed by employee relations strategies may direct the organisation towards:

□ changing forms of recognition, including single union recognition, or de-recognition

□ changes in the form and content of procedural agreements

□ new bargaining structures, including decentralisation or single-table bargaining

□ the achievement of increased levels of commitment through involvement or participation – giving employees a voice

- increasing the extent to which management controls operations in such areas as flexibility
- generally improving the employee relations climate in order to produce more harmonious and co-operative relationships
- developing a 'partnership' with trade unions recognising that employees are stakeholders and that it is to the advantage of both parties to work together (this could be described as a unitarist strategy aimed at increasing mutual commitment).

PART IV

THE PRACTICE OF STRATEGIC HRM

11 STRATEGIC HRM IN ACTION

As Armstrong and Long (1994) noted:

> On reading the literature we sometimes found the impression that the concept of HRM was invented by academics for academics. The rhetoric of strategic HRM does not seem to relate to what actually happens in offices, factories, shops and distribution depots.

Their research and the earlier research conducted by Armstrong (1989) did, however, indicate that there were organisations consciously developing and implementing HR strategies which bore at least some resemblance to the observations of academics, even if they did not call it strategic HRM.

Since 1994 a considerable amount of research as described in Chapter 7 has been carried out by British and US academics to demonstrate the link between HRM and business performance. Much has been discovered about what is actually going on and how well it works – even if it is not yet possible to describe with certainty *how* it works and *why* it works.

Further in-depth longitudinal studies are being carried out by a research team at Bath University led by Professor John Purcell and funded by the CIPD, designed to address and find answers to these questions. The CIPD has also funded an extensive research programme, many of the results from which are summarised in this book, in a bid to develop the body of evidence.

Our own recent research, which involved discussions with 15 senior HR practitioners and three chief executives, has aimed to provide further information and practical understanding to illustrate the academic material on how organisations set about developing and implementing integrated HR strategies.

This chapter aims to summarise what came out of our research and also out of the research undertaken by Marc Thompson, Ian Kessler and Kim Hoque (CIPD, 2000) for the CIPD, describing strategic HRM in action by reference to actual cases and, often, in the words of the key players. Action areas covered in the chapter are:

□ the characteristics of HR strategy
□ the overall content of HR strategy
□ the integration of HR and business strategy (vertical integration)
□ the integration of different areas of HR strategy (horizontal integration or 'bundling')
□ developing and implementing HR strategies.

The characteristics of HR strategy

A number of chief executives and heads of HR were asked to explain their concept of strategic HRM within their organisations. Their views are set out below. There was a considerable degree of consistency in the beliefs expressed about the need for integration between HR and business strategies.

The Children's Society

Geoff Hawkins, director of HR, recounted how:

Our emerging HR strategy is a development of the HR business plan, which in 2001 looked like this:

The Human Resources Division works with managers and staff of the Society to secure the following outcomes:

□ the development and continuous improvement of the human resources strategy for the Society
□ the development of the organisation in support of delivering the Corporate Plan and change management leadership
□ the promotion of an employee relations climate which facilitates the aims of The Children's Society to be a force for change in the lives of children and young people
□ the effective use of staff resources within The Children's Society

□ the commissioning of training and development programmes appropriate to business and employee needs.

There is a degree of flexibility which is dictated by the
demands that users of the service generate – a significant proportion of the human resources activity is reactive to management and staff needs.

The clients of the division include the Council, the Society
Management Team, managers and employees of the Society,
together with external organisations such as Government
departments and trade unions.

Determinants of workload include:

□ the extent to which the organisation currently complies
with the law or needs to change to do so
□ the industrial relations climate and the extent to which
there is a procedure-based culture or skilled managers and
leaders not dependent on procedure and schooled in the
application of best practice
□ the extent of the change agenda (eg the pace and depth of
change needed in culture, systems, process and structure
in order to implement the Corporate Plan; Social Work
projects opening and closing)
□ the extent to which the Society wishes to apply best practice
□ the extent to which the Society seeks to become effective
through innovative and modern management approaches
□ the extent of the investment in staff capability and
capacity
□ the interest among clients in using Human Resources to
improve performance skills.

As a support function its objectives and activities are intrin-
sically linked to the outcomes which other parts of the
Society are seeking to realise. The priorities are informed by
the Corporate Plan and the need to maintain effective support
services to managers in the deployment of the human
resources of the Society.

There will be increased demand for work in relation to
employee relations to support the organisational changes as a
consequence of the financial and organisational change

imperatives. There are existing pressures which are stretching the Division's resources – eg the expansion in Wales by 60 new posts. These have been reflected in the planned utilisation of staff resources.

Core values

The staff of the Human Resources Division fully subscribe to the values of the Society set out in its mission statement. The function is internally-focused and concerned with the management of the human resources of the Society. Nevertheless, all its work will be informed by the impact of its actions on our work with children and young people. Unlike our relationship with children and young people to whom the Society reaches out unconditionally, the relationship with its staff is conditional as determined by the Society's employment policies and procedures and its contracts of employment.

The Human Resources Division will:

☐ *reach out* – commit to respect all staff with respect for the personal and cultural backgrounds and regardless of their organisational position

☐ *involve and listen* – recognise the contributions which individuals can make to good decisions and take active steps to secure their participation

☐ *overcome injustice* – encourage fair and just processes within the Society and develop benchmarks against which human resource activity can be seen to meet best professional practice

☐ *recognise and nurture* – ensure that all staff and volunteers who add value to our work with children and young people are valued and rewarded and have opportunities for development to achieve business outcomes.

Priorities for the next financial year

The priorities for new activities in the next financial year are to:

☐ implement the rewards strategy of the Society to support the Corporate Plan and secure the recruitment, retention and motivation of staff to deliver its business objectives

- manage the development of the human resources information system to secure productivity improvements in administrative processes
- introduce improved performance management processes for managers and staff of the Society
- implement training and development which supports the business objectives of the Society and improves the quality of its work with children and young people
- develop and implement a revised Management Development Programme
- facilitate regional and local project groups that are relevant to the diversity and geographical spread of the Society in order to improve effective working between divisions, and thereby increase organisational capacity
- produce a new staff handbook to reflect the new management paradigm being developed within the Society
- maintain cost-effective support services for managers in ensuring the effective use of human resources within the Society
- assess the implications of the MacPherson Report and review current equal opportunities policy monitoring and implementation
- prepare a Human Resources Strategy for the Society.

Geoff Hawkins additionally commented:

> You have to get the fundamentals right. If they are not consistent with your overall strategy, you must do something about it. Ninety per cent of an organisation is what it has always been. There will always be routine. An organisation becomes dysfunctional if it is always doing new things because you never get consolidation and you never get processes embedded if you are always changing them. For example, you have to have well-established recruitment processes. You ought to be able to take the key objectives of the organisation and correlate HR practices with them, the routine maintenance activities as well as innovations.
>
> People frequently measure their success by what they have done differently. But often what you need is to do

the same thing well, to deliver the basic operations of the organisation effectively.

Unless HR delivers high-quality services, new offerings are a waste of time. If people perceive that the contribution of HR is second-rate, those offerings will not be valued however well designed they are. Our success in HR depends not on what new policies I design with my senior colleagues but on what our personnel and training consultants actually deliver to managers on a day-to-day basis.

Egg

Jean Tomlin, former HR director, explained the characteristics and aims of the Egg HR strategy. 'The major factor influencing business strategy was the need to attract, maintain and retain the right people.' In the light of Egg's successful creation, solutions from the past could in the main not be applied. How Egg treated and responded to its people would be reflected in the brand proposition offered to its customers, and vice versa.

Great Ormond Street NHS Trust

Sarah Bonham, training and development manager said to us that:

Our HR strategy is embedded in the business plan. There are a number of centrally-driven initiatives that are based on the performance framework for the Trust and that are in turn based on the government's performance frameworks. The plan covers such areas as the way doctors and nurses are trained, recruitment and retention, especially of nurses and other clinical staff, improving working lives, equal opportunities, personal development planning, and continuing professional development.

Lloyds TSB

In the opinion of Paul Turner, Group HR business director:

The criteria for a good HR strategy is the same as for business strategy. You must separate out objectives from strategy, mission and values. You need clearly articulated values, clear objectives, clear strategy and clear understanding of the resource allocation required.

If you accept that competitive advantage is achieved through people (and most senior managers now do) and this is a core component of HR strategy, then for example training strategy must be geared towards this.

New Forest District Council

Keith Ireland, former director of HR, commented that:

> The focus is on the organisation of excellence. That is our starting-point. We want to make sure that we have an excellent performance management system – we want to make sure that people achieve their full potential. These are the high-level HR strategies.

The Department of Health

Neil Offley and Steve Gosling of the Human Resources Directorate at the Department of Health believe that:

> Organisations deliver their purpose through people. What we seek is effective HR management and HR leadership as an integral part of overall organisation and effectiveness. To create a service strategy you have to look at HR and the organisational components. Otherwise, you will create the wrong focus for that service strategy.
>
> There are two iterative processes going on. You have a business strategy – the NHS plan – and there is a connection between the development of that business strategy and the development of an HR strategy that links with it, integrates with it, and reinforces it. They need to feed off one another. But there is also the implementation process which needs to constantly feed back to the policy-making process – this is working, that is not working, this would work better if you did this. So this feedback informs policy, and there needs to be a constant linking back between the two. To achieve this, the Modernisation Agency and the Leadership Centre have been set up to bring policy and development and policy implementation together so that the improvements are actually delivered on the ground.

Peabody Trust

Richard McCarthy, chief executive, told us that:

> First of all, you have your business strategy, which includes at management team level a review of what it is we expect our HR to deliver. We define what the strategy means in terms of its implications for us as individuals and for our employees. We decide what changes we have to effect and how we are going to communicate with and motivate the staff group to achieve these changes. The management team needs to be clear on what our vision for our people is, what we see our people doing, what we think they have to learn and what practices they need to change to effect the strategy we want. When you have answered these questions, then you can start to decide what the strategy is. The key to all this is that all our directors have to contribute. The most important thing is the corporate understanding and responsibility for HR strategy.
>
> A good HR strategy is one which actually makes people feel valued. It makes them knowledgeable about the organisation, and makes them feel clear about where they sit as a group, or team, or individual. It must show them how what they do either together or individually fits into that strategy. Importantly, it should indicate how people are going to be rewarded for their contribution and how they might be developed and grow in the organisation.

Ann Lewis, director of HR at the Peabody Trust, amplified these comments:

> HR has a major part to play in achieving the strategic aims. What we are seeking is to put into place a number of structures that will enable our people to understand the work of the organisation and contribute to it in a very fundamental way. At my request, we now have a Governor's Committee which is specific to HR.
>
> We want to make sure that our basic HR policies are as attractive to existing and potential staff as they need to be. We don't necessarily say that we are going to be out there a long way in front of everyone – we certainly need to balance costs with attractiveness.

The overall content of HR strategy

It was evident from our research that there was no standard model or framework for HR strategies. Each organisation tackled strategic HRM in its own way, although while the detail might vary, certain themes stand out, particularly those associated with culture change. As Thompson (2000) commented on the basis of the CIPD-sponsored research:

> Turning to the content of HR strategies across the various cases, it can be seen that there is surprising convergence on the objectives of the strategies – to modify values, behaviours and attitudes. However, the paths taken to get there were quite different.

Some examples are given below.

Civil Service College

Ewart Wooldridge, chief executive, described the college's HR strategy.

The key components of our HR strategy are:

- *investing in intellectual capital* – We have to improve the level of intellectual capital in the college, because if we don't, our customers will eventually lose faith in us.
- *performance management* – We have integrated into our performance management processes the values contained in the HR strategy, and performance reviews focus on how well people are performing on these values.
- *job design* – This is a key component and is concerned with how jobs are designed and how they relate to the whole business
- *the reward system* – This is crucial to the way we work. In developing reward policies we have to take into account that we are a very hard-driven business. We need a lot of contact time between lecturers and students. One of the issues is about team versus individual incentives.
- *the work–life balance* – Staff work long hours, but they can have a pretty flexible life.

We have to align all these components. If we don't, it is going to become dysfunctional.

New Forest District Council

Keith Ireland said that:

> We have broken the strategy down into eight sections: including employee relations, recruitment and retention, training, pay and benefits, health and safety, and absence management. We can link the HR strategy right back to the overall council policy. We have strong values and our strategy framework relates to those.
>
> We can see that some organisations have quite sophisticated approaches to HR but we've found that this just confuses people. What we need is simple things that enable people to associate their work programme with corporate objectives.

Peabody Trust

Richard McCarthy remarked that:

> I like the term 'HR' rather than 'Personnel' because it is about recognising that HR strategies and policies are more than just hours of work and your contract of employment, and even more than reward system and structure. I think that if you have good HR policies, you are thinking about reward, but also about communication and involvement. So I was very keen to introduce a staff council here, which I have never used before – there are very few in our sector and this will be one of them. We have had a reasonable first year, and I want to see if we can shift the discussion upwards and spend more time on strategy and employee input.

Smiths Industries

Annie Minto, HR director said that:

> One of the things I have learned is that you can't push on all fronts. You have to concentrate on a few things and do them well. We have recently focused on four main areas: health and safety, environment, succession planning and business-driven compensation packages.

Integrating the business and HR strategies

Differentis

Stephanie Bird, people and process leader, recalled that:

> At Differentis people management was inextricably linked with the overall aims and objectives of the business. They are essentially a knowledge business – their product is based on the knowledge and expertise of the people they employ. It is therefore necessary for those people to behave in a way that is compatible with the organisation's aims and to comply with the expectations of the kind of customers they are trying to attract.

The Children's Society

Geoff Hawkins explained that:

> I think it is very important to directly correlate any HR activity with the strategic intent of the organisation. So when I formulated our reward strategy, the paper I did for our management team and the trustees sought to make the connection between what was intended and what were, at that time, and remain, the priorities of the organisation. The aim of the HR strategy is to mirror the core values we set out in the Corporate Plan which are:
>
> □ to adopt a social justice attitude to all we do
> □ to be a child-centred organisation
> □ to concentrate on achieving change for children and young people throughout England and Wales
> □ to develop the necessary internal tools to align the organisation to our external aims.
>
> It is clearly under the last heading that most of the HR activities are focused.
>
> Similarly, involving and listening is a core value for the Society, and the Strategic Direction section of the Corporate Plan states that:
>
> □ We will develop a governance system that includes the participation of children and young people.

□ We will address the power relationship between the Society and children and young people.

□ We will ensure that children and young people have a direct and transparent involvement in the development of our programme and policy work.

An example of involving children and young people in the governance of the Society is in selecting staff. The Society when appointing a Director for Children and Young People – who heads the biggest unit of work in the organisation with 60 per cent of our staff based in it – required short-listed candidates to meet and make a presentation to a group of children and young people. They assessed the candidate's skills in both presenting and relating to them. Two young people were members of the final selection panel with our Trustees, and whilst they will have no formal vote, they will have as much right to participate as any other adviser on the panel. Their voices were heard.

So far as our staff are concerned, we relate to the core value of involving children and young people by saying that we recognise the contribution that individuals can make and that decisions are, in essence, better because of that contribution.

Another example is policies for nurturing our staff in which the driving force is that people have potential and we should try to realise it. This is consistent with what we are saying about children and young people. We believe very firmly that they all have potential and our task is to help realise that potential. In doing so, we recognise that in many instances they don't demonstrate the potential they've got because the system which impacts on them leads to alienation – dissociation from society.

Civil Service College

As described by Ewart Wooldridge:

The main elements of our HR strategy derive from a model of the environment we work in. The starting-point is our business objectives, but we have separated this out into two areas: supporting the business and culture change. We have a three-part vision on why we are here, but our strategy is actually change-driven. Our vision is eventually about changing the way people work and changing the way people connect. There is real integration between our business strategy, our values and our strategies for research and training. For example, an important business driver is the government's saying that the management of diversity is an overwhelming priority in changing the culture. In HR strategy terms it is then necessary to ensure that this place acts and behaves and models the very behaviour that we are talking about in diversity. There is a close link between the people involved in the diversity development work for our external customers and the team called the Equality and Diversity Group who are helping to improve diversity in the college.

Coventry Building Society

Julian Atkins made the point that:

We want to achieve consistency between the way we treat staff and the way we want them to treat customers. And if we are successful in achieving that consistently, then the customer will benefit even more and the staff will believe in the business because they are experiencing what we are delivering.

Egg

Jean Tomlin informed us that:

At Egg the HR strategy was designed in conjunction with key business leaders drawn from across the organisation. The business developed so fast it was impossible to focus on any issues peripheral to core demands. The days of developing five-year strategic plans and sticking to them have gone, and Egg was a visible example of how flexible strategic plans needed to be, to meet the rapidly changing demands of the business. The HR strategy cannot therefore be static; it should be dynamic and responsive without losing sight of the overall business strategy.

I feel strongly that a HR strategy has to be part of the business strategy. They are inextricably linked, moving forward the rather outmoded distinctions between the two becoming blurred over time. HR received a great deal of attention at Egg – it's just that activities did not always fall neatly under fixed functional banners. This is a good thing. The HR strategy should be what it needs to be to reflect the moment and maintain the longer-term strategic commitments.

The HR strategy should flow from the business strategy. But that is not to say that HR should not be inputting into the business strategy. For example, changing the culture at British Airways…was very much an HR piece.

Halifax plc

John Lee believes that:

The HR expert's responsibility is to make certain that the people strategy is absolutely in line with the business strategy. That gives you the core link between people management and business performance. If it is not lined up, two things happen: firstly, there is no chance of its contributing to business performance. However good it is, or however good the expert may be, it's not going to punch its weight, and that would be a massive shame. Secondly, you can't measure and assess the effects. So the kind of debate we now have about what good people management looks like becomes really a bit academic.

I am afraid that I see too many examples around where that alignment isn't in place for one or other of two reasons. Either there has been a people vacuum at the strategy formulation stage or you've got the personnel professionals preaching concepts of excellence, sometimes for the sake of it, which reflect their own value systems or what they have been taught, not what the business is actually there to do.

The oak tree in the middle of the forest is this core piece of alignment, If you haven't got that, then the rest is hot air.

Great Ormond Street NHS Trust

Sarah Bonham set the HR strategy of the Trust in the context of the business strategy.

The business strategy is contained in a large complex document which is derived from the business development plan. This is driven by central initiatives coming from government – the modernisation plan – and our strategy must reflect the NHS plan and the government's 'performance frameworks'.

The business strategy will be driven by fundamental concepts such as putting the child and family first, listening to parents and their families and then deciding to act upon what we hear. The strategy will be about developing clinical governance systems and dealing with such issues as waiting lists and waiting times. It incorporates strategies for investing in staff, which then become our HR strategy.

The Trust produces an annual business plan – a summary of which goes out to all members of staff telling them what we are doing in such areas as service effectiveness, creating capacity, quality, and research. Everyone therefore knows what the plan contains and it can be quoted when objective-setting takes place at a local level.

Lloyds TSB

Paul Turner believes that:

In HR there are some things you have to do anyway regardless of whether or not there is a link to business strategy. What you end up with is a matrix of people and business-centred activities. To some extent there is integration with business strategy in that certain information concerning strategic human resource forecasting has to be fed into the business strategy before a workable strategy can be developed.

Peabody Trust

The point of view of a chief executive was expressed by Richard McCarthy:

Business strategy comes first. We have a HR director on our management team. She is there to make sure that as we develop our business strategy we don't go off on the wrong course as far as the human resources are concerned. I would expect, if you like, the HR strategy and function to act as a rain-check, as would finance – 'a great idea but no chance to do it, no money'. What you need to come up with in terms of a business strategy is one that you have a chance of delivering because the resources are there.

Ann Lewis, director of HR at the Peabody Trust explained that:

My business plan is the part of the Trust's business plan which relates to us as an organisation. I think the whole point of HR, apart from the legal fire-fighting we have to do, is to make sure that the way we manage our people supports the way we want to be regarded as an organisation and how we work as an organisation. It is no good saying that the organisation is going to provide excellent customer service if you have people in HR who pick up the phone and say 'The answer is no – what is the question?'

Smiths Industries

Anne Minto, HR director, said to us:

I do not believe that you can have stand-alone HR strategies. You have to develop strategies that are an integrated part of the business objectives. I don't see HR standing alone in an ivory tower. Everything we do has to have a value-added benefit for the business. If it doesn't have a positive benefit for the business, we don't do it. If you can make a business case, then it will be supported.

There are issues where it is appropriate for the HR director to lead, but in the main we try to go for an integrated approach. If we are re-organising a business to respond to a particular market situation, then we would be developing strategies to help the managing director of that business to get to where he/she needs to be.

Integrating HR strategies

The integration of HR strategies (bundling or adopting a 'configurational' approach) was something that was in the minds of many of the HR leaders we met, although a deliberate attempt to link HR initiatives together in formulating strategies was not so common. The service industry case studies described by Thompson (2000) indicated that the importance of a systems perspective (ie the interdependencies between different policies and practices) only really came out in one public sector organisation. In this case, HR had created a visual map of the interlocking policies and was also developing a project management tool to co-ordinate HR activities during the change management programme. As Thompson commented:

> There was a recognition that a lack of fit could potentially derail and lengthen the change process. However, there was also a recognition that what may appear consistent and inter-related at the centre may not appear so to the troops on the ground, and the need to promote understanding of the change programme was highlighted as an important next step.

Children's Society

Geoff Hawkins told us that:

> The whole concept of bundling, to use a popular term, is an important one because there does need to be complementarity between the various HR activities. So although the priority has been a comprehensive review of the reward system, alongside that we are developing performance management processes because they complement the reward system. Things may be happening sequentially in time but in my mind there is a total concept of how they complement one another.

Coventry Building Society

Julian Atkins said that:

> From the start, I was keen to adopt a holistic approach. I really had to stress this point because I feel that the way

we treat our staff is so interrelated that we can't deal with things in isolation.

Great Ormond Street NHS Trust

Sarah Bonham remarked that:

> There are some stand-alone elements, but they all contribute to the bigger picture of investing in and retaining our staff. For example, we are looking at Individual Learning Accounts which focus on people who are not on a professional pathway that links in with recruitment and retention. And this is about getting them, retaining them, and making sure that they can do their job.

New Forest District Council

Keith Ireland said that:

> The actual ingredients of the bundles don't matter to us hugely. What matters is how they integrate together. For example, absence management is really important to us, and this is linked to the performance management system. On the one side we are pressing to make sure we get full attendance; on the other side we are pressing to ensure that everyone knows what they are doing – that they are focused on their objectives to maximise performance. A big issue we are addressing is that of career development within the confines of a rigid structure.

The formulation of HR strategy

Some of those we met – for example, Julian Atkins at the Coventry Building Society – emphasised the need to involve people in formulating the strategy. Others confirmed what they had already told us (see above) about the need to adopt an integrative approach

Coventry Building Society

Julian Atkins:

> We believed that if we wanted staff to achieve what we want them to achieve, they needed to be well-motivated and also have the ability to do the job. We wanted to

create a clear line of sight between what the business was trying to achieve and what every individual in the business did, so that we could harness their collective effort.

Great Ormond Street NHS Trust

Sarah Bonham:

Each director has the business plan which contains headings laid down centrally. The director of HR gets the senior HR team together and agrees how the HR plan will be laid out under these headings. Each team member then maps out the plan for his or her area of responsibility. The plan will also respond to the results of the annual staff attitude survey. HR contributes to the Trust business plan, bearing in mind the need to have hands on deck to actually care for the patients, and thinking about the expertise and skills mix of those people.

The Department of Health

Neil Offley and Steve Gosling:

Quite clearly, this is a public service and to some extent it is driven by the politicians of the day and what they believe to be both the current situation and the desired future position. There are a variety of think-tanks aligned to the political machinery, academic institutions or the NHS management infrastructure. They all gather data, form views and make suggestions. And there is an overarching management structure in the NHS. It's quite complex. We are the largest organisation or collection of organisations in Europe. Five per cent of the UK working population work in the health service. It's central to any political order of the day.

Increasingly, there is a desire and a requirement to modernise the health service. There will be lots of views that help to create some form of overall strategic direction. It's not a fixed model. Sometimes it will be very prescriptive from the centre. At other times it's quite open.

The implementation of HR strategy

Again, the consistent message was delivered to us that people have to be engaged not only in the process of formulating the HR strategy but also in delivering it.

Homebase

Judith Evans:

> What I have found out is that organisations can only take so much change at a time. My concern was to put in the mechanisms whereby you could engage people in the change process.

Great Ormond Street NHS Trust

Sarah Bonham:

> We have some key objectives to roll out, with target dates. We then decide who is going to be responsible for making it happen.

New Forest District Council

Keith Ireland:

> I run the chief executive's department and we aim to put best practice into place in that department and roll it out into the rest of the Council. We are trying to link it all together to high-level objectives in the HR strategy, the business plan which gives more detailed objectives and the procedures and reviews.
>
> We have got the performance management system in place and everyone is having monthly reviews with their managers. We have also created a manager's forum called the Chief Executive's Forum in which we are trying to empower middle managers to manage their own sections. The group focuses on corporate issues that are going to impact on their departments, and this group moves them forward. So they are the ones that influence how corporate issues are used within their departments, and people are quite excited about that.
>
> Our aim is to ensure that from the moment we fill a vacancy to the moment someone leaves the

organisation, they are covered within the HR framework. We have tried to make this as robust as possible – it's available on the intranet and in the packages we have developed. We want to make sure that we don't ignore the practical things such as communications and basic reporting.

We know that we do a lot of consultation – all our policies go out to the corporate management team and customer services. But what we really want to know is how they get down to managers and supervisors. So we have management advice notes which deal with how to apply policies.

The Department of Health

Neil Offley and Steve Gosling:

The policy idea has a lot of supporters – but how do you implement that on a practical level across thousands of organisations which will [each] have the best grasp of what works locally? It's an understatement to say that things are complex. The relationships and the account-abilities are many and varied. Sometimes they are perfectly aligned, and probably more often than not. But sometimes they are completely at odds with one another.

To help implementation we have the Modernisation Agency and an emphasis on strong leadership through the Leadership Centre.

The NHS plan has been well-communicated throughout the NHS. But the need is to translate national policies, and things get filtered and interpreted at local levels.

Conclusions

The conclusions that emerge from the research described above are that:

☐ There is strong evidence from all the organisations involved that a strategic approach is being adopted to the development of HR policies, processes and practices which will make a direct contribution to improving business performance. And most of those taking part in the survey believed that what they were doing was making a significant and measurable impact on the effectiveness of their organisations.

☐ A determined attempt is being made by many organisations to integrate the HR and the business strategy. This may be based on a 'big idea' such as a drive to improve performance, or it may take the form of ensuring that the HR strategy reinforces a corporate value such as customer service delivery.

☐ The HR leaders of the organisations covered by the research were generally aware of the need to link HR practices together. But only a few, such as Coventry Building Society, had consciously adopted a holistic approach.

☐ The need for the head of HR to act as a business partner was emphasised by a number of HR leaders. But some also recognised that the HR function had still to excel at service delivery to gain the respect and support of line managers.

☐ The relevance and impact of HR strategies were largely a function of the quality of the head of HR.

12 IMPROVING BUSINESS PERFORMANCE THROUGH STRATEGIC HRM

The constant theme throughout this book is that a strategic approach to human resource management can and does improve business performance. The evidence for this in the UK and the USA, as quoted in earlier chapters, is overwhelming. The chief executives and senior HR practitioners we talked to were all convinced that this is the case, and were taking well-planned steps to ensure that what they did generated improved performance. Frequently, what they were doing corresponded with the approach suggested by the CIPD (2001b). This is the 'high-performance management' model in which companies differentiate themselves through innovation and superior customer service. According to the CIPD, at the heart of the model is employee commitment: good people practices – including rigorous recruitment and selection procedures, extensive training and management development, incentive pay and performance management systems – generate greater satisfaction, satisfaction yields greater motivation, and greater motivation in turn is reflected in better performance.

But it is not enough to believe, however passionately, that the implementation of HRM policies and practices within the framework of integrated HR strategies will make a positive impact on results. Too often in the past personnel practitioners have had to attempt to justify their proposals by asking management to accept them as an act of faith: 'If it's good for our people, it must be good for the business.' The importance of defining how such proposals will meet business needs has not been generally accepted as positively as it was by the HR leaders we met. The fact that HR people should be concerned with deliverables rather than abstractions has been insufficiently recognised. Of course, all HR practitioners are aware of the current mantras 'Be strategic' and 'Be a business partner'. But *how* they should be strategic and *how* they should act as business partners has not always been explained by the academics who preach this gospel. The purpose of this chapter – indeed, the whole book – is to offer some guidelines. We are not offering prescriptions – things all depend on circumstances – but indications of the sort of strategic and businesslike approaches that, subject to fitting them within the context, are likely to assist in the delivery of sustained improvements in business performance.

The starting-point is a general assessment of the way forward, followed by analyses of the sort of HR policies and practices that will make an impact on performance and of the circumstances in which this impact is most likely to be made. Consideration should then be given to:

- the approach to incorporating these practices into HR strategies that will make an impact
- how integration can be achieved – vertical integration (linking HR strategies with business strategies) and horizontal integration ('bundling')
- how strategic plans can best be implemented.

The way forward

The way forward, as presented by Guest *et al* (2000a), is to focus on the business case for adapting human resource practices. This, they say, means that:

- managers should expand progressive people management practices
- the general principle should be 'the more the better', since the impact of any single practice in isolation is likely to be small
- the most attractive practices or combination of practices are those consistent with skills acquisition and development, knowledge management, motivation, commitment, job design and involvement
- effective execution of the practices is as important as their number, meaning that management skills are vital

☐ learning at all levels should be thought of as fundamental to people management processes, both as an outcome and as an input to the next round of continuous improvement and strategic capacity investment.

These prescriptions provide broad guidelines on the approach to the development and implementation of strategic HRM, although performance management processes and reward management policies might have been added to the list on the ground that the former are very much in the minds of chief executives (as established by Guest *et al*, 2001b) and the latter were frequently mentioned by the HR directors we saw as important elements in their strategic plans.

HR practices that improve business performance

To develop practices that make an impact on business performance it is necessary first to define the characteristics of such practices and then to identify the practices that meet those characteristics. In doing so, account should be taken of the concept of resource-based strategy which, as described in Chapter 2, suggests that the strategic capability of a firm depends on its resource capability, especially its distinctive resources. The concept is founded on the belief that competitive advantage is achieved if a firm can obtain and develop human resources which enable it to learn faster and apply its learning more effectively than its rivals (Hamel and Prahalad, 1989).

Characteristics of HR practices that make an impact on performance

To make an impact on business performance an HR practice should have a number of specific characteristics:

☐ The practice exists to meet a well-defined business need (a convincing business case has been made).

☐ *How* the practice meets that need has been specified.

☐ A determined effort has been made to define the impact the practice will make in terms of added value.

☐ Success criteria have been established to measure the impact.

☐ Steps have been taken to ensure that line managers and staff generally understand the reason for the practice, are aware of how it affects them and its benefits for them as well as the organisation, and have been given guidance and training in its application.

☐ The practice can be put into action by line management without relying on a vast amount of HR support and guidance.

☐ The practice is accepted – indeed, welcomed – by people generally following their involvement in its development.

☐ Constant effort is exerted by top management supported by HR to ensure that the practice works as intended.

☐ The impact of the practice is measured against the success criteria, and in the light of these measurements steps are taken to modify it if necessary.

HR practices most likely to impact on performance

The academic research to date has identified two main sets of HR practice that are most strongly associated with higher business performance. These are job design and skills development. However, case study work with senior executives (Guest *et al*, 2001) demonstrates that CEOs believe that selection and performance management are the key areas that can impact on business outcomes. Other studies have identified sets of higher-performance or sophisticated HR practices and demonstrated that using more of such practices raises performance levels. In the light of this knowledge, the main practice areas, how they make an impact and what impact they can potentially make are summarised in Table 4.

Table 4
HR PRACTICE AREAS THAT IMPACT ON PERFORMANCE

HR practice area	How it impacts	What impact it can make
Job design	By providing individuals with stimulating and interesting work and giving them the autonomy and flexibility to perform these jobs well	Enhancing job satisfaction and flexibility which encourages greater performance and productivity
Training and development	By developing the level of skill and competence in the workforce; management development programmes can also encourage managers to use more people management practices to encourage commitment and job satisfaction and encourage communication	Providing organisations with the skilled and committed people they need to achieve business objectives both in the present and the future; developing better management systems to ensure that these people are managed in such as way as to optimise their contribution to business performance
Culture change	Through culture change programmes which focus on the development of shared values and gaining commitment to them: these values are concerned with the sort of behaviour the management believes is appropriate in the interests of the organisation	Encouraging attitudes and behaviour that are orientated towards performance improvement, customer service, quality, continuous improvement and effective cost management
Attracting, developing and retaining high-quality people	By matching human resources to the strategic and operational needs of the organisation; it is concerned not only with obtaining and keeping the number and quality of staff required but also with selecting and promoting people who 'fit' the culture and the strategic requirements of the organisation	Ensuring the acquisition, development and retention of uniquely talented employees who can deliver superior performance, productivity, flexibility, innovation, and high levels of personal customer service
Managing knowledge and intellectual capital	By focusing both on organisational and individual learning and by providing learning opportunities and opportunities to share knowledge in a systematic way	Ensuring that vital stocks of knowledge are retained, and improving the flow of knowledge, information and learning within the organisation

HR practice area	How it impacts	What impact it can make
Increasing motivation, commitment and role engagement	(1) By developing intrinsic and extrinsic motivation processes through the use of a 'total reward' approach including both financial and non-financial rewards (2) By valuing people according to their contribution (3) By developing a commitment strategy (4) By job design and role-building processes which increase intrinsic interest in the work	Encouraging people to identify themselves with and act upon the core values of the organisation, and to willingly and effectively contribute to the achievement of organisational goals; developing a climate of co-operation and trust; clarifying the psychological contract
Empowering employees to exhibit the behaviours most closely associated with higher business performance such as leadership, risk-taking, innovativeness, sharing of knowledge, focusing on customers, and teamworking	By creating the organisational climate in which it is acceptable to exhibit these behaviours, reinforcing and rewarding such behaviours through the reward and performance management systems, and identifying and articulating the need for such behaviours	Fostering the development of well-motivated and committed staff who have the knowledge and leadership skills to manage themselves and others to exhibit higher levels of job satisfaction and hence productivity

An alternative framework for developing appropriate HR policies and practices – the 'four-task model' – was produced by Schuler, Jackson and Storey (2001):

□ Manage employee assignments and opportunities – get the right number of people at the right place at the right time.
□ Manage employee competencies – ensure that people have the needed skills, knowledge and abilities to perform successfully.
□ Manage employee behaviours – identify the appropriate behaviours and ensure that employees exhibit them.
□ Manage employee motivation – encourage willingness to perform, to stay with the firm, and to work at the agreed-upon time and place.

HR practice models

Another method of defining HR strategic policy and practice areas is to refer to the various strategic models as described in Chapter 5, summarised in Table 5.

Table 5
HRM MODELS

High-performance Buchanan (1987), Stevens 1998	High-commitment Beer et al (1984), Walton (1985)	High-involvement Pil and MacDuffie (1999)
☐ Management clearly defines what it needs in the form of new methods of working and the results expected from their introduction ☐ Management sets goals and standards for success ☐ Decision-making is devolved to those closest to the customer so as constantly to renew and improve the offer to customers ☐ People capacities are developed through learning at all levels, with particular emphasis on self-management and team capabilities to enable and support performance improvement and organisational potential ☐ Performance, operational and people management processes are aligned to organisational objectives to build trust, enthusiasm and commitment to the direction taken by the organisation	☐ The development of career ladders and an emphasis on trainability and commitment as highly-valued characteristics of employees at all levels in the organisation ☐ A high level of functional flexibility, and the abandonment of potentially rigid job descriptions ☐ The reduction of hierarchies and the ending of status differentials ☐ A heavy reliance on team structure for disseminating information (team-briefing), structuring work (teamworking) and problem-solving (quality circles) ☐ Job design as something management consciously does in order to provide jobs that have a considerable level of intrinsic satisfaction ☐ A policy of no compulsory layoffs or redundancies and permanent employment guarantees with the possible use of temporary workers to cushion fluctuations in the demand for labour ☐ New forms of assessment and payment systems and, more specifically, merit pay and profit sharing ☐ A high involvement of employees in the management of quality	☐ 'On-line' work teams ☐ 'Off-line' employee involvement activities and problem-solving groups ☐ Job rotation ☐ Suggestion programmes ☐ Decentralisation of quality efforts

HR 'best practice'

Although the existence of universal 'best' HR practices may be denied, there are a number of lists of good or high-performance people management practices which have been used to demonstrate the relationship between practice and performance. Some researchers such as Pfeffer (1994) argue that all practices must be implemented to achieve performance improvement, whereas other such as Guest claim that implementing more from a list of practices will lead to higher levels of business performance. Four of the best known of such lists are summarised in Table 6.

Table 6
HRM GOOD PRACTICES

Guest (1999)	Patterson et al (1997)	Pfeffer (1994)	US Department of Labor (1993)
☐ Selection and the careful use of selection tests to identify those with potential to make a contribution ☐ Training, and in particular a recognition that training is an ongoing activity ☐ Job design to ensure flexibility, commitment and motivation, including steps to ensure that employees have the responsibility and autonomy to use their knowledge and skills to the full ☐ Communication to ensure that a two-way process keeps everyone fully informed ☐ Employee share ownership programmes (ESOPs) to keep employees aware of the implications of their actions, including absence and labour turnover, for the financial performance of the firm	☐ Sophisticated selection and recruitment processes ☐ Sophisticated induction programmes ☐ Sophisticated training ☐ Coherent appraisal systems ☐ Flexibility of workforce skills ☐ Job variety on shop floor ☐ Use of formal teams ☐ Frequent and comprehensive communication to workforce ☐ Use of quality improvement teams ☐ Maintenance of harmonised terms and conditions ☐ Maintenance of basic pay higher than competition's ☐ Use of incentive schemes	☐ Employment security ☐ Selective hiring ☐ Self-managed teams ☐ High compensation contingent on performance ☐ Training to provide a skilled and motivated workforce ☐ Reduction of status differentials ☐ Sharing of information	☐ Careful and extensive systems for recruitment, selection and training ☐ Formal systems for sharing information with employees ☐ Clear job design ☐ High-level participation processes ☐ Monitoring of attitudes ☐ Performance appraisals ☐ Properly-functioning grievance procedures ☐ Promotion and compensation schemes that provide for the recognition and reward of high-performing employees

Cust/Add: 363610006/01   EBOV   NEWMAN COL
Cust PO No.   NW05000446   **Cust O**
BBS Order No: E439451   Ln: 1   Del: 1   **BBS O**
0852929234-10403828   **Sales Q**
(9780852929230)

Strategic HRM

Subtitle: the key to improved business performance   Stmt of Resp:

PAPERBACK   **Pub Year:** 2002   **Vol No.:**

Armstrong, Michael.   **Ser. Title:**

Chartered Institute of Personnel & Development
Acc Mat:

Tech Services Charges:
    Kapco UK   Date Due Slip UK
    Accession Stamp UK   Property Stamp UK
    Barcode Label   Security Device UK
    Base Charge Processing

Cust Fund Code: READL   **Cust Locati**
Stock Category: Standard Loan   **Cust Dept:**
STOCK CAT: Standard Loan **
Order Line Notes

Notes to Vendor   CUST. LOC - N <; 3 standard

Blackwell's Book Services

When HR practices contribute to improved business performance

Evidence from the research into strategic HRM suggests there are four factors that affect the degree to which HR practices improve business performance:

□ the organisational context

□ the views of top management

□ the competence of HR specialists, especially the HR leader

□ the attitudes and behaviour of line managers.

The context within the organisation

The organisational culture, especially its core values and beliefs, can provide an environment conducive to the development and implementation of high-performance HR practices or a climate which inhibits their effectiveness. Strategic HRM may well be concerned with culture change but it is a much longer haul when an inappropriate culture prevails.

The sector, market and economic climate in which an organisation operates largely determines the sort of HR strategies that will have greatest impact. Guest *et al* (2001) on further analysis of data from their cross-sector survey have found significant differences between sectors in the relationship between HR practice and business performance.

Generally, we can conclude from the evidence available that organisations that have made a conscious effort to identify the priority area in which HR will assist in the delivery of business objectives are most likely to recognise the impact of practices. Those that have made systematic efforts to articulate their business goals and objectives are thus more likely to view HR as a strategic delivery process. Businesses which employ a high proportion of knowledge workers, or are in the service sector where personal relationships with customers matter, will readily grasp the significance of HR practices which ensure that they have the committed and skilled people they need.

The views of top management

HR practices make a greater impact if top management appreciates their significance and potential. Well-informed managers may do this anyway, but the head of HR may have to enlighten those who do not – and such enlightenment may only take place if HR can produce a persuasive business case. However, CIPD research (Guest *et al*, 2001) demonstrates that many top managers believe they are already doing much to implement good HR practice and can see little room for improvement.

HR competence

A consistent message delivered by all those who participated in our research is that, ultimately, it is HR that makes the difference. If the head of HR and the HR team generally cannot convince top managers *and* line managers that what they have to offer will generate added value and will meet their needs, then little impact will be made.

The attitudes and behaviour of line managers

The best-laid plans of HR specialists will fail if they are not supported by line managers. Many an elegant performance management scheme has made no impact at all because line managers are not convinced that it is necessary for the organisation or for them. Their support cannot be taken for granted. It has to be won, earned, and fostered.

A practical approach to the development of HR strategies

We are often asked to provide a model of an HR strategy – a request to which we customarily answer in the negative. The HR strategy of an organisation *must* be contingent on the needs and circumstances of that organisation. Although it is possible to suggest headings under which a strategy might be expressed – as set out below – and to describe the process of strategy formulation, the actual identification and definition of strategic elements will depend on the requirements and context of the organisation.

Possible HR strategy headings

General headings under which an HR strategy could be expressed include:

☐ An overall analysis of the business needs, and how in

general the HR strategy should inform them and can help to meet them.

☐ The HR strategy areas: the 'hard' areas such as turnover, competence levels and payment systems, with an indication of the business needs they support and the impact they are expected to make on performance, and the 'softer' although equally important areas concerned with such matters as equal opportunities, the management of diversity, developing the employment relationship, the involvement of employees, and occupational health and safety

☐ A set of specific goals or targets

☐ An action plan containing a description of how it is proposed to implement the strategies, with an indication of priorities, schedules, and the steps to be taken to relate them to one another

☐ A definition of the critical success indicators to be used to evaluate progress in implementation and to assess the effectiveness of the strategy when it is finally in place

☐ A statement of the resources required (people and finance) and a summary of the added value the use of these resources will generate.

A practical approach

If you are asked to produce an HR strategy or have decided for yourself that a strategy is needed, what do you do? Your approach will depend on the circumstances, and the sort of questions you may have to answer are:

☐ Is this the first time a strategy is to be formulated, or is it an updating of an existing strategy?

☐ Does a well-defined business strategy or plan already exist? If not, what information can be obtained about intentions?

☐ What is your initial assessment of the key issues with which the HR strategy should be concerned?

☐ What is your initial view of the HR strategic intent – how are the key issues to be addressed?

☐ Are the resources available to develop and implement the strategy?

- ☐ To what extent is top management sympathetic to the idea of an HR strategy?
- ☐ What does top management hope to get out of it?
- ☐ Will line managers support strategy initiatives, and do they have the skills to implement them?
- ☐ How are staff generally likely to react to the strategy? Can any difficulties be anticipated, and if so, how can they be dealt with?
- ☐ Who should be involved in developing the strategy?

Equipped with the answers to these questions, you may then consider taking the steps shown in Figure 8 that are required to formulate the strategy.

Decide who is to be involved and how

It is important to identify key people in the organisation who can champion change and be involved in the formulation and

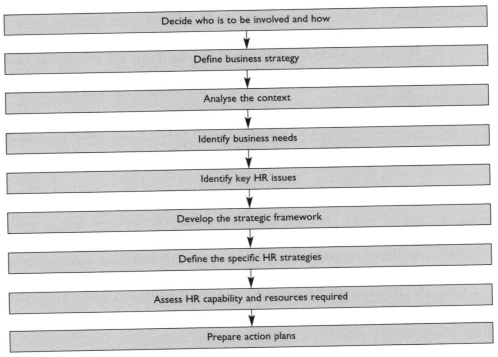

Figure 8
FORMULATING HR STRATEGY

Decide who is to be involved and how

Define business strategy

Analyse the context

Identify business needs

Identify key HR issues

Develop the strategic framework

Define the specific HR strategies

Assess HR capability and resources required

Prepare action plans

implementation of the strategy. Gratton (2000) emphasises the need to build a 'guiding coalition' involving line managers and others from all parts of the business and creating 'issue-based' cross-functional teams to define what has to be done, identify targets and stretch goals, and establish performance indicators.

Find out all you can about the business strategy

If you are on the board or are a member of the senior management team, this should not be too difficult. A long-term strategy may or may not have been committed to paper but it is highly probable that there will at least be a shorter-term business plan. If you have been an active member of the board and performing your role as a business partner, you should have been involved in the formulation of the business strategy, and an opportunity would have presented itself to ensure that the people issues were addressed during this process, thus making the HR strategy an integral part of the business strategy. In any case, it is helpful to take time to analyse the business strategy with a view to defining as precisely as possible the business needs with which the HR strategy should be concerned.

If, regrettably, you are not a member of the top team but still are charged with the responsibility for developing an HR strategy or, more probably, believe that such a strategy is required, then you have to make every effort to talk to those senior managers who have been involved to obtain an insight into where top management sees the organisation going.

If you are a member of the top team, you should bear in mind that acting as a business partner is not simply a matter of sitting on the board or a management committee. You have to take an active part and show that you not only understand the business issues but can also make a contribution to addressing them from an HR as well as a business perspective. If you are not a board member, your role as a business partner is still to ensure that you are aware of the business plans and their implications for human resource management by whatever means possible – talking, listening and reading.

Analyse the context

You must understand not only the provisions of the business strategy itself but also the context in which it has been prepared and will have to be implemented. This means appreciating the strengths and weaknesses of the organisation and the threats and opportunities it faces. It also means assessing the core competences of the organisation – what it is good at doing and has to continue to be good at doing – and identifying its critical success factors, especially those concerned with people.

Identify business needs

This is the crucial stage. Your task is to identify the business issues that should be addressed by the HR strategy. It is necessary to be as precise as possible. For example, the business strategy might include plans for product/market developments. In this situation, you need to find out what the resourcing implications are in terms of numbers and skills, and to devise plans to satisfy them. Or perhaps a merger or acquisition is proposed. In this case you may be involved in a 'due diligence' exercise to assess the human resource capabilities of the business that might be taken over. Whether or not you have been involved at this stage, you will need to develop a strategy for dealing with the human resource implications of the merger, such as rationalising pay structures.

In some circumstances there may only be some very broad-brush strategic intentions expressed by top management in relation to improving performance, productivity, quality or levels of customer service. You will have to be prepared to take this 'strategic intent' apart and assess how HR practices can make a specified and added-value contribution to achieving these broad goals.

Identify key HR issues

The key HR issues are those that directly affect the achievement of business goals under the general headings of organisation structure and development resourcing, human resource development, performance management, reward management, knowledge management and employee relations.

Develop the strategic framework

The strategic framework will define the main strategic goals, their interconnections and their priorities. The achievement of vertical and horizontal integration, as considered in the next section of this chapter, will be a major consideration. The links between them will have to be identified so that mutually supporting processes can be developed – for example, performance management processes, human resource development programmes and contribution-related pay. This will enable priorities to be established. In some cases, such as the example given above, the strategies would be bundled together. In other cases they might be implemented in sequence on the grounds that there is only so much innovation and change that an organisation can cope with at any one time. However, Andrew Pettigrew (1999) suggests on the basis of an international survey conducted by Warwick Business School that piecemeal changes – with the exception of IT – deliver little performance benefit and that higher-performing firms make organisational innovations in carefully aligned and complementary sets. He concludes that organisations should 'beware of attempts to improve performance by simple and singular changes', and that managements should 'deliver a complementary *and* contextually appropriate set of innovations and not the latest management fad'. He is, of course, not recommending that everything should be done all at once. What he does propose is that the interrelationships and sequencing should be considered with care, and that nothing should be done without assessing its consequences for other aspects of the business or HR strategy.

Define the specific HR strategies

You now need to amplify the strategic framework by statements of the business needs the various individual HR strategies are designed to satisfy, how they will meet the needs, the resources required, the programme for implementation (this will involve prioritisation) and their benefits in terms of added value. The strategy may be set out in outline with supporting material providing more detail. A summary of a strategy to develop contribution-related pay might be set out as shown in Table 7.

Table 7

A SUMMARY STATEMENT OF AN HR STRATEGY

Strategic goal	*To introduce contribution-related pay for all staff*
Business needs	Generally to develop a culture of continuous improvement in terms of both competence and performance. Specifically to enhance both levels of competence and performance, targeting particular areas in which performance must improve.
How the needs will be met	By developing performance management processes to define competence and output expectations. By paying consolidated increases up to the pay reference-point for the role to reflect growth in competence, and above the reference-point, paying cash bonuses to recognise exceptional achievements in targeted areas. The aim is to provide both incentives and rewards for improvement.
Resources required	Consultancy advice will be required to develop the performance management and contribution-related pay processes at a one-off cost of £a,000. There will be opportunity costs of the order of £b,000 for the time spent by staff involved in developing the schemes. Training and communication costs of £c,000 will be incurred in implementation. The implementation and management of the processes can be carried out by existing HR staff.
Development and implementation programme	The full performance management and contribution-related pay processes will take approximately two years to develop and implement.
Added value	The total cost of development and implementation is estimated at £A,000. It is anticipated that the improvement of performance resulting from the processes will generate added value of £B,000 over the first three years of operation. Thereafter, annual added value of about £C,000 should be maintained.

Assess HR capability and resources required

You now have a general idea about what actions are required to satisfy business needs. The next step is to assess the capacity of HR to do what has to be done. This means looking at two things. First, you have to subject what is happening now in HRM to close scrutiny to assess strengths and weaknesses in relation to the demands that will be made on existing policies and practices. The weaknesses may include inadequate processes or gaps in HR activities that will inhibit the ability to meet strategic goals. Second, you have to assess the extent to which the function itself – in the sense of how it is structured and the skills of its members – is capable of responding to new demands. The strategy you formulate has to be based on a realistic assessment of what can be achieved by using existing processes and resources and what additional resources may be required. If additions will have to be made, then a cost-benefit analysis must be carried out to answer the question 'What added value will be gained by this addition to HR resources?'

Prepare action plans

Your action plans should set out what has to be done, by whom, and by when. They should pay particular attention to the ways in which the implementation of the strategy can be forwarded and monitored. Project schedules will have to be developed which incorporate milestone reviews and the criteria (critical success indicators) to be used in order to check that satisfactory progress is being made. The plans should pay particular attention to the involvement of line managers and other staff in task forces, the means of communicating the strategy, and any training that may be required.

A strategic HRM checklist

To summarise, the questions to which answers are required when formulating HR strategies are:

☐ What are the key components of the business strategy?

☐ How can HR strategies support the achievement of the business strategy and thus secure vertical integration?

☐ What are the strengths and weaknesses of the organisation and the opportunities and threats it faces?

☐ What are the implications of the political, economic, social, technological, legal and environmental contexts in which the organisation operates?

☐ To what extent is the organisation in a stable or dynamic (turbulent) environment, and how will this affect our strategies?

☐ What is the nature of the corporate culture? Does it help or hinder the achievement of the organisation's goals?

☐ What needs to be done to define or redefine our values in such areas as quality, customer service, innovation, teamworking, and the responsibility of the organisation for its employees?

□ What do we need to do to increase commitment? How do we communicate our intentions and achievements to employees, and what steps do we take to give them a voice – obtaining feedback from them and involving them in the affairs of the organisation?

□ To what extent do we need to pursue a strategy of high-performance or high-commitment management, and what would be the main features of such a strategy?

□ How in general can we increase the resource capability of the organisation?

□ To what extent do existing HR practices meet future business needs? What should be done about any gaps or inadequacies?

□ In the light of this gap analysis, what specific aspects of HRM (processes and practices) do we need to focus on when formulating strategy?

□ How can we best 'bundle' together the various HR practices to achieve horizontal integration?

□ How can we achieve coherence in developing the different HR practices?

□ How can we achieve the flexibility required to cope with change?

□ What kind of skills and behaviours do we need now and in the future?

□ Are performance levels high enough to meet demands for increased profitability, higher productivity, better quality and improved customer service?

□ Will the organisation's structure and systems be able to cope with future challenges in their present form?

□ Are we making the best use of the skills and capabilities of our employees?

□ Are we investing enough in developing those skills and capabilities?

□ Are there any potential constraints in the form of skills shortages or employee relations problems?

□ Are our employment costs too high?

□ Is there likely to be any need for delayering or downsizing?

□ How should we involve people in developing the strategy?

- How can we ensure that strategic plans are implemented?

Example: the Higher Education Funding Council

The Higher Education Funding Council (HEFC) in 2001 produced a list of specific areas which the HR strategies of higher education institutions must cover in order to qualify for certain funds. The HEFC carefully stated that it did not want to prescribe a desired format for institutions' strategies but did indicate that strategies should include a set of institutional objectives for recruiting, retaining, rewarding and developing staff. The areas the HEFC suggested should be covered were:

- Address recruitment and retention difficulties in a targeted and cost-effective manner.
- Meet specific staff development and training objectives that not only equip staff to meet their current needs but also prepare them for future changes, such as using new technologies for learning and teaching. This would include management development.
- Develop equal-opportunities targets with programmes to implement good practice throughout the institution. This would include ensuring equal pay for work of equal value, using institution-wide systems of job evaluation, and could further involve institutions' working collectively – regionally or nationally.
- Carry out regular reviews of staffing needs, reflecting changes in market demands and technology. The reviews should consider overall numbers and the balance of different categories of staff.
- Conduct annual performance reviews of all staff, based on open and objective criteria, with reward connected to the performance of individuals including, where appropriate, their contribution to teams.
- Take action to tackle poor performance.

Example: a large not-for-profit organisation

A strategic review was conducted recently in a large not-for-profit organisation.

Background

A major strategic review has taken place and a new chief executive and other members of the senior management team have been appointed within the last two years. In essence, the review led to a business strategy which:

☐ redefined the purpose of the organisation

☐ emphasised that the core purpose continues to be given absolute priority

☐ set out the need to secure the future of activities outside its core purpose

☐ importantly, made proposals designed to shape and secure the financial future.

HR issues emerging from the strategic review

The key HR issues emerging from the strategic review are that:

☐ effectively, it declares an intention to transform the organisation

☐ the transformation will involve major cultural changes – for example:

– some change in the focus on activities other than the core activity

– a move away from a paternalistic command-and-control organisation

– introducing processes which enable the organisation to operate more flexibly

– clarifying expectations but simultaneously gaining commitment to managing and carrying out activities on the basis of increased self-regulation and decision-making at operational level rather than pressures or instructions from above

– more emphasis on managerial, as distinct from technical, skills for managers

– greater concentration on the financial requirement to balance income and expenditure while continuing to develop and improve service delivery

☐ a significant change in the regional organisation and the

roles of the management team and regional controllers/
managers is taking place; this means that new skills will
have to be used which some existing managers may not
possess

☐ from a human resource planning viewpoint, decisions will
have to be made on the capabilities required in the future
at managerial and other levels, and these may involve
establishing policies for recruiting new managerial talent
from outside the organisation rather than relying on promotion from within

☐ difficult decisions may have to be made on retaining some
existing managers in their posts who have not been successful in applying for new regional posts or lack the
required skills, and there may be a requirement to reduce
staff numbers in the future

☐ more positively, management development and career
planning activities will need to be introduced which
reflect the changing culture and structure of the organisation and the different roles managers and others will be
expected to play.

The provision of the core HR services, such as recruitment
and training, is not an issue.

Steps to address the issues

Steps have already been taken to address these issues – for
example:

☐ major communication initiatives introduced by the chief
executive

☐ a review of the pay system, specifically taking account of
the organisation's unsatisfactory experience in applying
performance management/pay procedures a few years ago

☐ decisions on the shape of the regional organisation

☐ an analysis and diagnosis of cultural issues – ie what the
present culture is and what it should become.

Future strategy

Against this background, it is necessary to build on the steps
already taken by:

□ adopting a systematic approach to the achievement of culture change, bearing in mind that it may be a long haul because it involves changing behaviour and attitudes at all levels and is difficult, if not impossible, to attain simply by managerial dictation

□ formulating an HR strategy which, as a declaration of intent, will provide a framework for the development of HR processes and procedures that address the issues referred to above; this will involve:

– strategic integration – matching HR policies and practices to the business strategy

– a coherent approach to the development of these processes so that HR activities are interrelated and mutually reinforcing

– a planned approach, but one that is not bureaucratic

– an emphasis on the needs to achieve flexibility, quality and cost-effectiveness in the delivery of HR services

□ focusing on the activities that will not only deal with the HR issues but will also help to achieve culture change:

– *resourcing* – deciding what sort of people are required, and ensuring that they are available

– *human resource development* – identifying the skills required, auditing the skills available, taking steps to match skills to present and future business requirements, and initiating processes for enhancing organisational and individual learning related to business needs

– *reward* – using reward processes to ensure that people are valued according to their contribution and to convey messages about the behaviour, capabilities and results expected of them

– *employee relations* – building on the steps already taken to communicate to employees and to involve them in decision-making processes on matters that concern them.

The HR strategy will have to establish priorities. Because the thrust of the strategic review initially makes most impact on managers, the priority may well be given to people at this level but without neglecting the needs of the rest of the staff. A model of the strategic review process is set out in Figure 9.

Figure 9
A STRATEGIC REVIEW MODEL

Achieving integration

One of the underlying aims of strategic HRM is to achieve vertical and horizontal integration.

Vertical integration

Vertical integration is achieved when there is fit between the business and the HR strategy. Fit is achieved by examining each aspect of the business strategy and then assessing its people management implications as the basis for formulating integrated HR strategies.

A competitive strategy approach as described by Schuler and Jackson (1987) identifies the different strategies for role behaviours shown in Table 8 and HR practices in relation to the three competitive strategies listed by Porter (1985).

Table 8

COMPETITIVE STRATEGIES, ROLE BEHAVIOUR AND HR PRACTICES

Type of strategy	Role behaviour	HR practices
Innovation strategy	□ a high degree of creative behaviour □ a longer-term focus □ a relatively high degree of co-operative, interdependent behaviour □ a greater degree of risk-taking □ a high tolerance of ambiguity and unpredictability	□ jobs that require close interaction between people □ jobs that allow people to develop skills that can be used in other positions in the firm □ broader career paths that reinforce the development of a wider range of skills. □ performance appraisals that are more likely to reflect longer-term and group-based achievements
Quality-enhancement strategy	□ a high concern for quality □ high concern for process (how goods and services are made or delivered) □ low risk-taking activity □ high levels of commitment	□ relatively fixed and explicit job descriptions □ relatively egalitarian treatment of employees and some guarantees of employment security □ high levels of employee participation on work issues □ extensive and continuous training
Cost-leadership strategy	□ primary concern for results, especially output quantity □ low risk-taking activity □ a relatively short-term focus □ modest concern for quality	□ narrowly-designed jobs and explicit job descriptions □ short-term results-orientated performance appraisals □ little training □ close monitoring of employee activities

Source: Schuler and Jackson, 1999.

An alternative formulation of the links between competitive strategies and various aspects of HR strategy (Armstrong, 2001) is shown in Table 9.

Table 9

LINKING HR AND COMPETITIVE STRATEGIES

	HR strategy		
	Resourcing	**HR development**	**Reward**
Achieve competitive advantage through innovation	Recruit and retain high-quality people with innovative skills and a good track record in innovation	Develop strategic capability and provide encouragement and facilities for enhancing innovative skills and increasing the intellectual capital of the organisation	Provide financial incentives and rewards and recognition for successful innovations
Achieve competitive advantage through quality	Use sophisticated selection procedures to recruit people who are likely to deliver quality and high levels of customer service	Encourage the development of a learning organisation; develop and implement knowledge management processes; support total quality and customer care initiatives with focused training	Link rewards to quality performance and the achievement of high standards of customer service
Achieve competitive advantage through cost-leadership	Develop core/periphery employment structures; recruit people who are likely to add value; if unavoidable, plan and manage downsizing humanely	Provide training designed to improve productivity; inaugurate just-in-time training that is closely linked to immediate business needs and can generate measurable improvements in cost-effectiveness	Review all reward practices to ensure that they provide value for money and do not lead to unnecessary expenditure
Achieve competitive advantage by employing people who are better than those employed by competitors	Use sophisticated recruitment and selection procedures based on a rigorous analysis of the special capabilities required by the organisation	Develop organisational learning processes; encourage self-managed learning through the use of personal development plans as part of a performance management process	Develop performance management processes which enable both financial and non-financial rewards to be related to competence and skills; ensure that pay levels are competitive

Horizontal integration

Horizontal fit occurs when the various HR strategies cohere and are mutually supporting. It can be achieved by the process of 'bundling' – ie the use of complementary HR practices, also known as 'configuration'.

Bundling implies the adopting of a holistic approach to the development of HR strategies and practices. No single aspect of HR strategy should be considered in isolation. The links between one area and other complementary areas must be established so that the ways in which they can provide mutual support to the achievement of the overall strategy can be ascertained. The synergy that can result from this process means that the impact of the whole bundle on organisational effectiveness can be greater than the sum of its parts. Bundling starts with a review of those HR practices which are likely to be mutually supportive or underpin a number of related practices. For example, the links might be established between the development of a job family structure based on competence analysis as a means of defining career and development paths and the superimposition of a pay structure on the job families with provision for contribution-related pay. The underpinning HR process might include competency frameworks which inform recruitment, job design, employee development and reward processes or performance management processes which can inform decisions on employee development and contingent pay. Examples of common requirements that can be met by initiatives in different areas of HR practice, as long as they are deliberately linked, are given in Table 10.

Table 10
COMMON ELEMENTS IN HR STRATEGY AREAS

Overall HR strategy	HR strategy area – common elements		
	Resourcing	HR development	Reward
Improve performance	Competence-based recruiting; assessment centres	Competence-based training; development centres.	Competence-related pay
Extend skills base	Identify skills development needs of recruits	Skills analysis; focused training in identified needs; accreditation of skills	Skills-based pay
Provide for competence and career development	Develop competency frameworks and profiles; identify competence levels and potential through performance management processes	Use performance management and personal development plans as basis for defining and meeting learning needs; establish broad 'career development' bands for mapping lateral development paths; identify career ladders in job families defined in competence terms	Develop broad-banded or job family structures defined in competence terms and which indicate clearly 'aiming points' (competence requirements in different roles within or outside job family); institute systems of career development pay for lateral progression through bands or vertical progression through job family levels

Overall HR strategy	HR strategy area – common elements		
	Resourcing	HR development	Reward
Provide for employability	Develop a positive psychological contract based on an undertaking to identify and develop transferable skills; provide scope for job enlargement/enrichment and opportunities to move into new roles	Identify skills development needs through personal development planning; institute programmes for developing transferable skills. Provide facilities for self-managed learning using e-learning processes and learning resource centres	Develop broad-banded/job family structures which identify competence levels for roles or job families and provide a basis for identifying learning needs
Increase commitment	Analyse characteristics of committed employees; use sophisticated selection methods to identify candidates who have these characteristics and are likely to be committed to the organisation; define and communicate organisational core values	On the basis of the analysis of the characteristics of committed employees, provide learning experiences which enhance understanding and acceptance of organisational core values and encourage value-driven behaviour	Reinforce value-driven behaviour by providing rewards based on evidence that core values are being upheld
Increase motivation	Analyse characteristics of well-motivated employees and structure selection interviews to obtain evidence of how well-motivated candidates are likely to be	Provide learning opportunities which reinforce characteristics of well-motivated employees and offer non-financial rewards	Use performance management processes as a basis for providing non-financial rewards related to opportunities for development and growth

Source: Michael Armstrong, *A Handbook of Human Resource Management Practice*, 8th edition, Kogan Page, 2001

Implementing HR strategies

The challenge

There is often a gap between the rhetoric of HR strategies and the reality of what happens subsequently. As stated by the CIPD (2001b):

The challenge (and the opportunity) is to turn the rhetoric into reality by putting people management at the heart of business concerns...Good management in these terms is not a mystery. Nor does it require huge financial investment. It:

□ supports and is based on a clear business strategy (the 'big idea' identified by the Bath researchers)

> □ builds competitive advantage by recruiting good people and developing the intellectual capital of the organisation
>
> □ selects and implements complementary sets of practices to recruit, develop and reward people
>
> □ monitors progress against analytical measures that support the business strategy
>
> □ places emphasis on line management's role in bringing people policies and practices to life
>
> □ is championed – and lived – by top management on the basis that it is people who execute business strategies and who make the difference between success and failure.

The issue of change management

Converting rhetoric to reality is essentially a change management issue. Everyone concerned with implementation, especially line managers, must be included in a change management programme. The main features of such a programme as described by Armstrong (2001) are:

□ The achievement of sustainable change requires strong commitment and visionary leadership from the top.

□ Understanding the culture of the organisation and the levers for change most likely to be effective in that culture is vital.

□ Those concerned with managing change at all levels should have the temperament and leadership skills appropriate to the circumstances of the organisation and its change strategies.

□ It is important to build a working environment that is conducive to change: this means developing the firm as a 'learning organisation'.

□ Commitment to change is improved if those affected by change are allowed to participate as fully as possible in planning and implementing it. The aim should be to get them to 'own' the change as something they want and will be glad to live with.

□ The reward system should encourage innovation and recognise success in achieving change.

□ Strategies for change must be adaptable – the ability to

respond swiftly to new situations and demands, which will inevitably arise, is essential.

□ Change will always involve failure as well as success. The failures must be expected and learned from.

□ Hard evidence and data on the need for change are the most powerful tools for its achievement, but establishing the need for change is easier than deciding how to satisfy it.

□ The emphasis must be on changing behaviour, not on trying to enforce corporate values.

□ It is easier to change behaviour by changing processes, structure and systems than to change attitudes.

□ It is necessary to anticipate problems of implementation – these will include resource dependency (shortages in the resources required, in people and time as well as in money, will inhibit change), the capacity and willingness of middle managers to support the change (without their co-operation, change strategies are likely to fail), and the capacity and will of HR to ensure that the change is embedded in spite of indifference or negative reactions (this includes the ability of HR to provide guidance, advice and training as well as to develop procedures that are user-friendly and not over-engineered).

□ There are usually people in organisations who can act as champions of change. They will welcome the challenges and opportunities that change can provide. These should be the ones chosen as change agents.

□ Resistance to change is inevitable if the individuals concerned feel that they are going to be worse off – implicitly or explicitly. The inept management of change will produce that reaction.

□ In an age of global competition, technological innovation, turbulence, discontinuity, even chaos, change is inevitable and necessary. The organisation must do all it can to explain why change is essential and how it will affect everyone. Moreover, every effort must be made to protect the interests of those affected by change.

Conclusions

There is overwhelming evidence that progressive HR practices improve business performance by helping to ensure that an organisation has the skilled, flexible, motivated and committed people it needs, and by improving job satisfaction, motivation and commitment to encourage productivity and hence profitability. To achieve the maximum benefit in terms of competitiveness and business success, organisations should ensure that their people management practices are:

☐ based on business-led strategies for creating a positive performance-orientated and customer-focused culture

☐ aimed at achieving competitive advantage by acquiring and developing high-quality people and enhancing the intellectual capital available to the organisation

☐ integrated with one another so that coherent and mutually supporting approaches are used to select, develop and reward people

☐ fully supported by top management on the understanding that it is people who implement the business plan and through whom competitive edge is achieved

☐ facilitated by an HR function whose members operate proactively as strategic business partners who can draw up a convincing business case for innovations that will add value, and who, in the words of Ulrich (1998), can 'impel and guide serious discussion of how the company should be organised to carry out its strategy'.

REFERENCES

Andrews K. A. (1965) *The Concept of Corporate Strategy.* Georgetown, Ontario, Irwin.

Ansoff H. I. (1965) *Corporate Strategy.* New York, McGraw-Hill.

Argyris C. (1992) *On Organizational Learning.* Cambridge, Mass., Blackwell.

Argyris C. *and* Schon D. A. (1996) *Organisational Learning II: Theory, method and practice.* New York, Addison Wesley.

Armstrong M. (1987) 'Human resource management: a case of the emperor's new clothes'. *Personnel Management.* August. pp30–35.

Armstrong M. (1989) *Personnel and the Bottom Line.* London, Institute of Personnel Management.

Armstrong M. (2000a) 'The name has changed but has the game remained the same?' *Employee Relations.* Vol. 22, No. 6. pp576–589.

Armstrong M. (2000b) *Strategic Human Resource Management.* London, Kogan Page.

Armstrong M. (2001) *A Handbook of Human Resource Management Practice.* 8th edition. London, Kogan Page.

Armstrong M. *and* Long P. (1994) *The Reality of Strategic HRM.* London, Institute of Personnel and Development.

Armstrong M. *and* Murlis H. (1998) *Reward Management.* 4th edition. London, Kogan Page.

Arthur J. B. (1990) *Industrial Relations and Business Strategies in American Steel Minimills.* Unpublished PhD dissertation, Cornell University.

Arthur J. B (1992) 'The link between business strategy and

industrial relations systems in American steel mills'. *Industrial and Labor Relations Review*. Vol. 45, No. 3. pp488–506.

Arthur J. B. (1994) 'Effects of human resource systems on manufacturing performance and turnover'. *Academy of Management Review*. Vol. 37, No. 4. pp670–687.

Arthur J. B. (1999) 'Human resource practices in US mini-mills'. In P. Cappelli (ed.) *Employment Policies and Business Strategy*. New York, Oxford University Press.

Barney J. (1991) 'Types of competition and the theory of strategy: towards an integrative approach'. *Academy of Management Review*. 11(4). pp791–800.

Barney J. (1995) 'Looking inside for competitive advantage'. *Academy of Management Executive*. Vol. 9, No. 4. pp49–61.

Baron A. *and* Walters J. (1994) *The Culture Factor – Corporate and International*. London, Institute of Personnel and Development.

Becker B. E. *and* Gerhart B. (1996) 'The impact of human resource management on organisational performance, progress and prospects'. *Academy of Management Journal*. Vol. 39, No. 4. pp779–801.

Becker B. E., Huselid M. A., Pickus P. S. *and* Spratt M. F. (1997) 'HR as a source of shareholder value: research and recommendations'. *Human Resource Management*. Spring. Vol. 36, No. 1. pp39–47.

Beckhard R. (1989) 'A model for the executive management of transformational change'. In G. Salaman (ed.) *Human Resource Strategies.* London, Sage.

Beer M., Spector B., Lawrence P., Quinn Mills D. *and* Walton R. (1984) *Managing Human Assets*. New York, The Free Press.

Blackler F. (1995) 'Knowledge, knowledge work and organisations'. *Organisation Studies*. Vol. 16, No. 6. pp16–36.

Blake P. (1998) 'The knowledge management explosion'. *Information Today*. Vol. 15, No. 1. pp12–13.

Blyton P. *and* Turnbull P. (eds) (1992) *Reassessing Human Resource Management*. London, Sage.

Bontis N. (1996) 'There's a price on your head: managing intellectual capital strategically'. *Business Quarterly.* Summer. pp4–47.

Bontis N. (1998) 'Intellectual capital: an exploratory study that develops measures and models'. *Management Decision.* Vol. 36, No. 2. pp63–76.

Bontis N., Dragonetti N. C., Jacobsen K. *and* Roos G. (1999) 'The knowledge toolbox: a review of the tools available to measure and manage intangible resources'. *European Management Journal.* Vol. 17, No. 4. pp391–402.

Bower J. L. (1982) 'Business policy in the 1980s'. *Academy of Management Review.* Vol. 7, No. 4. pp630–638.

Boxall P. F. (1992) 'Strategic HRM: a beginning, a new theoretical direction'. *Human Resource Management Journal.* Vol. 2, No. 3. pp61–79.

Boxall P. F. (1993) 'The significance of human resource management: a reconsideration of the evidence'. *The International Journal of Human Resource Management.* Vol. 4, No. 3. pp645–665.

Boxall P. F. (1994) 'Placing HR strategy at the heart of the business'. *Personnel Management.* July. pp32–35.

Boxall P. F. (1996) 'The strategic HRM debate and the resource-based view of the firm'. *Human Resource Management Journal.* Vol. 6, No. 3. pp59–75.

Brewster C. (1993) 'Developing a "European" model of human resource management'. *The International Journal of Human Resource Management.* Vol. 4, No. 4. pp765–784.

Brown D. (2001) *Reward Strategies: From intent to impact.* London, Chartered Institute of Personnel and Development.

Buchanan D. (1987) 'Job enrichment is dead: long live high-performance work design!'. *Personnel Management.* May. pp40–43.

Burgoyne J. (1999) 'Design of the times'. *People Management.* 3 June. pp39–44.

Burns B. (1992) *Managing Change.* Pitman, London.

Burns J. M. (1978) *Leadership.* Harper & Row, New York.

Caldwell R. (2001) 'Champions, adapters, consultants and

synergists: the new change agents in HRM'. *Human Resource Management Journal*. Vol. 11, No. 3. pp39–52.

Cappelli P. (1999) *Employment Practices and Business Strategy*. New York, Oxford University Press.

Cappelli P. (2000) 'Managing without commitment'. *Organizational Dynamics*. Spring. pp11–24.

Cappelli P. *and* Crocker-Hefter A. (1996) *Organizational Dynamics*. Winter. pp7–22.

Carter A. *and* Robinson D. (2000) *Employee Returns – Linking HR performance indicators to business strategy*. Institute of Employment Studies.

Caulkin S. (2001) 'The time is now'. *People Management*. 30 August. pp32–34.

Chadwick C. *and* Cappelli P. (1998) 'Alternatives to generic strategy typologies in human resource management'. In P. Wright, L. Dyer, J. Boudreau and G. Milkovich (eds) *Research in Personnel and Human Resource Management*. Greenwich, Conn., JAI Press.

Chandler A. D. (1962) *Strategy and Structure*. Boston, Mass., MIT Press.

CIPD (2001a) *Raising UK Productivity: Why people management matters*. London, Chartered Institute of Personnel and Development.

CIPD (2001b) *The Change Agenda: People management and business performance*. London, Chartered Institute of Personnel and Development.

Coleman J. S. (1990) *Foundations of Social Theory*. Cambridge, Mass., Harvard University Press.

Daft R. L. *and* Weick K. E. (1984) 'Towards a model of organisations as interpretation systems'. *Academy of Management Review*. Vol. 9. pp284–295.

Dale M. (1994) 'Learning organizations'. In C. Mabey and P. Iles (eds) *Managing Learning*. London, Routledge.

Davenport T. H. (1996) 'Why re-engineering failed: the fad that forgot people'. *Fast Company*. Premier issue. pp70–74.

Davenport T. H. *and* Prusak L. (1998) *Working Knowledge:*

How organizations manage what they know. Boston, Mass., Harvard Business School Press.

Davenport T. O. (1999) *Human Capital*. San Francisco, Jossey Bass.

Delaney J. T. *and* Huselid M. A. (1996) 'The impact of human resource management practices on perceptions of organizational performance'. *Academy of Management Journal*. Vol. 39, No. 4. pp949–969.

Delery J. E. *and* Doty H. D. (1996) 'Modes of theorizing in strategic human resource management: tests of universality, contingency and configurational performance predictions'. *International Journal of Human Resource Management*. Vol. 6. pp656–670.

Digman L. A. (1990) *Strategic Management – Concepts, Decisions, Cases*. Georgetown, Ontario, Irwin.

Drucker P. E. (1955) *The Practice of Management*. London, Heinemann.

Dyer L. (1984) 'Studying human resource strategy: an approach and an agenda'. *Industrial Relations*. Vol. 23, No. 2. pp156–169.

Dyer L. *and* Holder G. W. (1988) 'Strategic human resource management and planning'. In L. Dyer (ed.) *Human Resource Management: Evolving roles and responsibilities*. Washington, D.C., Bureau of National Affairs.

Dyer L. *and* Reeves T. (1995) 'Human resource strategies and firm performance: what do we know and where do we need to go?'. *The International Journal of Human Resource Management*. Vol. 6, No. 3 September. pp656–670.

Edvinson L. *and* Malone M. S. (1997) *Intellectual Capital: Realizing your company's true value by finding its hidden brainpower*. New York, Harper Business.

Ehrenberg R. G. *and* Smith R. S. (1994) *Modern Labor Economics*. New York, HarperCollins.

Elliott R. F. (1990) *Labor Economics – A Comparative Text*. Maidenhead, Berks., McGraw-Hill.

Faulkner D. *and* Johnson G. (1992) *The Challenge of Strategic Management*. London, Kogan Page.

Fitz-enj J. (2000) *The ROI of Human Capital*. New York, American Management Association.

Fombrun C. J., Tichy N. M. *and* Devanna M. A. (1984) *Strategic Human Resource Management*. New York, Wiley.

Fowler A. (1987) 'When chief executives discover HRM'. *Personnel Management*. January.

French W. L. *and* Bell C. H. (1990) *Organization Development*. Englewood Cliffs, N.J., Prentice-Hall.

Furnham A. *and* Gunter B. (1993) *Corporate Assessment*. London, Routledge.

Garvin D. A. (1993) 'Building a learning organization'. *Harvard Business Review*. July–August. pp78–91.

Gennard J. *and* Judge G. (1997) *Employee Relations*. London, Institute of Personnel and Development.

Geppert M. (1996) 'Parts of managerial learning in the East German context'. *Organisation studies* 17(2), pp249–268.

Ghoshal H. *and* Bartlett C. A. (1999) *The Individualised Corporation*. New York, Harper Perennial.

Goold M. *and* Campbell A. (1986) *Strategies and Styles: The role of the centre in managing diversified corporations*. Oxford, Blackwell.

Grant R. M. (1991) 'The resource-based theory of competitive advantage: implications for strategy formulation'. *California Management Review*. Vol. 33, No. 3. pp114–135.

Grant R. M. (1998) *Contemporary Strategic Analysis*. 3rd edition. Malden, Mass., Blackwell.

Gratton L. (1999) 'People processes as a source of competitive advantage'. In L. Gratton, V. H. Hailey, P. Stiles and C. Truss (eds) *Strategic Human Resource Management*. Oxford, Oxford University Press.

Gratton L. (2000) 'A real step change'. *People Management*. 16 March. pp27–30.

Gratton L., Hailey V. H., Stiles P. *and* Truss C. (1999) *Strategic Human Resource Management*. Oxford, Oxford University Press.

Guest D. E. (1987) 'Human resource management and industrial relations'. *Journal of Management Studies*. Vol. 14, No. 5.

Guest D. E. (1989a) 'Human resource management: its implications for industrial relations and trade unions'. In J. Storey (ed.) *New Perspectives in Human Resource Management*. London, Routledge.

Guest D. E. (1989b) 'Personnel and HRM: can you tell the difference?' *Personnel Management*. January. pp48–51.

Guest D. E. (1991) 'Personnel management: the end of orthodoxy'. *British Journal of Industrial Relations*. Vol. 29, No. 2. pp149–176.

Guest D. E. (1993) 'Current perspectives on human resource management in the United Kingdom'. In C. Brewster (ed.) *Current Trends in Human Resource Management in Europe*. London, Kogan Page.

Guest D. E. (1997) 'Human resource management and performance: a review of the research agenda'. *The International Journal of Human Resource Management*. Vol. 8, No. 3. pp263–276.

Guest D. E. (1999) 'Human resource management: the workers' verdict'. *Human Resource Management Journal*. Vol. 9, No. 2. pp5–25.

Guest D. E. *and* Conway N. (1997) *Employee Motivation and the Psychological Contract*. London, Institute of Personnel and Development.

Guest D. E. *and* King Z. (2001) 'Personnel's paradox'. *People Management*. 27 September. pp24–27.

Guest D. E., Michie J., Sheehan M., Conway N. *and* Metochi M. (2000a) *Effective People Management*. London, Chartered Institute of Personnel and Development.

Guest D., Michie J., Sheehan M. *and* Conway N. (2000b) *Employee Relations, HRM and Business Performance: An analysis of the 1998 Workplace Employee Relations Survey*. London, Institute of Personnel and Development.

Guest D., Conway N., King Z., Michie J. *and* Sheehan M. (2001) *Voices from the Boardroom*. London, Chartered Institute of Personnel and Development.

Guile D. *and* Fonda N. (1999) *Managing Learning for Added Value*. London, Institute of Personnel and Development.

Gunnigle P. *and* Moore S. (1994) 'Linking business strategy and human resource management: issues and implications'. *Personnel Review*. Vol. 23, No. 1. pp63–83.

Hailey V. H. (1999) 'Managing culture'. In L. Gratton, V. H. Hailey, P. Stiles and C. Truss (eds) *Strategic Human Resource Management*. Oxford, Oxford University Press.

Hall R. (1992) 'The strategic analysis of intangible resources'. *Strategic Management Journal*. Vol. 13. pp135–144.

Hamel G. *and* Prahalad C. K. (1989) 'Strategic intent'. *Harvard Business Review*. May–June. pp63–76.

Hansen M. T., Nohria N. *and* Tierney T. (1999) 'What's your strategy for managing knowledge?'. *Harvard Business Review*. March–April. pp106–116.

Harrison R. (1997) *Employee Development*. 2nd edition. London, Institute of Personnel and Development.

Hay Group (2001) *Engaged Performance: Strategies for success*. unpublished.

Heller R. (1972) *The Naked Manager*. London, Barrie & Jenkins.

Hendry C. *and* Pettigrew A. (1986) 'The practice of strategic human resource management'. *Personnel Review*. Vol. 15. pp2–8.

Hendry C. *and* Pettigrew A. (1990) 'Human resource management: an agenda for the 1990s'. *International Journal of Human Resource Management*. Vol. 1, No. 3. pp17–43.

Hermanson R. (1964) *Accounting for Human Assets*. Bureau of Business and Economic Research, Michigan State University, Occasional Paper, November.

Herriot P., Hirsh W. *and* Riley P. (1998) *Trust and Transition: Managing the employment relationship*. Chichester, Wiley.

Hofer C. W. *and* Schendel D. (1986) *Strategy Formulation: Analytical concepts*. New York, West Publishing.

Hope-Hailey V., Gratton L., McGovern P., Stiles P. *and* Truss C. (1998) 'A chameleon function? HRM in the '90s'. *Human Resource Management Journal*. Vol. 7, No. 3. pp5–18.

Huselid M. A. (1995) 'The impact of human resource management practices on turnover, productivity and corporate financial performance'. *Academy of Management Journal.* Vol. 38, No. 3. pp635–672.

Huselid M. A. *and* Becker B. E. (1995) 'High-performance work practices and the performance of the firm: the mediating effects of capital structure and competitive strategy'. Paper presented at the Academy of Management Conference, Vancouver, 6–9 August.

Ichkinowski C. *and* Kochan T. A. (1995) 'What have we learned from workplace innovations?'. Unpublished type-script.

Iles P. (2001) 'Employee resourcing'. In J. Storey (ed.) *Human Resource Management: A critical text.* 2nd edition. London, Thompson Learning.

Institute of Personnel and Development (1994) *People Make the Difference.* London, Institute of Personnel and Development.

Johnson G. *and* Scholes K. (1993) *Exploring Corporate Strategy.* Hemel Hempstead, Prentice Hall.

Kamoche K. (1996) 'Strategic human resource management within a resource capability view of the firm'. *Journal of Management Studies.* Vol. 33, No. 2. pp213–233.

Kanter R. M. (1984) *The Change Masters.* London, Allen & Unwin.

Kay J. (1999) 'Strategy and the illusions of grand designs'. *Mastering Strategy.* Financial Times, pp2–4.

Keenoy T. (1990a) 'HRM: a case of the wolf in sheep's clothing'. *Personnel Review.* Vol. 19, No. 2. pp3–9.

Keenoy T. (1997) 'HRMism and the images of re-presentation'. *Journal of Management Studies.* Vol. 4, No. 5. pp825–841.

Keenoy T. (1999) 'HRM as a hologram, a polemic'. *Journal of Management Studies.* Vol. 36, No. 1. pp1–23.

Keep E. (1989) 'Corporate training strategies'. In J. Storey (ed.) *New Perspectives on Human Resource Management.* Oxford, Blackwell.

Kotter J. J. (1995) *A 20 per cent Solution: Using rapid re-design to build tomorrow's organization today.* New York, Wiley.

Lawson P. (1995) 'Performance management: an overview'. In M. Walters (ed.) *The Performance Management Handbook*. London, Institute of Personnel and Development.

Le Blanc P. V., Mulvey P. W. *and* Rich J. (2000) 'Improving the return on human capital: New metrics'. In *Compensation and Benefits* Review. January/February, pp13–20.

Legge K. (1989) 'Human resource management: a critical analysis'. In J. Storey (ed.) *New Perspectives in Human Resource Management*. London, Routledge.

Legge K. (1995) *Human Resource Management: Rhetorics and realities*. London, Macmillan.

Legge K. (1998) 'The morality of HRM'. In C. Mabey, D. Skinner and T. Clark (eds) *Experiencing Human Resource Management*. London, Sage.

Legge K. (2000) 'Personnel management in the lean organisation'. In S. Bach and K. Sissons (eds) *Personnel Management: A comprehensive guide to theory and practice*. Oxford, Blackwell.

Legge K. (2001) 'Silver bullet or spent round? Assessing the meaning of the "high-commitment management"/performance relationship'. In J. Storey (ed.) *Human Resource Management: A critical text*. 2nd edition. London, Thompson Learning.

Lengnick-Hall C. A. *and* Lengnick-Hall M. L. (1990) *Interactive Human Resource Management and Strategic Planning*. Westport, Quorum Books.

Likert R. (1961) *New Patterns of Management*. New York, McGraw-Hill.

Mabey C. *and* Salaman G. (1995) *Strategic Human Resource Management*. Oxford, Blackwell Business.

Mabey C., Skinner D. *and* Clark T. (1998) *Experiencing Human Resource Management*. London, Sage.

MacDuffie J. P. (1995) 'Human resource bundles and manufacturing performance'. *Industrial Relations Review*. Vol. 48, No. 2. pp199–221.

Marchington M. *and* Wilkinson A. (1996) *Core Personnel and Development*. London, Institute of Personnel and Development.

Mayo A. (1999) 'Making human capital meaningful'. *Knowledge Management Review*. January–February. pp26–29.

McGregor D. (1960) *The Human Side of Enterprise*. New York, McGraw-Hill.

Mecklenberg S., Deering A. *and* Sharp D. (1999) 'Knowledge management: a secret engine of corporate growth'. *Executive Agenda*. Vol. 2. pp5–15.

Miles R. E. *and* Snow C. C. (1978) *Organizational Strategy: Structure and process*. New York, McGraw Hill.

Miller A. *and* Dess G. G. (1996) *Strategic Management*. 2nd edition. New York, McGraw Hill.

Miller P. (1987) 'Strategic industrial relations and human resource management: distinction, definition and recognition'. *Journal of Management Studies*. 24. pp101–109.

Miller P. (1989) 'Strategic human resource management: what it is and what it isn't'. *Personnel Management*. February. pp46–51.

Miller P. (1991) 'Strategic human resource management: an assessment of progress'. *Human Resource Management Journal*. Vol. 1, No. 4. pp23–39.

Mintzberg H. (1978) 'Patterns in strategy formation'. *Management Science*. May. pp934–948.

Mintzberg H. (1987) 'Crafting strategy'. *Harvard Business Review*. July–August. pp66–74.

Mintzberg H. (1994) 'The rise and fall of strategic planning'. *Harvard Business Review*. January–February. pp107–114.

Mintzberg H., Quinn J. B. *and* James R. M. (1988) *The Strategy Process: Concepts, contexts and cases*. New York, Prentice-Hall.

Mintzberg H., Ahlstrand B. *and* Lampel J. (1998) *Strategic Safari: A guided tour through the wilds of strategic management*. New York, The Free Press.

Moore J. (1992) *Writers on Strategic Management*. London, Penguin Books.

Murlis H. (ed.) (1996) *Pay at the Crossroads*. London, Institute of Personnel and Development.

Nahpiet J. *and* Ghoshal S. (1998) 'Social capital, intellectual capital and the organizational advantage'. *Academy of Management Review*. Vol. 6, No. 2. pp242–266.

Nonaka I. (1991) 'The knowledge-creating company'. *Harvard Business Review*. November–December. pp96–104.

Nonaka I. *and* Takeuchi H. (1995) *The Knowledge-Creating Company*. New York, Oxford University Press.

Noon M. (1992) 'HRM: a map, model or theory?'. In P. Blyton and P. Turnbull (eds) *Reassessing Human Resource Management*. London, Sage.

OECD (1998) *Human Capital Investment: An international comparison*. Paris, Organisation for Economic Co-operation and Development.

Pascale R. (1990) *Managing on the Edge*. London, Viking.

Pascale R. *and* Athos A. (1981) *The Art of Japanese Management*. New York, Simon & Schuster.

Patterson M. G., West M. A., Lawthom R. *and* Nickell S. (1997) *The Impact of People Management Practices on Business Performance*. London, Institute of Personnel and Development.

Pearce J. A. *and* Robinson R. B. (1988) *Strategic Management: Strategy formulation and implementation*. Georgetown, Ontario, Irwin.

Pedler M., Boydell T. *and* Burgoyne J. (1989) 'Towards the learning company'. *Management Education and Development*. Vol. 20, No. 1. pp1–8.

Peters T. *and* Waterman R. (1982) *In Search of Excellence*. New York, Harper & Row.

Pettigrew A. (1999) *Organising to Improve Company Performance*. Warwick, Warwick Business School.

Pettigrew A. *and* Whipp R. (1991) *Managing Change for Strategic Success*. Oxford, Blackwell.

Pfeffer J. (1994) *Competitive Advantage Through People*. Boston, Harvard Business School Press.

Pil F. K. *and* MacDuffie J. P. (1996) 'The adoption of high-involvement work practices'. *Industrial Relations*. Vol. 35, No. 3. pp423–455.

Pil F. K. *and* MacDuffie J. P. (1999) 'Organizational and environmental factors influencing the use and diffusion of high-involvement work practices'. In P. Cappelli (ed.) *Employment Practices and Business Strategy*. New York, Oxford University Press.

Porter M. E. (1980) *Competitive Strategy*. New York, The Free Press.

Porter M. E. (1985) *Competitive Advantage: Creating and sustaining superior performance*. New York, The Free Press.

Prahalad C. K. *and* Hamel G. (1990) 'The core competences of the organization'. *Harvard Business Review*. May–June. pp79–93.

Purcell J. (1989) 'The impact of corporate strategy on human resource management'. In J. Storey (ed.) *New Perspectives on Human Resource Management*. London, Routledge.

Purcell J. (1993) 'The challenge of human resource management for industrial relations research and practice'. *The International Journal of Human Resource Management*. Vol. 4, No. 3. pp511–527.

Purcell J. (1999) 'Best practice or best fit: chimera or cul-de-sac'. *Human Resource Management Journal*. Vol. 9, No. 3. pp26–41.

Purcell J. (2001a) 'The meaning of strategy in human resource management'. In J. Storey (ed.) *Human Resource Management: A critical text*. 2nd edition. London, Thompson Learning.

Purcell J. (2001b) 'People mean business'. Presentation at the CIPD National Conference, Harrogate, October.

Purcell J. *and* Ahlstrand B. (1994) *Human Resource Management in the Multidivisional Company*. Oxford, Oxford University Press.

Purcell J., Kinnie N., Hutchinson S. *and* Rayton B. (2000) 'Inside the box'. *People Management*. 26 October. pp30–38.

Putnam R. (1996) 'Who killed civic America?'. *Prospect*. March. pp66–72.

Quinn J. B. (1980) *Strategies for Change: Logical incrementalism*. Georgetown, Ontario, Irwin.

Quinn Mills D. (1983) 'Planning with people in mind'.

Harvard Business Review. November–December. pp97–105.

Rajan A., Chapple K. *and* van Eupen P. (1999) *Building Capability for the 21st Century.* London, Investors in People UK.

Richardson R. *and* Thompson M. (1999) *The Impact of People Management Practices on Business Performance: A literature review.* London, Institute of Personnel and Development.

Sackmann S., Flamholz E. *and* Bullen M. (1989), 'Human asset accounting'. *Journal of Accounting Literature.* Vol. 5. pp235–264.

Sako M. (1994) 'The informational requirement of trust in supplier relations: evidence from Japan, the UK and the USA'. Unpublished.

Salaman G. (2001) 'The management of corporate culture change'. In J. Storey (ed.) *Human Resource Management: A critical text.* 2nd edition. London, Thompson Learning.

Scarbrough H. *and* Carter C. (2000) *Investigating Knowledge Management.* London, Chartered Institute of Personnel and Development.

Scarbrough H., Swan J. *and* Preston, J. (1999) *Knowledge Management: A literature review.* London, Institute of Personnel and Development.

Schein E. H. (1985) *Organization Culture and Leadership.* New York, Jossey Bass.

Scott A. (1994) *Willing Slaves? British Workers Under Human Resource Management.* Cambridge, Cambridge University Press.

Schuler R. S. (1992) 'Strategic human resource management: linking people with the strategic needs of the business'. *Organizational Dynamics.* Vol. 21, No. 1. pp18–32.

Schuler R. S. *and* Jackson S. E. (1987) 'Linking competitive strategies with human resource management practices'. *Academy of Management Executive.* Vol. 9, No. 3. pp207–219.

Schuler R. S. *and* Jackson S. E. (1999) *Strategic Human Resource Management: A reader.* London, Blackwell.

Schuler R. S., Jackson S. E. *and* Storey J. (2001) ' HRM and its link with strategic management'. In J. Storey (ed.) *Human Resource Management: A critical text.* 2nd edition. London, Thompson Learning.

Schuller T. (2000) 'Social and human capital; the search for appropriate technomethodology'. *Policy Studies.* Vol. 21, No. 1. pp25–35.

Schultz T. W. (1961) 'Investment in human capital'. *American Economic Review.* Vol. 51. March. pp1–17.

Schultz T. W. (1981) *Investing in People: The economics of population quality.* Sacramento, University of California.

Senge P. (1990) *The Fifth Discipline: The art and practice of the learning organization.* London, Doubleday.

Sisson K. (1990) 'Introducing the Human Resource Management Journal'. *Human Resource Management Journal.* Vol. 1, No. 1. pp1–11.

Sloman M. (1999) 'Seize the day'. *People Management.* 20 May. p31.

Smith A. (1776) *An Inquiry into the Nature and Causes of the Wealth of Nations.* Oxford, Clarendon, 1976.

Stevens J. (1998) *High-Performance Working Is for Everyone.* London, Institute of Personnel and Development.

Storey J. (1989) 'From personnel management to human resource management'. In J. Storey (ed.) *New Perspectives on Human Resource Management.* London, Routledge.

Storey J. (1993) 'The take-up of human resource management by mainstream companies: key lessons from research'. *The International Journal of Human Resource Management.* Vol. 4, No. 3. pp529–557.

Storey J. (2001) *Human Resource Management: A critical text.* 2nd edition. London, Thompson Learning.

Tan, J. (2001) 'Knowledge management: Just more buzz-words?'. *British Journal of Administrative Management.* March–April, pp37–44.

Teece D., Pisano G. *and* Shuen A. (1997) 'Dynamic capabilities and strategic management'. *Strategic Management Journal.* Vol. 18. pp509–533.

Thompson M. (1998a) 'Trust and reward'. In S. Perkins and S-J. Sandringham (eds) *Trust, Motivation and Commitment: A reader.* Faringdon, Strategic Remuneration Research Centre.

Thompson M. (1998b) 'Jet-setters'. *People Management.* 16 April. pp38–41.

Thompson M. (2000) *Comments on the Outcomes of CIPD-Sponsored Research on Strategic HRM.* London, CIPD, unpublished.

Torrington D. P. (1989) 'Human resource management and the personnel function'. In J. Storey (ed.) *New Perspectives on Human Resource Management.* London, Routledge.

Townley B. (1989) 'Selection and appraisal: reconstructing social relations?'. In J. Storey (ed.) *New Perspectives in Human Resource Management.* London, Routledge.

Truss C. (1999) 'Soft and hard models of HRM'. In L. Gratton, V. H. Hailey, P. Stiles, and C. Truss (eds) *Strategic Human Resource Management.* Oxford, Oxford University Press.

Trussler S. (1998) 'The rules of the game'. *The Journal of Business Strategy.* Vol. 19, No. 1. pp16–19.

Tyson S. (1985) 'Is this the very model of a modern personnel manager?'. *Personnel Management.* 26. pp35–39.

Tyson S. (1997) 'Human resource strategy: a process for managing the contribution of HRM to organizational performance'. *The International Journal of Human Resource Management.* Vol. 8, No. 3. pp277–290.

Tyson S. *and* Witcher M. (1994) 'Human resource strategy emerging from the recession'. *Personnel Management.* August. pp20–23.

Ulrich D. (1997) *Human Resource Champions.* Boston, Harvard Business School Press.

Ulrich D. (1998) 'A new mandate for human resources'. *Harvard Business Review.* January–February. pp124–134.

US Department of Labor (1993) *High-Performance Work Practices and Work Performance.* Washington, D.C., US Government Printing Office.

Walker J. W. (1992) *Human Resource Strategy.* New York, McGraw-Hill.

Walton R. E. (1985) 'From control to commitment in the workplace'. *Harvard Business Review*. 63. pp76–84.

Wenger E. *and* Snyder W. M. (2000) 'Communities of practice: the organizational frontier'. *Harvard Business Review*. January–February. pp33–41.

West P. (1996) 'The learning organisation: losing the luggage in transit?'. *Journal of European Industrial Training*. Vol. 18, No. 11. pp30–38.

Whittington R. (1993) *What is Strategy, and Does it Matter?* London, Routledge.

Wick C. W. *and* Leon L. S. (1995) 'Creating a learning organization: from ideas to action'. *Human Resource Management*. Summer. pp299–311.

Wickens P. (1987) *The Road to Nissan*. London, Macmillan.

Willmott H. (1993) 'Strength is ignorance, slavery is freedom: managing culture in modern organizations'. *Journal of Management Studies*. Vol. 29, No. 6. pp515–552.

Wood S. (1996) 'High-commitment management and organisation in the UK'. *The International Journal of Human Resource Management*. February. pp41–58.

Wood S. *and* Albanese M. (1995) 'Can we speak of a high-commitment management on the shop floor?'. *Journal of Management Studies*. March. pp215–247.

WorldatWork (2000) *Total Rewards: From strategy to implementation*. Scottsdale, Ariz., WorldatWork.

Wright P. M. *and* McMahan G. C. (1992) 'Theoretical perspectives for SHRM'. *Journal of Management*. Vol. 18, No. 2. pp295–320.

Wright P. M. *and* Snell S. A. (1991) 'Towards an integrative view of strategic human resource management'. *Human Resource Management Review*. Vol. 1, No. 3. pp203–225.

Wright P. M. *and* Snell S. A. (1998) 'Towards a unifying framework for exploring fit and flexibility in strategic human resource management'. *Academy of Management Review*. Vol. 23, No. 4. pp756–772.

Youndt M. A. (2000) 'Human resource considerations and value creation: the mediating role of intellectual capital'. Paper delivered at the National Conference of the US Academy of Management, Toronto, August.

AUTHOR INDEX

SUBJECT INDEX